ENLISTMENT

INTERVENTIONS: NEW STUDIES
IN MEDIEVAL CULTURE
Ethan Knapp, Series Editor

ENLISTMENT

Lists in Medieval and Early Modern Literature

∼

**Edited by Eva von Contzen
and James Simpson**

THE OHIO STATE UNIVERSITY PRESS
COLUMBUS

Copyright © 2022 by The Ohio State University.
All rights reserved.

Library of Congress Cataloging-in-Publication Data
Names: Contzen, Eva von, editor. | Simpson, James, 1954– editor.
Title: Enlistment : lists in medieval and early modern literature / edited by Eva von Contzen and James Simpson.
Other titles: Interventions: new studies in medieval culture.
Description: Columbus : The Ohio State University Press, [2022] | Series: Interventions: new studies in medieval culture | Includes bibliographical references and index. | Summary: "Unearths the cultural significance of medieval and early modern lists from Chaucer's and Spenser's epic catalogues of trees, to household vocabulary, to genealogies and bestiaries"—Provided by publisher.
Identifiers: LCCN 2022006922 | ISBN 9780814215227 (cloth) | ISBN 081421522X (cloth) | ISBN 9780814282212 (ebook) | ISBN 0814282210 (ebook)
Subjects: LCSH: Lists in literature. | Literature, Medieval—History and criticism. | Literature, Modern—15th and 16th centuries—History and criticism. | Literature, Modern—17th century—History and criticism.
Classification: LCC PN56.L54 E55 2022 | DDC 821/.209—dc23/eng/20220421
LC record available at https://lccn.loc.gov/2022006922
Other Identifiers: 9780814258378 (paper) | 0814258379 (paper)

Cover design by Laurence J. Nozik
Text design by Juliet Williams
Type set in Adobe Minion Pro

CONTENTS

~

List of Illustrations   vii

INTRODUCTION   Enlistment as Poetic Stratagem
               EVA VON CONTZEN AND JAMES SIMPSON   1

CHAPTER 1   "He should not overlook anything that could ever be of
               significance": Knowledge and Vocabulary in *Gerefa*
               ALEXIS KELLNER BECKER   15

CHAPTER 2   In the Space of a List—*Widsith*'s Global Modernism
               ANDREW JAMES JOHNSTON   35

CHAPTER 3   Listing Divine Names: A Study in Liturgical Form
               KATHRYN MOGK WAGNER   55

CHAPTER 4   Naming the Children of Jacob: The Shape of Negative
               Theology in the *Benjamin Minor*
               SUZANNE CONKLIN AKBARI   75

CHAPTER 5   Out of Eden and Back Again: Following the Flow of
               Concepts, Categories, and Lists in the Four Rivers of Paradise
               MARTHA RUST   97

CHAPTER 6   Epic Lists: The Matter of Troy and the Catalogue Form
               in Middle English Literature
               EVA VON CONTZEN   115

CHAPTER 7	Performing Generic Exhaustion: Implosive Households in Gavin Douglas's *Palice of Honour*	
	WOLFRAM R. KELLER	135
CHAPTER 8	The Epic Tree Catalogue from Chaucer to Spenser	
	INGO BERENSMEYER	155
CHAPTER 9	What's in a List? Erasmus, Cromwell, Bale	
	ALEX DAVIS	173
CHAPTER 10	Reformation Lists: Syntax, the Sacred, and the Production of Junk	
	JAMES SIMPSON	195
List of Contributors		213
Index		217

ILLUSTRATIONS

FIGURE 4.1	British Library, Harley MS 674, fol. 112r	79
FIGURE 4.2	Harvard University, Houghton Library, MS Richardson 22, fol. 54r	88
FIGURE 4.3	Harvard University, Houghton Library, MS Richardson 22, fol. 54v	89
FIGURE 5.1	Diagram of concept, category, and category members	102
FIGURE 5.2	HM 1086, f. 97, The Huntington Library, San Marino, California	106
FIGURE 5.3	Princeton University Library, Special Collections, Taylor MS 17, f. 9v	111
FIGURE 5.4	Princeton University Library, Special Collections, Taylor MS 17, f. 9	112
FIGURE 8.1	Tree species featured in Sidney's, Spenser's, and Chaucer's tree catalogues	164
TABLE 8.1	Semantic agreement among shared tree species epithets in Sidney, Spenser, and Chaucer	166
FIGURE 8.2	Distribution of shared tree epithets	167
FIGURE 10.1	"A Lively Picture, Describing the Weight and Substaunce of God's Most Blessed Word Against the Doctrines and Vanities of Mans Traditions," in John Foxe, *Actes and Monuments of the English Church* (London, 1576), Book 6, 795	206

INTRODUCTION

Enlistment as Poetic Stratagem

EVA VON CONTZEN AND JAMES SIMPSON

The noun *enlistment* dates to the eighteenth century and means the action of enrolling someone on the 'list' of a military body. In Western literature, literary listing begins with the act of enlisting someone: one of the oldest forms of the list in European poetry is the muster of armies, as in the second book of Homer's *Iliad*. More than forty leaders of the Greek army are enumerated here, accompanied by various ethnonyms and toponyms. Used in a broader sense, to enlist someone means to win their support in joining or supporting something or someone, voluntarily. It is an action and a practice that highlights the potential of the list as a form to include and exclude, to create a sense of belonging, of exclusivity, of demarcation. As a poetic stratagem, enlistment directs our attention to the ways in which enumerative, list-like practices of ordering implicate audiences in the sense-making process. Through the various forms of enumeration medieval authors could draw on, they attempt to align—to 'enlist,' indeed—readers with their projects. Such strategies of enlisting audiences are especially pertinent in contexts in which enumerative principles do not fulfill any immediate practical functions. As a strategic undertaking, the kind of enlistment we are interested in is intimately tied to poetic functions and purposes and manifests itself at the intersections of the structural arrangement of a text, its content and context, and the cognitive processes of meaning making that are evoked in the reception process.

In this volume, we conceive of the 'list' in a broad and abstract sense. We use it as an umbrella term for various practices and principles of ordering that are characterized by enumerative and/or sequential patterns. What these enumerative practices have in common is that one cannot ignore them; the list form draws attention to itself and calls for an in-depth study of its implications. It may be true that lists are the one formal element in texts that (modern) readers are most likely to skip, but in a context of oral-aural reception, there is no escape from the list. The many examples of lists in medieval and early modern literature strongly suggest that enumerative forms seem to have exerted a special power. Audiences must have taken delight in enumerations—how else could we explain their proliferation? What is called for is a nuanced analysis of the specific forms and functions of lists within medieval and early modern literature in general and within individual works in particular. Our volume is the attempt to take the list as a *Denkform*—a way of thinking—seriously and to scrutinize its manifestations and functions in order to better understand how and why premodern audiences were prone to be 'enlisted.'

LISTS EVERYWHERE: CONTEXTS AND SCHOLARSHIP

In the Greek context, the term used for the list of leaders and ships is 'catalogue,' from the Ancient Greek verb *katalegein,* meaning both 'to enumerate' and 'to narrate.' The term was known by medieval English authors, as were other rhetorical devices derived from the classical tradition, such as enumeration, frequentation, accumulation, and amplification. In Middle English, the verb *enrollen* was used in a broad sense to denote the action of entering or recording someone's name, or a deed or contract, in an official list.[1] An *enrolment* thus implied the medium on which the action is performed: the roll, also known as a scroll. The scroll format was suited exceptionally well to make lists: one could easily add items so that they form a continuous line and thereby store practical information.[2] The term 'list' has a similar etymology: as David Matthews has pointed out with reference to Chaucer, for medieval users, a list "was the piece of paper or perhaps cloth on which a series of items were written down, *not* the words on the paper themselves or the concept of a rank of similar or related items."[3] A 'list' was something material, not conceptual.

---

1. See *OED*, entry "Enlistment, n. 1"; *MED*, entry "enrollen v."
2. See Thomas Forrest Kelly, *The Role of the Scroll* (New York / London: Norton, 2019).
3. David Matthews, "Enlisting the Poet: The List and the Late Medieval Dream Vision," *Style* 50, no. 3 (2016): 280–95, here 285.

Due to their flexible format, late medieval lists served first and foremost practical purposes: they were used for administrative, legal, or financial ends, and they were most certainly not meant to be read in their entirety.[4] The need to manage and order knowledge was a major incentive for making lists, which was coupled with an understanding of gathering and collecting as much material as possible on a certain topic. The aim was for totality, wholeness. This accumulation of knowledge led to the production of encyclopedias, as well as to manifold specialized works: bestiaries, lapidaries, lunaries, herbals, books on hunting, fishing, language learning, cooking, and many more.[5] In medieval schooling, lists of vocabularies and technical terms combined the encyclopedic with the educational, the strife for total knowledge with the particulars of step-by-step learning.

These practical lists—encyclopedias, vocabularies, administrative lists, and so forth—often heavily overlap with the kinds of lists we encounter in medieval poetry and imaginative literature.[6] L. R. Poos and Martha Rust have recently shown how reading administrative lists can shed light on *Piers Plowman,* and Sarah Stanbury has demonstrated how the use of the word "lists" informed Chaucer's poem "The Former Age."[7] The use of encyclopedic knowledge is another productive means of incorporating practical lists into literary texts. Thus, Jean de Meun's continuation of the *Roman de la Rose* with its overabundance of scientific knowledge, often in list form, attests to his

---

4. Lucie Doležalová begins her edited collection on *The Charm of the List* with the claim that the list "is most frequently a tool—a table of contents, dictionary, phone book, etc. One does not *read* but only *uses* a list: one looks up the relevant information in it, but usually does not need to deal with it as a whole—and is happy about this fact" ("Introduction: The Potential and Limitations of Studying Lists," in *The Charm of a List: From the Sumerians to Computerised Data Processing,* ed. Lucie Doležalová [Newcastle upon Tyne: Cambridge Scholars Publishing, 2009], 1–8, here 1).

5. See George R. Keiser, *Works of Science and Information: A Manual of the Writings in Middle English, 1050–1500,* vol. X (New Haven: Connecticut Academy of Arts and Sciences, 1998) on the rich tradition of practical and scientific works in the Middle English period, as well as Lisa H. Cooper, "The Poetics of Practicality," in *Middle English,* ed. Paul Strohm (Oxford: Oxford University Press, 2007), 491–505.

6. See Umberto Eco on the distinction between practical and poetic lists—a distinction which is not as neat as Eco suggests, as poetic lists often draw heavily on practical lists: *The Infinity of Lists: From Homer to Joyce,* trans. Alastair McEwen (London: MacLehose, 2009), 113–18.

7. L. R. Poos and Martha D. Rust, "Of *Piers,* Polltaxes and Parliament: Articulating Status and Occupation in Late Medieval England," *Fragments* 5 (2016): 96–127, and Sarah Stanbury, "Multilingual Lists and Chaucer's 'The Former Age,'" in *The Art of Vision: Ekphrasis in Medieval Literature and Culture,* ed. Andrew James Johnston, Ethan Knapp, and Margitta Rouse (Columbus: The Ohio State University Press, 2015), 36–54.

encyclopedic approach to narrative.[8] Practical lists, too, can acquire poetic dimensions, especially when lists cease to enumerate and begin to evoke or create narratives.[9]

Even though lists proliferate in the literatures of the Middle Ages and the early modern period, they have not received much attention from scholars.[10] Charles Muscatine's remarks on the many lists in Chaucer are telling in this regard. He singles out list-making as one of Chaucer's "large stylistic traits" and then muses on the rationale behind the heavy use of this feature.[11] On the one hand, Muscatine argues, Chaucer "in his use of the catalogue follows antique literary tradition and also a number of typically medieval impulses"; Chaucer attests to "a kind of lay encyclopaedism, a symptom of the secularisation of learning in the Middle Ages." On the other hand, Muscatine also admits, rather carefully, that at certain points one "can sense Chaucer's curving of the figure toward functional literary use."[12] Then all of a sudden everything in the *Canterbury Tales* becomes a catalogue:

> In a certain sense the sequence of portraits in the *General Prologue* (and even the sequence of *The Canterbury Tales* as a whole) has the form of a catalogue; it is possible that Chaucer's liking for this form is related ultimately to the enumerative, processional, paratactic quality that pervades the structure of *The Canterbury Tales* in large and small. The individual portraits are themselves composed of catalogues of traits.[13]

We can witness here the shift from a general scepticism, perhaps even contempt, for the list form towards the recognition that the list as a figure of

---

8. Mary Franklin-Brown, *Reading the World: Encyclopedic Writing in the Scholastic Age* (Chicago / London: University of Chicago Press, 2012), 183–214.

9. See Cooper, "Poetics," 497.

10. Literary lists in general have not been discussed much. Robert Belknap's book on lists in Emerson, Whitman, Melville, and Thoreau contains a useful introduction on literary lists (*The List: The Uses and Pleasures of Cataloguing* [New Haven: Yale University Press, 2004]). Sabine Mainberger's *Die Kunst des Aufzählens: Elemente zu einer Poetik des Enumerativen* (Berlin: De Gruyter, 2003) is a broad introduction to various kinds of lists and their functions in literature, focusing mainly on German and French modern and postmodern literature. Umberto Eco's *The Infinity of Lists* also contains useful starting points for thinking about literary lists more generally. It is based on his exhibition on lists at the Louvre in 2009. On lists from the perspective of literary history, see Eva von Contzen, "The Limits of Narration: Lists and Literary History," *Style* 50, no. 3 (2016): 241–60.

11. Charles Muscatine, "*The Canterbury Tales*: Style of the Man and Style of the Work," in *Medieval Literature, Style, and Culture: Essays by Charles Muscatine* (Columbia: University of South Carolina Press, 1999), 1–25, here 7.

12. Muscatine, "*The Canterbury Tales*," 7.

13. Muscatine, "*The Canterbury Tales*," 8.

thought may indeed underlie Chaucer's work as a whole. If anything, we can take from Muscatine's comments that there is an urgent need to take the list as a form seriously, and to tease out its functions within a specific work, but also across different works.

Almost twenty years after Muscatine (his article was first published in 1966), Stephen Barney wrote what is still the crucial article for anyone interested in Chaucer's lists.[14] It also contains fruitful material for the study of medieval lists in general because Barney approaches the list form from a systematic angle. Barney sets lists apart from narration and argues that lists are smaller than stories; are adjectival (that is, the list's elements modify the conceptual category under which they are gathered); follow some principle of order; are symmetrical and intransitive (the items must be of the same status); and are, in Roman Jakobson's terms, metaphoric and paradigmatic.[15] Barney's approach is clearly influenced by structuralism, and the binaries he creates may not always be the most viable categories when it comes to analyzing lists, which tend to thwart neat distinctions. Yet they offer a useful starting point for thinking about what lists as a form can afford.

In a second step, Barney points to seven strands of tradition that inform Chaucer's use of lists (which, he notes, are obviously interwoven). These are: wisdom literature, oral poetry, rhetoric, satire, encyclopedic literature, moral and homiletic literature, and technological literature, especially scientific writing.[16] It goes without saying that these traditions are not exclusive to Chaucer's list-making. They have influenced medieval and early modern literary production more generally, as the contributions in our volume demonstrate (see in more detail below). More recently, the lists in the *House of Fame* have been discussed in greater depth, and linked to memory work, and the undermining of literary authority.[17] David Matthews has discussed lists in later medieval dream visions (John Skelton in particular) and argued that with Stephen Hawes's neglect of the list form, the genre of dream vision has come to an

---

14. Stephen A. Barney, "Chaucer's Lists," in *The Wisdom of Poetry: Essays in Early English Literature in Honor of Morton W. Bloomfield*, ed. David C. Benson and Siegfried Wenzel (Kalamazoo, MI: Medieval Institute Publications, 1982), 189–223.

15. Barney explicates Jakobson's terms as follows: "Metaphoric or paradigmatic discourse associates things non-temporally, quasi-spatially. Our image is the vertical row (*cata-logue*: 'downward word')." He also stresses that the metaphoric is based on substitution and that it specifies the thing by what it is not ("Chaucer's Lists," 193). Its counterparts are the metonymic and the syntagmatic respectively, which are characteristics of a story.

16. Barney, "Chaucer's Lists," 194.

17. See T. S. Miller, "Forms of Perspective and Chaucer's Dream Spaces: Memory and the Catalogue in *The House of Fame*," *Style* 48, no. 4 (2014): 479–95, and Lara Ruffolo, "Literary Authority and the Lists of Chaucer's *House of Fame*: Destruction and Definition through Proliferation," *The Chaucer Review* 27, no. 4 (1993): 325–41.

end.[18] The extent to which lists played an important role in distinguishing the necessary from the superfluous, especially in contexts that were critical of plenitude, such as Reformation and Lollard writing, has been analyzed by Anke Bernau.[19] In addition, there are only a handful of book-length publications that approach lists as a fundamental formal feature of medieval literature. For Old English, Nicholas Howe's study the *Old English Catalogue Poems* remains important.[20] With respect to the medieval French context, Madeleine Jeay has provided a detailed study on enumeration as a literary principle. She attributes to the medieval period an aesthetics of discontinuity and enumeration, of which lists are an integral part—and makes a plea for taking enumerations and their effects seriously.[21]

The overall scarcity of scholarship on the topic may be indicative of modern readers' discomfort with the form: lists have the curious capacity to challenge our categories of thinking and ordering the world. Jorge Luis Borges's famous example of a (fictitious) Chinese encyclopedia illustrates this perfectly. According to this encyclopedia,

> animals are divided into (a) those that belong to the Emperor, (b) embalmed ones, (c) those that are trained, (d) suckling pigs, (e) mermaids, (f) fabulous ones, (g) stray dogs, (h) those that are included in this classification, (i) those that tremble as if they were mad, (j) innumerable ones, (k) those drawn with a very fine camel's hair brush, (l) others, (m) those that have just broken a flower vase, (n) those that resemble flies from a distance.[22]

How can we make sense of the categories that do not in the least correspond to our expectations of how one could or should classify animals—not to speak of entry (h), which renders the whole list ad absurdum? The latter is an example of Russell's paradox, but even this recognition does not help us to *think* by means of the list.[23] Michel Foucault adduces Borges's classification as an example of a totally different—in his terms, 'monstrous'—system of thought in the preface to *The Order of Things*.[24] He, too, discusses the uneasiness the

---

18. Matthews, "Enlisting the Poet."
19. Anke Bernau, "Enlisting Truth," *Style* 50, no. 3 (2016): 261–79.
20. Nicholas Howe, *The Old English Catalogue Poems* (Copenhagen: Rosenkilde and Bagger, 1985).
21. Madeleine Jeay, *Le commerce des mots: L'usage des listes dans la littérature médiévale (XIIe–XVe siècles)* (Genève: Droz, 2006), 45.
22. Jorge Luis Borges, "The Analytical Language of John Wilkins," in *Other Inquisitions 1937–1952*, trans. Ruth L. C. Simms (London: Souvenir, 1973), 101–5, here 103.
23. See Eco, *Infinity*, 324–7; 395–6, on Russell's paradox.
24. Michel Foucault, *The Order of Things: An Archaeology of the Human Sciences* (London: Tavistock, 1970), xvi.

list evokes, and argues that it is the lack of a common ground that causes our uneasiness. The individual entries are linked by the order of the alphabet, but there is no

> site on which their propinquity would be possible. . . .—where could they ever meet, except in the immaterial sound of the voice pronouncing their enumeration, or on the page transcribing it? Where else could they be juxtaposed except in the non-place of language? Yet, though language can spread them before us, it can do so only in an unthinkable space.[25]

Turning Foucault's argument around and focusing on the productivity of the list form, we can highlight the capacity of lists to create spaces of and for thought. They depict and generate order(s), which are culturally embedded. The lists we encounter in medieval and early modern literature, especially in imaginative literature, can thus be seen as seismographs of cultural knowledge, but also as testing grounds for that which is otherwise unthinkable or ineffable or unfathomable, or too dangerous to express in a different form.

THE LIST AS *DENKFORM*

Borges's encyclopedic entry also highlights the political dimension of enumerative forms. As a classification, the content of the list appears to be authoritative. We accept its truth claims because the form—the neat arrangement of fourteen categories—propels us to do so. Discussing modern enumerative practices, sociologists have pointed out the potentially dangerous undercurrent of lists: often, the processes that precede the making of a list are not made transparent; the reasoning behind an item's inclusion or exclusion is not laid bare. Yet, the effect of truth and authority remains unaffected by the lack of transparency. As Urs Stäheli explains,

> list-making is not only a problem of selection, but it is necessarily a transformative and performative practice: it produces the items which the list will comprise. It is the epistemic power of these practices which I call the invisible politics of lists.[26]

Discussing lists as a means to express key tenets of Thing Theory, Object Oriented Ontology, and other new materialist theories, Katherine Little has argued

---

25. Foucault, *Order*, xvi–xvii.
26. Urs Stäheli, "Indexing—The Politics of Invisibility," *Environment and Planning D: Society and Space* 34, no. 1 (2016): 14–29, here 14.

recently that it is "the inherent poetry of the list" which may at times work against the seeming transparency of the list form: "Grouping various things together can have an ideological function, mystifying the relationships between things; it can also generate suspicion, demystifying the same relationships."[27] Stäheli and Little's work draws attention to the charged relationship between an enumerative or list-like passage, its function, and the processes of sense-making on the part of the reader or listener. In order to grasp these processes adequately, we regard the list (understood in a broad sense) first and foremost as a form or way of thinking, a *Denkform*. It functions as a shorthand for different kinds of enumerative ordering principles, and provides a dynamic entryway into coming to terms with the purposes and effects of such systems of order. Put differently, how do medieval and early modern people think with and through lists? How do their lists reveal the limits of thought?

Our approach to the list is indebted to recent discussions on formal approaches to literary (and also social) forms, in particular that of Caroline Levine. According to Levine, the flexible and portable nature of form can be captured by the notion of 'affordance,' a term that derives from gestalt theory and draws attention to the cognitive basis of formal elements.[28] A list, then, may be understood as a form of thought, as a cognitive structure that plays out differently in different contexts. Levine suggests asking, 'What is a form capable of doing?'[29] Against this backdrop, the essays in this volume offer answers to the question, 'What are lists capable of doing in medieval and early modern literature?'

PARAMETERS FOR THEORIZING LISTS

In the ten contributions,[30] which focus on texts from the early English period to the aftermath of the Reformation, different kinds of lists take center stage, such as the catalogue, enumeration, various phenomena of *copia,* accumulation, proliferation, *distinctiones,* genealogies, and household vocabulary. The breadth of enumerative practices attests to the flexibility of the form, as well

---

27. Katherine C. Little, "The Politics of Lists," *Exemplaria* 31, no. 2 (2019): 117–28, here 118; 119.

28. Caroline Levine, *Forms: Whole, Rhythm, Hierarchy, Network* (Princeton: Princeton University Press, 2015), 6–11. See also Eva von Contzen, "Die Affordanzen der Liste," *Zeitschrift für Literaturwissenschaft und Linguistik* 3 (2017): 317–26.

29. Levine, *Forms,* 6.

30. The contributors come from the Anglo-American and German tradition of medieval and early modern studies respectively, reflecting the editors' backgrounds. The volume thus pays tribute to our scholarly exchange across the Atlantic.

as to its iterability. All of the practices and principles of order under discussion share the trait that they offer an abstract perspective on whatever they enumerate, and the individual items or entries are only loosely or not at all embedded syntactically. Sometimes, the syntactic links with the surrounding discourse also tend to be tenuous. Four parameters of analysis can be singled out that run like golden threads through the essays in the volume. These are in/completeness, dis/ordering knowledge, un/familiarity, and boredom/play. Each of these pairs is best understood not in strictly binary terms but as opening up a range of possibilities between two poles.

In/Completeness

Completeness—or the impossibility of achieving it—is the central concern in the material Kathryn Mogk Wagner looks at in her essay: how can one name or address God, whose absolute completeness makes all human words inadequate? The solution medieval authors found was addressing by approximation: lists of names that in their capaciousness could at least approximate the unfathomable divine completeness.

The Old English poem *Widsith*, as Andrew James Johnston argues, creates an effect of completeness, fullness, even timelessness through its long lists of places and people, even though these lists appear random and impossible at first sight.

In Ingo Berensmeyer's essay, the poetic tradition of the catalogue of trees becomes an issue of completeness: which trees are enumerated in a given catalogue, which are altered, which are referenced differently from Chaucer to Sidney and Spenser?

Wolfram Keller argues that chaos and effects of fullness and totality dominate in the many lists included in Chaucer's *House of Fame*. Gavin Douglas, by contrast, constructs his *Palice of Honour* around enumerative principles of harmony, restoration, and balance, even though he ultimately fails in managing his literary 'household.'

In the Middle English theological treatise *Benjamin Minor*, the closed framework of a genealogy is exploited to maximize affective piety, as Suzanne Akbari shows in her contribution: through a diagrammatic structure of the family tree of Jacob, the text combines a linear with a cyclical approach to lineage and ultimately to practicing one's faith.

A similar closed system that nevertheless becomes remarkably flexible is the tradition of the four rivers of Eden: starting from the four rivers, as Martha Rust demonstrates, we can follow their interpretive expansion across a wide range of exegetical and allegorical contexts. While the number four remains consistent, the associations and interpretations bring forth a variety of new sets of four.

Questions of completeness or incompleteness are frequently raised in contexts of epic catalogues of warriors. Eva von Contzen asks in her essay, 'Who should be listed, and in which order?' Poets and scribes in the medieval Troy tradition comment on their decision to complete or break off the enumeration of names, thus drawing attention to the catalogue form itself.

The Old English *Gerefa*, a text about managing land as a reeve, is of encyclopedic scope. Yet the author, as Alexis Becker illustrates, questions the completeness of the work so that there is an imbalance of knowledge between the reeve mentioned in the text and the author who describes his tasks.

James Simpson discusses open-ended lists which form part of a sentence and may be potentially infinite—and which fulfill crucial functions in the context of 'cultural road cleaning' during and after the Reformation.

Erasmus's *De Copia*, as Alex Davis demonstrates in his contribution, is characterized by a strife for open-ended variation. The sheer endless possibilities, however, are threatened by their conceptual Other, the heap or pile, which are no longer ordered and therefore sensible in any way. Here, the category of in/completeness is intimately linked with that of dis/ordering knowledge.

Dis/Ordering Knowledge

In *Widsith*, knowledge about the world appears to be arranged epistemologically arbitrarily, unless one approaches the seeming disorder of the lists in terms of an alternative temporality: the flattening of time and history becomes a strategic act of poetic appropriation (Johnston).

The attempts at approximating God's name by means of reordering and reassembling names can bring forth liturgical sequences in which names and typologies are deliberately broken up and disordered to heighten the effect of sacrality and performativity (Wagner).

In the *House of Fame,* Chaucer's lists gesture towards processes of *oikonomia* and good household management; they are a means for organizing knowledge and, especially, memory (Keller).

The poet of *Gerefa* puts his own knowledge behind that of the reeve whose tasks he is describing, thus complicating notions of labor and knowledge. This becomes especially pertinent in two lists of vocabulary (Becker).

In the early modern period, Erasmus's *De Copia* was commonly used in the schoolroom as a means of teaching rhetoric; the lists were useful as didactic devices to teach the practical knowledge of linguistic variation (Davis).

James Simpson's essay demonstrates how attacks from both Protestants and Catholics to offend and criticize one another often take the form of the list—and these lists highlight the downside of every collection: what one side may deem precious, the opposing side may deem junk.

Even in the highly conventionalized tradition of the tree catalogue, the symbolic meaning of the trees is aligned with traditions of the actual and ecological significance of trees, which are inscribed into the catalogues (Berensmeyer).

In Philo's *Allegorical Interpretations of Genesis 2*, the four rivers of Eden are reinterpreted and realigned with different allegorical meanings that lead to new functions; the effect is one of a mental 'flow' chart that is based on the associative power of interpretation in enumerative sequences (Rust).

Thomas Cromwell relied fundamentally on administrative lists in order to reorganize and reshape the nation in the aftermath of the English Reformation, which highlights the transformative power of the list form (Davis).

Un/Familiarity

In *Widsith*, many familiar places and people are mentioned, yet their idiosyncratic arrangement renders them strange and unfamiliar (Johnston).

The tradition of enumerating the four rivers of Eden functions as a familiar heuristic device, which by association and allegorical extension acquires new meanings in contexts of affective piety (Rust).

In the transmission history of the names of God medieval authors enumerated to approximate God's true name, the names can move from the known and familiar to the utterly strange and arcane; rather than identifiable names or concepts, performative aspects can take precedence (Wagner).

The epic catalogues included in Middle English narratives about the Trojan War become sites for expressing skepticism about the genre of epic and poetic tradition, which demonstrates the poets' awareness of the metareflexive potential of the catalogue form (von Contzen).

In the early modern period, poets fundamentally relied on their audiences recognizing the familiar tradition of the catalogue of trees, which required them to identify both the intertextual reference and the changes made to the ancient or medieval sources used (Berensmeyer).

Similar patterns of recognition also underlie the reception of Douglas's *Palice of Honour* and his intertextual references to the *House of Fame*. Seeing the known and familiar in that which is strangely unfamiliar becomes particularly visible in Douglas's use of lists (Keller).

The odd intersection of different kinds of labor and struggles of authority in *Gerefa* renders the activities of a reeve strange and opens up a poetic dimension of interpretation (Becker).

The Middle English *Benjamin Minor* presents an unusual because positive reading of Dyna in the genealogy of Jacob's children. The list form subtly rearranges familiar patterns of knowledge (Akbari).

By means of apposition (making items equal), lists in the context of the Reformation render that which they enumerate meaningless. The result can be an alienation effect that ascribes new meanings to old concepts and contexts (Simpson).

Boredom/Play

Some Middle English narratives of the Trojan War bear witness to the boredom and tediousness which the form of the epic catalogue may elicit: scribes refrain from reproducing or translating the many names of the Catalogue of Ships, for instance, and replace it with a brief reference to the catalogue in the sources (von Contzen).

The many and varied lists in Chaucer's *House of Fame* demonstrate the entropic character of enumerations and highlight the playful dimension of the list form (Keller).

A playful dimension is discernible also in hymns, sequences, and litanies that enumerate God's names in a performative way, that is, for sound effects rather than meaning (Wagner).

The tree catalogues in Sidney's *Old Arcadia* and Spenser's *Faerie Queene* fulfill overt metareferential and metapoetic functions. The audience is invited to read the catalogues differently (through recognition) from the rest of the narratives, the effect of which, however, may also be one of boredom (Berensmeyer).

In humanist circles, the excessive enumerations in texts such as *De Copia* were held in high esteem as the creative, imaginative dimension of the form was much appreciated (Davis).

In the anonymous text *The Ymage of Ipocrisy*, the production of verbal and syntactic junk in the form of lists is carried to the extreme, the effect of which is both playful and hugely polemic (Simpson), quite similar to John

Bale's exhaustive use of the list form in his satiric attacks against the Catholic Church and its traditions (Simpson; Davis).

Our choice of essays lays open the richness and the potential of enumerative practices and principles of order at the intersection of practical list-making and lists as a poetic means. Lists are not only a tool for managing, ordering, and accumulating knowledge; they also become generators of poetic meaning when put in the hands of poets who exploit (whether successfully or not) the capacity of lists to be all and nothing. As a *Denkform,* the various kinds of the list offer insights into how to make sense of the world through enumerations in medieval and early modern texts. Ultimately, lists both promise satisfying completeness and order and threaten the reverse. Literary discourse is always centrally concerned with wholeness, or the lack thereof, but literary criticism tends especially to focus on the ways in which completeness is achieved through specific rhetorical means, notably synecdoche, a part for the whole, and formal verbal patterning that evokes completion (e.g., the stanza, or 'room'). In this volume we look instead at the undervalued, often unnoticed, even dismissed dimensions of the list. We look at the ways in which the list as a cognitive form might promise satisfying completeness, might shed light on practices of knowledge and principles of order, might enlist our sympathies or thwart them, and might also be used to underline the entropic impossibility of satisfying wholeness.

CHAPTER 1

"He should not overlook anything that could ever be of significance"
Knowledge and Vocabulary in Gerefa

ALEXIS KELLNER BECKER

At the end of an Old English manuscript that comprises mostly law-codes, a self-conscious author lists the things the reeve of an estate needs to have and to know, while insisting that he, the author, does not and cannot fully know these things. *Gerefa*, the Old English guide for the reeve of an estate,[1] also referred to after its first line, *Be gesweadan gerefan* (*Concerning the wise reeve*), is the only extant Old English text of its kind.[2] There is only one manuscript witness for *Gerefa*, Cambridge, Corpus Christi College, MS 383 (c. 1100).[3] It is included as part of the only English version of *Rectitudines singularum personarum* (*RSP*), a text on the rights and duties of various estate personnel, excluding the reeve (*RSP* ff. 63v–66v; *Gerefa* ff. 66v–69r). Particularly remarkable is *Gerefa*'s use of lexical lists, which emphasize

---

1. See Rosamond Faith, *The Moral Economy of the Countryside: Anglo-Saxon to Anglo-Norman England* (Cambridge: Cambridge University Press, 2020), esp. 24; 40; 82, for various meanings of *gerefa*.

2. Thomas Gobbitt, introduction to *RSP/Gerefa*, http://www.earlyenglishlaws.ac.uk/laws/texts/rspger. Gobbitt's Early English Laws online edition of *RSP* and *Gerefa* is excellent and includes a manuscript facsimile, transcription, translation, and commentary; all quotations from the text, and translations except for where otherwise noted, are Thom Gobbitt's. I also thank Thom for his generous help with this project.

3. See the manuscript description in Orietta Da Rold, Takako Kato, Mary Swan, and Elaine Treharne, *The Production and Use of English Manuscripts 1060 to 1220* (https://www.le.ac.uk/english/em1060to1220/mss/EM.CCCC.383.htm) and its full digitization in Parker Library on the Web, https://parker.stanford.edu/parker/catalog/mv340ty8592.

the linguistic knowledge inherent in the reeve's duties. The *Gerefa*-author uses the compilation of an always-incomplete reevish vocabulary to identify the tensions and conjunctions between authorial and managerial labor.

Gerefa may be based on a classical model, although it has no completely clear classical antecedent.[4] Yet its intense focus on Old English vocabulary suggests that it was inspired by, rather than translated from, any earlier sources. As Thomas Gobbitt puts it, *Gerefa* "is primarily a literary rather than a practical piece based on a possibly classical model and with emphasis given to alliterative and rhythmical form and philosophical musings. As such, *Gerefa* contrasts with the technical tone and close administrative focus of *RSP*."[5] Called a "literary exercise" by both P. D. A. Harvey and Christopher Dyer, there is no other extant text in quite the same genre as *Gerefa* until the emergence of Latin and Anglo-Norman estate management treatises in the mid-thirteenth century.[6] In Dyer's words, "The treatise resembles a literary exercise rather than a practical handbook, the list of implements being designed to show off the author's encyclopaedic knowledge and wide vocabulary."[7] At the same time as *Gerefa* does, indeed, "show off" the author's "encyclopaedic knowledge and wide vocabulary," it repeatedly gestures toward the reeve's greater knowledge and wider vocabulary.

In the thirteenth and particularly in the fourteenth century, peasant-born reeves' access to literacy and literate forms made them liminal figures with divided loyalties in that century's conflicts between lords and laborers.[8] The eleventh century's different social and economic structures, as well as the lack of clear evidence concerning the literacy of the *gerefa*, make it difficult to establish whether any similar dynamics may have been at work for *Gerefa's* wise reeve. The *Gerefa*-author's references to the gaps in his own knowledge, and therefore the incompleteness of his text, open up a fissure between the forms of knowledge such a text, or any text, can capture, and the forms of

---

4. P. D. A. Harvey suggests Columella's *Rei rusticae libri* and Cato's *De agri cultura* as likely partial sources. Harvey, "*Rectitudines Singularum Personarum* and *Gerefa*," *The English Historical Review* 108, no. 426 (1993): 1–22, here 9–12.

5. Gobbitt, *Rectitudines*.

6. Harvey, "*Rectitudines*," 9. For thirteenth-century estate management treatises, see Dorothea Oschinsky, *Walter of Henley and Other Treatises on Estate Management and Accounting* (Oxford: Clarendon Press, 1971).

7. Christopher Dyer, *Making a Living in the Middle Ages: The People of Britain, 850–1520* (New Haven: Yale University Press, 2002), 34–5.

8. See, for example, M. B. Parkes, "The Literacy of the Laity," in *The Medieval World*, ed. David Daiches and Anthony Thorlby (London: Aldus Books, 1973), 555–77; Miriam Müller, "The Aims and Organizations of a Peasant Revolt in Early Fourteenth-Century Wiltshire," *Rural History* 14, no. 1 (2003): 1–20.

knowledge a reeve both has and embodies. *Gerefa*'s lexical lists of tools and other objects demonstrate the limits of authorial knowledge.

THE MANUSCRIPT

Gerefa is a pre-Conquest text, imagining and preserving a pre-feudal reeve, redacted into and preserved in a post-Conquest legal manuscript.[9] While *RSP* is a much more straight-forwardly administrative text than *Gerefa*, the compilator/scribe of CCCC 383 clearly meant to present *Gerefa* as part of the same text as *RSP*. Thom Gobbitt has shown how, in CCCC 383, *RSP* and *Gerefa* were stylistically assimilated with each other in phrasing and tone, forming what he calls a "redacted collection."[10] Directly following the final part of *RSP*, the heading of *Gerefa* imitates the form of sections that describe the perquisites owed to the estate's workers: "Be sceadwisan gerefan" (cf., for example, "Be oxan hyrde"). In addition, there are repeated phrases throughout the two texts. Although *Gerefa* fills an obvious gap in *RSP*, scholars agree that it is a differently authored text written for a different purpose, used later to fill the gap in *RSP*.[11] Harvey has suggested that reeves were the intended audience of *RSP*, hence the reeve's exclusion; its eleventh-century redactor "saw that by supplying this omission it could be turned into a little treatise on rural society in general."[12] *RSP* begins with a section on the "law of the thegn" followed by the duties of the tenant, the cottager, the peasant, the beekeeper, the tenant, and the bound swineherd; the perquisites the estate owes its workers, including the swineherds; the provisions due to men and to women; the perquisites owed to the follower [of the plough], the sower, the oxherd, the cowherd, the shepherd, the goatherd, the cheese-wright, the barley-keeper, the beadle, and the forester. The text concludes with the author's reminder that practices and customs vary in different places. In its list of personnel, with their duties and perquisites, *RSP* does not mention the reeve or estate manager who, as *Gerefa* will make clear, is responsible for almost every aspect of the functioning of the estate. *RSP*'s Latin translation was included in five of the eleven extant copies of the collection of legal texts known as the *Quadripartitus*, the largest surviv-

---

9. See Rosamond Faith, *The Moral Economy of the Countryside: Anglo-Saxon to Anglo-Norman England* (Cambridge: Cambridge University Press, 2020), for a clear picture of how the early medieval English agrarian economy is non-feudal.
10. Gobbitt, *Rectitudines* (Introduction).
11. Harvey, "*Rectitudines*," 12.
12. P. D. A Harvey, "The Manorial Reeve in Twelfth-Century England," in *Lordship and Learning: Studies in Memory of Trevor Aston*, ed. Ralph Evans (Woodbridge: Boydell Press, 2004), 125–38, here 125.

ing collection of pre-Conquest law. None of these include *Gerefa*, of which no Latin translation exists.

Thomas Gobbitt has suggested that "the contents of CCCC 383 imply a MS intended for the use of a reeve (or perhaps the supervisor of a reeve) and embedded in a literate context."[13] The law-codes copied in the MS "supply the knowledge of the law that the competent reeve requires": the "land riht" and the "folces gerihtu" that *Gerefa* claims the reeve must know.[14] The inclusion of a charm against theft, among the law-codes, supports the idea of CCCC 383 as a manuscript for the practical use of a reeve.[15] In this interpretation, it is not only *Gerefa*'s insistent vernacularity that prevented its inclusion in the *Quadripartitus*; *Gerefa* was included in CCCC 383 to mark that manuscript's specific intended audience. In the context in which we now read it, its CCCC 383 redaction, *Gerefa* would be a text meant to be read by its own central character.

CCCC 383 may have been produced at St. Paul's Cathedral, London.[16] The other large post-Conquest manuscript that contains Old English legal texts is the *Textus Roffensis* (MS DRc/R1), the two parts of which were probably compiled at Rochester Cathedral in the first quarter of the twelfth century. The *Textus Roffensis* and CCCC 383 share a number of Old English materials, including a charm against cattle theft, but the *Textus Roffensis* does not include *RSP* or either of the texts with which *RSP* appears in the British Library, Royal MS 11 B. II manuscript of the *Quadripartitus*, *II Æðelræd*, and *Dunsæte*. Like CCCC 383, part one of the *Textus Roffensis* ends with "a series of lists of West Saxon kings, popes, emperors, eastern patriarchs, English archbishops and bishops, elders, and archangels," although CCCC 383's West Saxon Genealogy is truncated.[17] Part two consists primarily of the cartulary for the Rochester

---

13. Thomas Gobbitt, "The Production and Use of MS Cambridge, Corpus Christi College 383 in the Late Eleventh and First Half of the Twelfth Centuries," Ph.D. diss., University of Leeds, 2010, 46.

14. Gobbitt, "Production," 45.

15. This charm, or ritual, was, however, included in several manuscripts of Old English legal texts. See Andrew Rabin, "Ritual Magic or Legal Performance? Reconsidering an Old English Charm Against Theft," in *English Law Before Magna Carta: Felix Lieberman and 'Die Gesetze der Angelsachsen,'* ed. Stefan Jurasinski, Lisi Oliver, and Andrew Rabin (Leiden: Brill, 2010), 177–95.

16. See Patrick Wormald, *The Making of English Law: King Alfred to the Twelfth Century* (Oxford: Blackwell, 1999), 233–4 and Kathryn Powell, "The 'Scipmen' Scribe and Cambridge, Corpus Christi College 383," *The Heroic Age* 14 (2010), https://www.heroicage.org/issues/14/powell.php.

17. Bruce O'Brien, "*Textus Roffensis*: An Introduction," in *Textus Roffensis: Law, Language, and Libraries in Early Medieval England*, ed. Bruce O'Brien and Barbara Bombi (Turnhout: Brepols, 2015), 2.

Cathedral priory, of which pre- and post-Conquest forged charters make up a part.[18] The creation of manuscripts like CCCC 383 and the *Textus Roffensis* suggests a strong post-Conquest interest in copying, recording, compiling, and, in some cases, generating pre-Conquest law and record.[19] Pollock and Maitland describe *RSP* as belonging to the class of documents "which are not known ever to have had any positive authority, but appear to have been put together with a view to practical use, or at least to preserve the memory of things which had been in practice, and which the writer hoped to see in practice again."[20]

In Latin translation in the *Quadripartitus* and in Old English in CCCC 383, *RSP* (and in the case of CCCC 383, *Gerefa*) traveled with two other texts: *II Æðelræd* (994) and *Dunsæte* (c. 926–1000). *II Æðelræd* is a treaty between Æðelræd and Viking leaders after the battle of London in 994.[21] *Dunsæte* is a treaty on the terms for legal interactions between the English and the Welsh in a specific border area. All three texts, Stanley Lemanski argues, share a theme of intercultural contact and negotiation.[22] *RSP* was likely included in a post-Conquest legal manuscript like CCCC 383 in order to preserve, or at least teach a new audience about, the forms and customs of the early English

---

18. Simon Keynes, "King Æðelræd the Unready and the Church of Rochester," in *Textus Roffensis*, ed. O'Brien and Bombi, 315–62. At the end of the cartulary is a book-list of Rochester Cathedral's library. See Mary P. Richards, "The *Textus Roffensis*: Keystone of the Library at Rochester," in *Textus Roffensis*, ed. O'Brien and Bombi, 29–34.

19. See, for example, Mary Swan and Elaine Treharne, eds., *Rewriting Old English in the Twelfth Century* (Cambridge: Cambridge University Press, 2000), especially the introduction, 1–10 and Susan Irvine, "The Compilation and Use of Manuscripts Containing Old English in the Twelfth Century," 11–40; Mary Swan, "Imagining a Readership for Post-Conquest Old English Manuscripts," in *Imagining the Book*, ed. Stephen Kelly and John J. Thompson (Turnhout: Brepols, 2005), 145–57; Julia Crick, "Conquest and Manuscript Culture," in *Conquests in Eleventh Century England: 1016, 1066*, ed. Laura Ashe and Emily Joan Ward (Woodbridge: Boydell, 2020), 123–39; and Bruce O'Brien, "Pre-Conquest Laws and Legislators in the Twelfth Century," in *The Long Twelfth-Century View of the Anglo-Saxon Past*, ed. Martin Brett and David A. Woodman (Farnham: Ashgate, 2015), 229–74.

20. Frederick Pollock and Frederic William Maitland, *The History of English Law*, vol. 1 (Cambridge: Cambridge University Press, 1968), 27.

21. See Gobbitt, "Production" and "The Other Book: Cambridge, Corpus Christi College, MS 383 in Relation to the *Textus Roffensis*," in *Textus Roffensis*, ed. O'Brien and Bombi, 69–82, as well as Stanley Lemanski, "The *Rectitudines Singularum Personarum*: A Pre- and Post-Conquest Text," Ph.D. diss., University of Akron, 2009, for more on the contents of CCCC 383.

22. Lemanski describes this theme as "the coexistence of legal traditions of different ethnic groups and the provision of mechanisms that allow them to interact when necessary, whether it be Anglo-Saxon vis-à-vis Welsh, Anglo-Saxon vis-à-vis Danes, or (within its early post-Conquest context) Normans vis-à-vis Anglo-Saxons. The inclusion of the *Rect.* highlights the need that the pre-Conquest customs and arrangements of estates (now owned by Normans who barely understood these arrangements) should remain in place." See Lemanski, "*Rectitudines*," 224.

estate and its personnel. As Rosamond Faith says, *RSP* "seems to describe an idealized world which was thought to be in jeopardy."[23] Its place in its manuscripts reconciles historical customs with new forms.[24] In their Old English form in CCCC 383, *II Æðelræd*, *Dunsæte*, *RSP*, and *Gerefa* all address, in the vernacular, the difficulties inherent in communicating and interacting across often hostile cultural and linguistic boundaries—the former two explicitly, the latter two by their very presence in a post-Conquest manuscript.

Gerefa is the last text in CCCC 383 by the manuscript's main scribe. It is followed by two lists in a different hand.[25] A list with the heading "Scipmen" catalogues the estates of St. Paul's with their naval levies.[26] Following the *Scipmen* list is a truncated version of the West Saxon Genealogy of kings, saints, and bishops also found in the *Textus Roffensis*. These additions are slightly later than the other part of the manuscript, dating to the first half of the twelfth century. Gobbitt has suggested that these might represent the remnants or beginnings of an administrative expansion of CCCC 383.[27] *RSP* is the kind of administrative list that models administration, as opposed to texts like the polyptyques of the French monasteries, the memoranda from Ely Abbey, or the *Scipmen* list, which are the products or byproducts of administration.[28] *Gerefa* unmoors itself from the administrative function of the list; while the non-list parts of *Gerefa* make the reeve's job as a manager of people clear, its own lists focus on actions and lexemes, not people. If we read the final four texts of CCCC 383 in sequence, then, we see a miniature miscellany of work the list form can do: model administration; reflect on the differences between scribal/authorial and administrative labor; actually administrate; and proliferate narratives of power.

THE OBJECT-LISTS

I will focus on two occasions where the *Gerefa*-author explicitly draws our attention to his failure to know what the reeve knows. They both, in some capacity, serve to introduce the text's lists of objects, places where the practical/

---

23. Faith, *Moral Economy*, 54.
24. Lemanski, "*Rectitudines*," 224.
25. Gobbitt, "Production," 183–6. For evidence that these were intended to be additions to *this* MS, rather than an opportunistic use of parchment, 236–7.
26. See Powell, "The *Scipmen* Scribe."
27. Gobbitt, "The Other Book," 80.
28. For why there are no polyptyques from early medieval England, see Rosamond Faith, "Social Theory and Agrarian Practice in Early Medieval England: The Land Without Polyptyques," *Revue Belge de Philologie et d'Histoire* 90 (2012): 299–331.

material and imaginative/poetic coalesce. In *The Infinity of Lists,* Umberto Eco articulates the difference between two types of list-poetics: "etcetera" and "everything included."[29] An "everything included" list, like a shopping list, the list of attendees at an event, or a manorial account, is bounded by itself. It contains all of its potential items. The poetics of "etcetera," on the other hand, open up infinite possibilities of inclusion. These types of list-poetics are often in tension with each other in the list form. As James Simpson and Eva von Contzen write in their introduction to this volume, lists "both promise satisfying completeness and threaten the reverse."[30] In *Gerefa,* the claims of incompleteness—of the inadequacy of the *Gerefa*-author's, and possibly everyone but the reeve's, knowledge or memory—opens these lists up to the possibility of openness, of expansion, even while their specificity, length, and occasional repetition suggest finitude. The first of these lists comes at the end of the following calendar of the reeve's duties:

> On længene eregian . 7 impian . beana sawan . wingeard settan . dician . deorhege heawan . 7 raðe æfter ðam gif hit mot gewiderian . mederan settan . linsed sawan . wadsæd eac swa . wyrtun plantian . 7 fela ðinga . ic eal getellan ne mæig þæt god scirman bycgan sceal.

> During the spring to plough and busy oneself with sowing beans, setting the vineyard, making dikes, cutting the animal hedge, and soon after that if the weather may be fair to sow madder, sow linseed, sow woad and likewise to plant the garden and [do] many things. I cannot recount all that a good shireman must do. (27)

We cannot expect this calendar to be comprehensive, the author tells us. Indeed, as Debby Banham has pointed out, it even omits when farmers sow their seed.[31] This is because the author is not able (*ne mæig*) to *getellan* all (*eal*) that the *god scirman* must (*sceal*) *bycgan*.[32] Gobbitt translates *getellan* as recount, which captures some of the ambiguity inherent in the verb. The verb (*ge*)*tellan* certainly contains the present-day English translations of *tell* or *recount,* but also *enumerate, count, include,* or *give order to.* In the very word

---

29. Umberto Eco, *The Infinity of Lists* (New York: Rizzoli, 2009), 7.
30. See p. 13.
31. Debby Banham and Rosamond Faith, *Anglo-Saxon Farms and Farming* (Oxford: Oxford University Press, 2014), 57. For the *gerefa*'s calendar, see David Hill, "Eleventh Century Labours of the Months in Prose and Pictures," *Landscape History* 20, no. 1 (1998): 29–39.
32. The *scir* (shire) here refers to the territory of his administration. See Charles McLean Andrews, *The Old English Manor: A Study in English Economic History* (Baltimore: Johns Hopkins University Press, 1892), 55.

recount we can see that a present day English lexis, too, associates telling with counting. But the word leaves the sentence ambiguous: perhaps he cannot tell us all that a good shireman must do, perhaps he cannot remember it, or, perhaps, he cannot put all of the things in order. Initially, this gesture seems simply to underline the magnitude and variety of the *gerefa*'s tasks. But the author's use of the word *getellan* suggests his awareness of his own managerial inadequacy: if he does not have the language, he cannot create order.[33]

After a brief excursus on what the reeve must do in the town and indoors, he offers his first alliterative list of items that the reeve must procure and have: "He sceal fela tola to tune tilian . 7 fela and lomena to husan habban." (*He must procure many tools for the estate and have many utensils (/implements) for the house*) (27.2).

> Æsce . adsan . bil . byrse . scafan . sage . cimbiren . tigehoc . næfebor . mattuc . ippingiren . scear . culter . 7 eac gadiren . siðe . sicol . weodhoc . spade . scofle . wadspitel . bærwan . besman . bytel . race . geafle . hlædre . horscamb . 7 sceara . fyrtange . wæipundern . 7 fela towtola . flexlinan . spinle . reol . gearnwindan . stodlan . lorgas . presse . þihten . timplean . wifte . wefle . wulcamb . cip . amb . crænc stæf . sceaðele . seam sticcan . scearra . hædle . slic .

> axe . adze . pruning-hook . boring-tool . saw . joining-iron . dragging-hook . auger . mattock . crowbar . plowshare . coulter . and also a goad-iron . scythe . sickle . weed-hook . spade . shovel . woad-spade . hand-barrow . broom . mallet/hammer . rake . pitchfork . ladder . horse-comb . and scissors . firetongs . scale . and many textile-tools . flax-line . spindle . reel . yarn-winder . loom-uprights . heddle rods . cloth-press . comb-beater . temples . weft thread . warp thread . wool-comb . rod. beater . crank rod . sheath . seampicks . shears . needle . mallet/wooden hammer. (27.3)[34]

---

33. Gobbit translates *bycgan* as *do*. In all of its definitions and attestations in the *Dictionary of Old English*, this verb has to do with buying (obtaining/procuring) or selling. Liebermann translates it "besorgen" (get) but also suggests the possibility that *bycgan* might be a scribal error for *began*, which has, among its meanings, *undertake, till, cultivate, tend to, look after, care for, perform, do*. Felix Liebermann, ed., *Die Gesetze der Angelsachsen*, vol. 1 (Halle: M. Niemayer, 1903–16), 454.

34. The translations of the object-lists are mostly mine, with great help from Thom Gobbitt's edition and translation and R. G. Poole, "The Textile Inventory in the Old English *Gerefa*," *The Review of English Studies* 40, no. 160 (1989): 469–78. Translations for some of the items are only approximate. See also Swanton's translation of *RSP* and *Gerefa* as "Two Estate Memoranda" in *Anglo-Saxon Prose* (London: Dent, 1975), 21–7.

This list consists, primarily, of outdoor tools and textile tools. It begins with two alphabetical alliterative pairs before taking its reader through a selection of tools for carpentry, farming, housekeeping, husbandry, and textile working.

The author's other admission of ignorance, forgetting, or incompleteness comes directly before the text's other list of objects. This second list, which alliterates inconsistently, focuses primarily on cooking and food-storage. Its words, as far as their definitions can be known, vary in specificity, and sometimes multiple words seem to mean the same thing or almost the same thing. For example, this list contains a large number of dishes and vessels, many of which could plausibly be translated simply as "vessel." From a vantage point of a millennium into the future, it is hard to know whether the exhaustiveness is the point, or if there are subtleties of definition and connotation that are now inaccessible.[35] My reading of the list suggests a combination of the two.

The earlier admission of ignorance, depending on how one interprets *bycgan*, either ends a description of actions or takes the place of a description of purchasing. This admission, on the other hand, is paraleptic: "Ælc weorc sylf wisað hwæt him to gebyreð . nis ænig man þæt atellan mæge ða tol eall ðe man habban sceal." (*He must know himself what each type of work entails. There is not any man who may recount all the tools a man must have*) (29.1). The author does list many of the materials and apparatus that the reeve must recount, first apologizing for the incompleteness of the list; then he goes forward with a list of almost comic specificity and what could be mistaken for comprehensiveness.

> Man sceal habban wænge wædu. Sulhgesidu . Egeðgetigu . 7 fela ðinga . ðe ic nu genæmnian ne can ge eac mete . awel . to odene fligel . and lamena fela . Hwer . lead . cytle . hlædel . pannan . Crocca . brandiren . dixas stelmelas . cyfa . cyflas . cyrne . cysfæt . ceodan . wilian . windlas . Syftras . syfa . Sædleap . hriddel . hersyfe . Tæ mespilan . fanna . trogas . æscena . Hyfa hunigbinna . beorbydene . bæðfæt . beodas . butas . bleda . melas . cuppan . seohhan . candelstafas . Sealtfæt . Sticfodder . Piperhorn . Cyste . mydercan . bearmteage . hlydan . Sceamelas . Stolas . læflas . leohtfæt . blacern . cyllan . Sapbox. Camb . yrsebinne . fodderhec . Fyregebeorh . meluhudern . ælhyde . ofn race . mexscofle .
>
> One must have a wagon-cover . the appurtenances of a plough . apparatus for harrowing . and many things . which I cannot name now, nor can I mea-

---

35. See Christine Fell, "Some Domestic Problems," *Leeds Studies in English* 16 (1985): 59–82, for an attempt to reconcile the omissions and apparent repetitions.

sure them : awl . and a flail for the threshing floor . and many clay loomweights . pot . cauldron . kettle . ladle . pans . crockery . iron for cooking pots above a fire . dishes with handles . tub . buckets . churn . cheese vat . bag . rolled basket . basket . sieves . sieve . seed basket . coarse sieve . hair sieve . sieve-stake . winnowing fan . ash-wood bucket . bee-hive . honey-bin . beer-vessel . bathtub . dishes . earthenware vessels . goblets . bowls, cups . sieve . candlesticks . salt cellar . spoon case[36] . pepper horn . chest . money chest . yeast-box . seats . benches . stools . bowls . lantern . lamp . leather bag[37] . box for resin . comb . iron-box . manger . fire-protector . meal-storehouse . eel-box[38] . oven fork . dung shovel. (29.2)

The author is confident about his memory for most general terminology for the agricultural equipment that "man sceal habban": wagon-cover, plow-appurtenances, barrow-apparatus. Then, he says, one must have "fela ðinga ðe ic nu genæmnian ne can ge eac mete": *many things that I cannot name now nor measure.* He then lists a number of items, which are either (some of) the items that fall under the heading "many things I cannot name or measure now" or a surplus set of items, beyond that category.

Both lists invite the reader into the project of developing an organizational schema for their contents. The reeve is responsible for several kinds of management: of words, of the objects they signify and their appropriate uses and locations, and of the people associated with them. Christine Fell argues that the objects are organized by type/function; in her analysis of part of the list, she sees the items categorized into sections of cooking equipment, storage, dairy equipment, herb and garden harvesting equipment, honey and fermentation, tableware, and storage containers.[39] Mark Gardiner has suggested that the organization of items in this list ("List B") is dependent on the organization of the seigneurial farmstead. Roughly, the groups of words are objects we would find in, respectively, the kitchen, the dairy, the granary, the buttery, the pantry or spence, and the bakehouse and brewhouse.[40]

Fell and Gardiner's readings of these lists are, in many ways, supported by the *Gerefa*-author's admonition that if the reeve is *too proud or neglects things*

---

36. Other possibilities include a case for pegs, a case for sticks, or a case made out of twigs.
37. Or wineskin.
38. Other possibilities include eel-skin, fire-cover, awl-hide. See my discussion of *ælhyde* on p. 27, this volume.
39. Fell, "Some Domestic Problems," 77–8.
40. Mark Gardiner, "Implements and Utensils in *Gerefa* and the Organization of Seigneurial Farmsteads in the High Middle Ages," *Medieval Archaeology* 50 (2005): 260–7, here 266–7; 264–5.

which are to be done and attended to, that which belongs in the cattle-shed or to the threshing floor will soon turn up in the barn:

> Forðam to soðe to secge . oferho|gie he . oððe forgyme ða ðing tobeganne 7 to bewitanne ðe to scipene oððe to odene be limpað . sona hit wyrð on ber|ne þæt to ðam belimpað. (22.4)

This vision of hypothetical disorder revolves around objects being in the wrong places: something that belongs in the *scipen* (cattle-shed), like the *scofel* (shovel) from list A, or something that belongs to the *oden* (threshing floor), like the *fligel* (flail) from list B, turning up in the *bern* (barn). The reeve's humility and attention keep words in their lists and objects in their right places. *Bern* is the shortened form of *bere-ern*, literally a "barley-building," used to refer to any grain-storage building in the Old English period.[41] While this passage suggests that the three places mentioned are three distinct buildings, indoor threshing floors were often in barns. And while the Old English word *bere-ern* or *bern* was not, to my knowledge, used to refer to cattle-sheds or other habitations for animals, the Middle English *bern* would be by the thirteenth century.[42] If it were already making that move in spoken English at the time of *Gerefa*'s composition, the *Gerefa*-author might be pointing toward the confusion that can arise when knowledge of words is not supported by experiential and material knowledge, as well as an ability to make subtle distinctions between both words and places.[43]

In order to prevent the wrong things turning up in the barn, the reeve must "*take care of both the better and of the worse so that nothing go wrong if he may prevent it: not corn nor sheaf, nor flesh nor morsel of fat, nor cheese nor rennet, nor any of those things which may ever be of note*" (22.5). *Any of those things which may ever be of note*: "ne nan ðera ðinga ðe æfra to note mæge." The small things the *Gerefa* chooses as examples of things that may ever be of note alliterate: "necorn . nesceaf . ne flæsc . ne slot smeru . ne cyse . ne cysclyb." Alliteration in Old English prose is common; Wulfstan, with

---

41. Banham and Faith, *Anglo-Saxon Farms and Farming*, 27. The word *bern* translates *horreum* in Ælfric's *Glossary*.

42. See *MED*, entry "*bern*, n.(2)."

43. Although this passage strongly suggests that cattle accommodation, threshing, and grain storage took place in different buildings, the archaeological record is inconclusive; buildings of wood are transient, and there is a notable shortage of grain storage buildings in the record. See Helena Hamerow, *Rural Settlements and Society in Anglo-Saxon England* (Oxford: Oxford University Press, 2012), 50–2, and Nicholas Howe, *Writing the Map of Anglo-Saxon England: Studies in Cultural Geography* (New Haven: Yale University Press, 2008), 48–56.

whom the authorship of *Gerefa* has been associated, was a prodigious author of alliterative prose, and much other Old English prose participated in sonic patterning, usually in less regular forms than, but on the model of, Old English poetry.[44] The lists in *Gerefa* are marked particularly by their vernacularity and by their participation in alliterative style; *Gerefa*'s "formidable lists of implements,"[45] so necessary to the management of the land, insist upon their local language. While the person-catalogue of the *RSP* was easily Latinized, *Gerefa*'s lists are insistent in their vernacularity for reasons both poetic and practical. They alliterate: "critics have pointed to the use of alliteration, rhyme and of two-stress phrase, arguing that the author was striving at least as much for literary effect as practical instruction. It seems that *Gerefa* is more the product of the scriptorium than of the farmyard."[46] The items' Latin translations would not alliterate. At the same time, the specificity of some of the items—and the author's claim of his own ignorance—conveys a familiarity on the part of the reeve (or the ideal reeve) that is both intimate and learned. Management is a special kind of practical knowledge of objects and words. In this case, this specialized knowledge is peculiarly vernacular. The *Gerefa*-author organizes the reeve's estate knowledge according to poetic principles. The reeve is responsible for the management of an estate, its spaces and people as well as its language.

As Harvey has pointed out, these alliterative lists of objects are good evidence for original vernacular composition of at least these parts of *Gerefa*.[47] *Gerefa*, as far as we know, was never translated into Latin, and it is not included in the *Quadripartitus*. Harvey reasons that

> the author of the *Quadripartitus* may have felt that when the text passed from enumerating rights and obligations to describing the reeve's agricultural management it no longer fell within the scope of a collection of legal

---

44. Janet Bately, "The Nature of Old English Prose," in *The Cambridge Companion to Old English Literature*, ed. Malcom Godden (Cambridge: Cambridge University Press, 1991), 71–87, here 83. Dorothy Bethurum has argued that *Gerefa* was, in fact, written by Wulfstan (*The Homilies of Wulfstan* [Oxford: Clarendon Press, 1957]), and her argument has been taken up by a number of scholars, including P. D. A. Harvey. Among recent scholars, Rosamond Faith has picked up on Wulfstan or Wulfstan-adjacent authorship (*Moral Economy*), while Andrew Rabin argues against it (*The Political Writings of Archbishop Wulfstan of York* [Manchester: Manchester University Press, 2015]). *Gerefa*'s use of two-stress units is, in fact, one of the reasons this text has been connected to Wulfstan. While authorship by Wulfstan or a member of his circle is compelling, I remain unconvinced by the evidence. See also Wormald, *The Making of English Law*, 388–9.

45. Harvey, "Rectitudines," 4.
46. Gardiner, "Implements," 260.
47. Harvey, "Rectitudines," 11–12.

texts, or he may, reasonably enough, have been daunted by the thought of putting into Latin its formidable lists of implements.[48]

The reeve knows these things, these items, these words, in English. He does not need this knowledge in Latin. The sound and the content of the lists both draw attention to their untranslatability. CCCC 383's *RSP/Gerefa* redaction moves from a linguistically translatable, if culturally and historically specific, catalogue of duties, rights, and perquisites, to a text that revels in its own untranslatability. Not only do its words never make their way into Latin— some of them, the *Gerefa*-author tells us, never even make their way from the reeve's field of knowledge into the author's own.

The third to last item, *ælhyde*, one of several hapax legomena in the lists, is translated by Gobbitt as "eel-box(?)" and by Liebermann, likewise, as "aalbehalter(?)." Meritt suggests that it is actually two words, an awl and a hide.[49] The *DOE* calls it "an obscure compound, or perhaps to be taken as two words." Among the possibilities they suggest: an *eel-skin*, perhaps used to link two parts of a flail; *eel receptacle*; *fire cover*; or, as Meritt has proposed, two separate words, *awl* and *hide*, the hide belonging to the trade of a shoemaker.[50] Throughout the Middle Ages, and especially in the tenth and eleventh centuries, people across the island paid rent in eels.[51] The farming memoranda of Ely Abbey, the only extant Old English vernacular farm accounts, include the rental of a fen for 26,275 eels.[52] Located where it is in the *Gerefa* list, between the meal storage house and the oven-rake (a fork or a rake for stirring the fire in a furnace for cooking), the *ælhyd*, if an eel box or receptacle, likely held the estate's store of dried eels, for consumption and other purposes. If it were a fenland estate, the eel-box could have held fresh eels as well. Was there, in the early medieval household, a special box for eels and only eels? While *arca anguillarum* even alliterates, it is not found, to my knowledge, in any extant early medieval Latin texts.[53] The presence of such an ambiguous hapax lego-

---

48. Harvey, "*Rectitudines*," 4.

49. Herbert Dean Meritt, "Conceivable Clues to Twelve Old English Words," in *Anglo-Saxon England*, vol. 1 (Cambridge: Cambridge University Press, 1972), 193–205, here 194.

50. See Angus Cameron et al., eds., *The Dictionary of Old English: A to I* (Toronto: Dictionary of Old English Project, 2018), https://tapor.library.utoronto.ca/doe/.

51. See John Wyatt Greenlee's *Eel-Rents Project*, http://historiacartarum.org/eel-rents-project/.

52. See R. G. R. Naismith, "The Ely Memoranda and the Economy of the Late Anglo-Saxon Fenland," *Anglo-Saxon England* 45 (2017): 333–77. See also Banham and Faith, *Anglo-Saxon Farms and Farming*, 8–9, and M. T. Clanchy, *From Memory to Written Record: England 1066–1307* (Chichester, West Sussex: Wiley-Blackwell, 2013), 32.

53. A Google search for "*arca anguillarum*" finds one (translated as "eel ark") in *The Register of the Great Seal of Scotland, 1306–1424*.

menon aligns the reader more closely with the author and his clerical peers, with their simultaneous scribal surplus and managerial lack of knowledge, than with the reeve.

Many plausible readings of the lists require that items that appear not to belong are reinterpreted until they do. R. I. Page, for example, reads *ælhyd* as "fire-cover" and *mexscofel* as "ember-shovel" because he reads the last five items of the list as having to do with fire and cooking.[54] The lists, it seems, invite projects of cognitive organization, rather than arriving with predetermined shapes. This may be their point: the "wise reeve" would be able to discern the lists' organization or lack thereof, as well as supply any missing words; any other reader is left guessing.

Much of the scholarship on these lists focuses on either fixing or exploring the definitions of the words the *Gerefa*-author uses.[55] The lists, however, are ambivalent about their own direct practicality. Both of the lists, as I mentioned before, are preceded by a claim, by the *Gerefa*-author, of ignorance or incomplete knowledge. Through this insistence, he is not only emphasizing his own ignorance and/or forgetfulness in comparison with that of the reeve; he is also insisting that he is not naturalized into the reeve's particular body of knowledge and its attendant language, even as he offers that body of knowledge, and its language, up for the reader.

Maitland imagined the *Gerefa*-author as a church reeve, who "might even write a tract on the management of manors."[56] Yet the author's insistence on the difference between the parameters of his knowledge and the reeve's shows the *Gerefa*-author explicitly presenting himself as neither the absolute authority on reeves' labor nor a reeve himself, recording the contours of his duties for posterity. To whatever extent it may have been intended to serve as a partial practical guide for real reeves and/or served as a nostalgic reminder of the duties of a prior age of manorial administration, the text uses lexical lists to explore the differences and the overlap between the labor of the writer and the labor of the reeve. If, as Thomas Gobbitt has argued, CCCC 383 is a compilation intended for the use of a reeve, *Gerefa*'s inclusion might be less about instructing the reeve about his duties and more about helping him imagine his own relationship to language and to written texts.

---

54. Rosamond Faith has shown the enormous symbolic and practical importance of the hearth to the early medieval English household, and, furthermore, the presence of an additional oven aside from the hearth, just for cooking, was a sign of prestige. Faith, *Moral Economy*, 58–69.

55. See, for example, the essays by Fell, Meritt, Gardiner, Page, and Poole.

56. Frederic William Maitland, *Domesday Book and Beyond: Three Essays in the Early History of England* (Cambridge: Cambridge University Press, 1921), 392.

OTHER LISTS

These vocabulary lists—in particular List A, with its alphabetical beginning—may have been, in Gardiner's words, "a play upon the idea" of glossaries.[57] Fell points out *Gerefa*'s semantic overlap with Latin lexical texts; book 20 of Isidore of Seville's *Etymologies*, for example, included whole lists of receptacles.[58] *Gerefa*'s rough contemporary Ælfric of Eynsham's Latin and Old English glossary organized its words by category. Within these categories, words often alliterated. Ælfric's *Glossary* also uses the same conventions of punctuations as the lists in *Gerefa* do, with a *punctus circumflexus* between each item. The *Glossary* concludes, "We ne magan swa þeah . ealle naman gewritan . ne forþon geþencan."[59] (*However we cannot write down all of the words, nor even think of them.*) This is a gesture much like the *Gerefa*-author's gestures of ignorance. But unlike in *Gerefa,* the lexical field here is *all of the words,* not just the *gerefa*'s.

In one manuscript, Ælfric's *Glossary* traveled with his *Grammar* and his *Colloquy*. The *Colloquy*, like *Gerefa,* is interested in the relationship between lexical knowledge and managerial power. It is meant for use in the monastic classroom, to teach the monastery's new oblates how to speak—and how to be—in Latin. Like *RSP,* it lists the personae one might find on an estate; unlike *RSP,* it describes them in their "own" voices. The *Colloquy* imagines plowmen, oxherds, bakers, and other laborers conversing fluently in Latin; this fiction of elite language's practical use inducted a text's readers or users or actors into its linguistic world, with all of that world's social meanings. This dialogue, extant in three copies across four manuscripts, is written out in continuous Latin prose and glossed completely in Old English in one copy and partially in another copy. The Old English glosses share some of the *Gerefa*'s material vocabulary, such as a few of the parts of a plough.[60] As Lisa Cooper points out, the *Colloquy* links the arts of discourse inextricably "to labour and to the practical knowledge that makes that labour efficacious in the world."[61] In order to learn Latin, the students of the *Colloquy* perform the roles of lay laborers: plowmen, shepherds, oxherds, hunters, fishermen, fowlers, merchants, shoemakers, salt-workers, bakers.

---

57. Gardiner, "Implements," 263.
58. Fell, "Some Domestic Problems," 62–3.
59. Robert George Gillingham, "An Edition of Abbot Ælfric's Old-English Latin Glossary with Commentary," Ph.D. diss., The Ohio State University, 1981, 294.
60. Banham and Faith, *Anglo-Saxon Farms,* 48.
61. Lisa Cooper, "Poetics of Practicality," in *Middle English,* ed. Paul Strohm (Oxford: Oxford University Press, 2007), 491–506, here 491.

While *RSP* and the *Colloquy* are extremely different texts, it is striking that neither includes a reeve in its list of personae. Monks who served as wardens of monastic estates would likely have worked closely with reeves.[62] Although the fluent Latinity of all of the *Colloquy*'s laborers is, of course, a fiction, I wonder if Ælfric, like the translators and compilers of the *Quadripartitus*, also saw something untranslateable about the reeve's relationship to language. While Ælfric's *Colloquy* makes a certain kind of (Latin) knowledge of land-labor necessary for membership in a linguistically marked, sanctified otiose class, *Gerefa* uses an Old English lexicon of specific and discrete estate materials to differentiate its author (possibly a member of Ælfric's monastic class) from its reeve. The *Colloquy*'s oblate ventriloquizes the plowman in the Latin words a real plowman would not speak; the *Gerefa*-author lists the English words only a reeve can truly know.

The St. John's manuscript at Oxford, from around the beginning of the eleventh century, has the version of the *Colloquy* most heavily revised by Ælfric's student Ælfric Bata; this is the only manuscript in which the *Colloquy* traveled with the *Grammar* and the *Glossary*. The text of the original *Colloquy* in this MS includes multiple editorial additions, such as several additional kinds of prey for the hunter, including elephants, camels, lions, and snails. At the end of the hunter's list of animals, he adds, "aliaquae . . . quae enumerare non possum hac uice nec cogitare" (*and others which I can't enumerate or think of right now*).[63] In this case, Bata has made the failure of recollection and expression the failure of the practical knowledge-keeper, the (fictional) hunter (who is meant to be ventriloquized by a monastic oblate). But in both cases, the lists are made *etcetera*. *Enumerare* is the closest Latin equivalent of *getellan*, that which the *Gerefa*-author cannot do.

The *Colloquy* was composed for a class at an elementary stage of Latin. Monks were supposed to avoid the vernacular, so lists of words, with their English equivalents, were drawn up, and pupils committed them to memory. Ælfric's *Glossary* was an example of one of these word-lists, drawn up to form an appendix to his *Grammar*. The word-lists in *Gerefa* are a kind of inversion of this form. The reeve (the possible audience for the text) already knows the words in its word-lists, and they are very much vernacular words, some without, to my knowledge, Latin equivalents.

---

62. See Sherri Olson, *Daily Life in a Medieval Monastery* (Santa Barbara: Greenwood, 2013), 184–7.

63. See David Porter, trans., and Scott Gwara, ed., *Anglo-Saxon Conversations: The Colloquies of Ælfric Bata* (Suffolk: Boydell and Brewer, 1997), 58.

Ælfric's texts' practical, pedagogical use and monastic context are clear and clearly different from *Gerefa*'s, but the areas of overlap are striking.[64] Ælfric's *Glossary* concludes its long list of words with an admission of its own incompleteness: "However, we cannot write down all of the words, nor even think of them." This is Ælfric's gesture toward the expansive world of words; a glossary cannot be complete or comprehensive, nor can a glossarian's mind.[65] Ælfric Bata's hunter concludes his list of Latin words for animals with "others which I can't enumerate or think of right now." These gestures toward *etcetera* are different from *Gerefa*'s. In both cases, the word-knower and the word-sayer are identical: in Ælfric's case, the glossarian himself, and in Ælfric Bata's case, the fictional character of the hunter (whose part would be read by a monastic oblate learning these Latin words). In *Gerefa*, on the other hand, the author is working to approximate the reeve's knowledge, with the admission that such a thing is impossible. The speaker, the *Gerefa*-author, is the inadequate knowledge-haver; the subject of his text, the reeve, must have the knowledge the author does not.

KNOWLEDGES

The fissure between textual and practical knowledge becomes most evident in the item lists. Even to an audience used to alliterative prose, "lists that sound good can prevent apprehension of the singular object and even rob words of some or all of their meaning."[66] It is for the reeve to know and to have the objects in *Gerefa*'s lists; the author, or the non-reeve reader, only has access to an (incomplete) list of words. Redacted together and included in CCCC 383, *RSP* and *Gerefa* participate in the confrontation of cultures that Lemanski describes as happening in the manuscript context. But the confrontation in CCCC 383 is not only between English and Norman forms of legal custom and estate governance; it is also between the forms of knowledge that are authorial (that is, scribal and literate), and the forms that are concrete and embodied.

In this way, *Gerefa* contains an implicit critique of textual authority. Its author, its *auctor*, only has expertise as far as it can be known, remembered, and written by him. As such, the text can only offer this much knowledge. The reeve's knowledge is different; it is greater, and it cannot be precisely captured

---

64. Eco writes that "the voraciousness of the list often prompts us to interpret practical lists as if they were poetic lists—and in effect what often distinguishes a poetic list from a practical one is only the intention with which we contemplate it" (*The Infinity of Lists*, 171).
65. See Eco, *The Infinity of Lists*, 59, on ineffability topoi.
66. Katherine C. Little, "The Politics of Lists," *Exemplaria* 31, no. 2 (2019): 117–28, here 119.

by the text. The author can list the names of implements, but they are only ever words. This is made especially apparent when, in between lists A and B, the author says that the *gerefa* must supply tools to any skilled artisan he has, and that "he must know what each type of work entails, [as] there is not anyone who may recount all the tools one must have" (29.1).⁶⁷ The reeve knows (*witan*) while the *Gerefa*-author can only recount (*atellan*).

Although we cannot know what the unredacted version of *Gerefa* might have looked like, the effect of reading *RSP* and *Gerefa* in sequence, or as two parts of the same text, is almost kaleidoscopic. From a catalogue of people we are slowly ushered into catalogues of things, *things,* it is made very clear, that are also *words.* The *Gerefa*-author's claims of his own ignorance in the face of specialized vocabulary bring the relationship between language and management into clear and complicated focus. In addition, John Sabapathy has suggested that the *RSP* is written in the "voice" of a reeve or over-reeve (*ealdorman*).⁶⁸ This would explain the omission of the reeve from the *RSP*'s catalogue of offices; he is the one keeping track of all of the people. In this case, rather than filling in an omission in *RSP, Gerefa* could be seen as deepening, expanding, and meditating on how the functional operation of the estate depends upon linguistic categorization, precision, *and* expansiveness. If that is the case, *Gerefa* is a break with that voice, replacing the perspective of the reeve with that of the scribe-author.

Andrew Cole writes, about clerical forms of composition, that in "the processes that go into constructing (and reading) lists, accounts, registers, and so forth [. . .] items or entries accumulate in lists but lists of course never follow the unfolding logics of narrative or allegory; even so, we still do learn something about writing and recording—the memorial and accumulative practices of scribal culture."⁶⁹ The *Gerefa*-author, a scribal laborer, recognizes the overlap, one of cataloguing, between himself and his subject. In ancient South West Asia, lists seem to have been a central part of early scribal training.⁷⁰ This may have also been the case for early medieval English scribes. With his lists of items—perhaps marked by a *punctus circumflexus,* which "separates

---

67. I have changed Gobbitt's translation of *man* from "a man" to *one,* for the sake of clarity and to match *"man sceal habban,"* one must have, in the section immediately following.

68. John Sabapathy, *Officers and Accountability in Medieval England 1170–1300* (Oxford: Oxford University Press, 2014), 56.

69. Andrew Cole, "Scribal Hermeneutics and the Genres of Social Organization in *Piers Plowman,*" in *The Middle Ages at Work: Practicing Labor in Late Medieval England,* ed. Kellie Robertson and Michael Uebel (New York: Palgrave Macmillan, 2004), 179–206, here 186.

70. Jack Goody, *The Domestication of the Savage Mind* (Cambridge: Cambridge University Press, 1977), 93–8, and William W. Schniedewind, *The Finger of the Scribe: How Scribes Learned to Write the Bible* (Oxford: Oxford University Press, 2019).

smaller syntactic units," as they are in this manuscript[71]—the *Gerefa*-author draws attention to the overlap between scribal and managerial labor: both require lists. He is calling attention to the memorial and accumulative practices of the reeve—in particular, to the ways in which the reeve's memorial and accumulative practices, his professional lexis, are superior to and more specialized than the author's own.

The reeve's knowledge requires an attention to detail that sets him apart from the other estate personnel in *RSP* and both differentiates him from and draws him into kinship with the *Gerefa*-author.

> Hit is earfoðe eall to gesecganne þæt se beðencan sceal ðe scire healt . ne sceolde he nan ðing . Forgyman ðe æfre to note mehte . ne forða musfellan. ne þæt git læsse is to hæpsan pinn . fela sceal to holdan hames gerefan . 7 to gemetfæstan manna hyrde . ic gecende be ðam ðe ic cuðe . se ðe bet cunne gecyðe his mare

> It is difficult to say everything that one who runs a shire must keep in mind; [but] he should not overlook anything which might ever be of significance, not even a mouse trap even though it be as insignificant as a fastening peg. Many things are needed of a faithful reeve, and a responsible overseer of men. I have spoken about that which I know; he who knows better should make known more. (30–30.10)

Again, the wise reeve understands the "significance" of objects, objects that are only words in the text. This moment invites its reader to ask: what is the significance of a mouse trap? What is the significance of a "fastening peg"? (What, I find myself asking, is a fastening peg?) These items' significance is in the reeve's realm of knowledge. Indeed, his job is to know what might "ever be of significance" (or *ever of use*—"æfre to note"), and, therefore, to not overlook or forget it. His job is to manage both the material and the epistemological organization of the estate: what might matter? What needs to be kept in mind? "When made of language, lists remind the literary-obsessed that the stuff of things is many."[72] The *gerefa*, *Gerefa* suggests, does not need to be reminded of this.

As ever, in the text's concluding sentences, the *Gerefa*-author points toward the limitations of his authorial knowledge in comparison with the practical

---

71. Daniel Donoghue, *How the Anglo-Saxons Read Their Poems* (Philadelphia: University of Pennsylvania Press, 2018), 56.

72. Ian Bogost, *Alien Phenomenology, or, What It's Like to Be a Thing* (Minneapolis: University of Minnesota Press, 2012), 14.

knowledge of the reeve. When he says that "he who knows better should make known more," the *Gerefa*-author gestures toward a greater authority than himself; this is perhaps the reeve, or a possible future *Gerefa*-author or redactor who has the knowledge both of the author and the reeve. The object-lists make this more than a rhetorical gesture of modesty or ineffability; they cannot be complete, fully organized, or appropriately administrated inside of a text.

CHAPTER 2

In the Space of a List—*Widsith*'s Global Modernism

ANDREW JAMES JOHNSTON

The Anglo-Saxon poem *Widsith*—named after its highly conspicuous poet-narrator, literally "Long Journey"—is primarily organized as a long list—or, strictly speaking, three consecutive lists—of historical and legendary rulers and peoples. Most of these lists are connected by the travels of the self-identified poet-narrator, a famed poet showered with gifts by the various monarchs he visits, most notably Eormanric, king of the Ostrogoths.

Like many another premodern poetic list, *Widsith* has provoked a certain degree of critical bafflement. Scholars have found the poem and its list(s) oddly monotonous. Frequently, the text has evoked a sense of vague aesthetic and/or intellectual insufficiency. Attempts to account for and (sometimes) aesthetically justify the poem's striking characteristics have centered, for instance, on its being a repository of historical knowledge or on its encyclopedic nature.[1] Alternatively, the poem has been seen as an example of wisdom

---

Some of the research that went into writing this chapter was funded by the Deutsche Forschungsgemeinschaft (DFG, German Research Foundation) under Germany's Excellence Strategy, more precisely within the context of the Cluster of Excellence *Temporal Communities: Doing Literature in a Global Perspective*, EXC 2020, project number 390608380.

1. Raymond Wilson Chambers, *Widsith: A Study in Old English Heroic Legend* (Cambridge: Cambridge University Press, 1912), 179; Kemp Malone, ed., *Widsith* (Copenhagen: Rosenkilde and Bagger, 1962), 105; Nicholas Howe, *The Old English Catalogue Poems* (Copen-

poetry[2] or else as a wide-ranging celebration of the power of poetry, including poetry's didactic function.[3] A further explanation has been to see in the text's sheer endless number of peoples, rulers, and heroic warriors, some of them unidentifiable or even utterly fictitious, a display of a particularly *literate* virtuosity unfolding against the backdrop of an older oral tradition.[4] Yet another prominent approach to *Widsith* has been a combination of the sociological with the anthropological, which considers the poem as a format for expressing and negotiating the values and ideology of the society that it was written for, thus making it possible for the members of that society to engage in societally meaningful action.[5] For John D. Niles, "both *Widsith* and *Beowulf* exemplify the capacity of poetry to promote social reproduction."[6]

While all these contributions provide interesting insights into the text, their readings tend to privilege a wider cultural purpose outside the poem, rather than focus on the text's specifically literary resources for generating meaning—in this case, above all, the formal characteristics of poetic list-making as displayed in the poem. What deserves greater attention is the manner in which the poem employs a particular aesthetic of the list to develop a unique perspective, a manner that transcends the boundaries of the, by no means unimportant, cultural issues mentioned above. The present chapter seeks to intervene, therefore, in the debates on *Widsith,* with the aim of showing how the text's specific selection and combination of themes and structures within its list(s) generates a larger view on questions of culture, history, and, most importantly, temporality. This approach will put a special emphasis on a poetic understanding of "global modernism/global modernity," a more detailed discussion of which will be provided below.

Before we proceed, a caveat seems to be in order. I have called Widsith the 'poet-narrator.' The use of the term is deliberate: it highlights the fact that the text's main narrator reveals himself to be a character within the poem, who claims to be a poet, that is, Widsith, and who narrates in the first person singular. By no means is the term 'poet-narrator' meant to refer to the poem's

---

hagen: Rosenkilde and Bagger, 1985), 169; Renée R. Trilling, *The Aesthetics of Nostalgia: Historical Representation in Old English Verse* (Toronto: University of Toronto Press, 2009), 209.

2. Michael D. C. Drout, *Tradition and Influence in Anglo-Saxon Literature: An Evolutionary, Cognitivist Approach* (New York: Palgrave Macmillan, 2013), 140; 252; endnote 26.

3. David A. Rollman, "*Widsith* as an Anglo-Saxon Defense of Poetry," *Neophilologus* 66 (1982): 431–9, here 432.

4. R. D. Fulk and Christopher M. Cain, *A History of Old English Literature* (Malden, MA: Blackwell Publishing, 2013), 316.

5. John D. Niles, "*Widsith* and the Anthropology of the Past," *Philological Quarterly* 78 (1999): 171–213.

6. Niles, "Anthropology of the Past," 199.

empirical poet—of whom we know nothing and who, in any case, should never be confused with the poem's narrator, an entity to be considered, first and foremost, as a poetic construct. On the contrary, the following observations are based on the fundamental premise that the poem's sophisticated artistry derives, to a large extent, from the creation of an utterly fictional, but highly specific narrative voice,[7] a voice that establishes specific perspectives the audience are invited to understand as strategically facilitating a particular process of poetic meaning-making. I prefer the term 'poet-narrator' to simply speaking of the 'narrator' because the poem employs a frame, consisting of an introductory prologue and an epilogue, as one of its more important devices, and—as far as we can judge by the poem's structure—that frame is not spoken by Widsith, the poet-narrator. Of the relation between frame and list-narrative proper, more will be said further below.

In order to understand the global modernism of *Widsith*, this essay takes as its point of departure a brief but highly perceptive observation made by John D. Niles in 1999, an observation he did not pursue at any length due to the specific nature of his sociological and anthropological concerns. Niles has drawn attention to one of the poem's most conspicuous effects, one that he calls a temporal "flattening."[8] This "flattening" is the result of the decidedly achronological way that the poem's lists of rulers and peoples are organized. Traditionally, that is, ever since Raymond Wilson Chambers's study of the text in 1912, the poet-narrator's narrative is considered to be divided into three lists or thulas:[9] the first, ll. 10–49, is a list of rulers and their nations that ends with a brief historical sketch of the deeds of Offa and then with an equally brief reference to Hrothulf and Hrothgar. Here, in the first of his lists, the poet-narrator does not actually claim to have visited the rulers and peoples in question. But from l. 50 onwards he begins to mention nations that he supposedly has visited, amongst them not only the Greeks ruled by Caesar, whom he already referred to in the first list, but also a number of nations belonging to Biblical history. Roughly the second half of this section is concerned with his experience at the court of Eormanric and his interaction with Ealhhild, Eormanric's bride, whom the poet-narrator has accompanied from Angeln to the court of the Gothic king, as the prologue has already informed us. Line 109 witnesses the start of the third thula, as the poet-narrator begins to describe his travels amongst the Goths, listing a number of Eormanric's

---

7. Mark C. Amodio, *The Anglo-Saxon Literature Handbook* (Chichester: Wiley-Blackwell, 2014), 240.
8. Niles, "Anthropology of the Past," 198.
9. Chambers, *Widsith: A Study*, 127–8.

retainers. The poet-narrator's speech ends with l. 134 and is succeeded by an epilogue.

While it is possible to identify a clear structure to the succession of lists interspersed with narrative, that structure is completely oblivious to historical chronology. It looks as if, by blithely ignoring received historical sequence, the poem were intent on removing any sense of chronology from history, on downright erasing, from the landscape of history, the very notion of the temporal. Placing in poetic contiguity historical and/or legendary events, figures, and nations that, according to historical record, could never have had anything to do with each other, the text, at first glance, appears deliberately to be employing the list as a means of envisioning a paradoxically atemporal concept of history. Available to the poet-narrator in glorious spatial co-presence, the past—or, indeed, various pasts, such as those of Alexander the Great, Julius Caesar, Attila, and the Langobardian king, Alboin ("Ælfwine") respectively—all seem to be merging into a vast and undifferentiated field every corner of which may be accessed simultaneously. Consequently, Rolf H. Bremmer Jr.'s perceptive designation of Widsith as a time-traveler does not quite capture the aesthetic effect the text produces:[10] rather than witnessing Widsith as a time-traveler, we are left with the impression that time has fully been absorbed into space. To put it differently, as far as the reader's initial experience is concerned, Widsith does not have to travel through time, because time as an independent category appears to have vanished, to have "flattened," as John D. Niles has put it.[11]

---

10. Rolf H. Bremmer, Jr., "Anglo-Saxon England and the Germanic World," in *The Cambridge History of Early Medieval English Literature*, ed. Clare Lees (Cambridge: Cambridge University Press, 2013), 198.

11. In some ways, the poem's list-like arrangement appears to resemble the annalistic fashion of representing history that occurred with considerable frequency in the early Middle Ages. In an insightful article on medieval annals and chronicles, Hayden White actually refers to the annalistic ordering of time as a "list," not least because he considers annals to be utterly devoid of a "narrative component" (Hayden White, "The Value of Narrativity in the Representation of Reality," *Critical Inquiry* 7 [1980]: 9). While it seems quite possible that the *Widsith*-poet may have been responding to the particular representational aesthetic encapsulated in annalistic practices, it is also clear that the text very much seeks to differentiate its conception of history from that to be found in annals. To point out only two of the major differences: Whereas annals tend to observe a strict chronology—often to such a degree that they even list years for which they cannot provide entries—in *Widsith* there is a deliberate rejection of chronological order. And even more importantly, annals tend to lack any personal or subjective traces, but *Widsith*'s narrative construction is indissolubly linked to the poet-narrator's particular perspective. So, it is probably best to see annals as an implicit foil before which *Widsith*'s eccentricities can unfold all the more glaringly.

At the very beginning of the reader's experience, at least, *Widsith*'s temporality appears to resemble the kind of past that François Hartog has identified with the past produced by the Homeric bard:

> His particular task is to celebrate the renown (*kleos*) of those who have died, and in ensuring their *kleos*, to perpetuate their memory. In praising those who have passed on, he fabricates a past, but a past without duration, a past which is simply over. It is a past on demand, generated by the gap introduced by the bard as soon as he breaks into song.[12]

This impression of a temporal flattening,[13] "a past without duration," is further increased by the fact that nearly each and every one of the peoples and nations listed in the first thula is represented by exactly one ruler only. Reigning in supreme singularity, that ruler comes to embody his nation and its history, a history thereby condensed to the fame and achievements of a single, emblematic individual. In his odd historical isolation, each monarch in question resembles an exemplary character rather than an active participant in his nation's fate. The rare departures from this scheme leave an all the more striking impression, as, for instance, when the poet-narrator draws attention

---

12. François Hartog, *Regimes of Historicity: Presentism and Experiences of Time*, trans. Saskia Brown (New York: Columbia University Press, 2015), 55.

13. At this point, it is worth stressing again that the effect of "temporal flattening" Niles has identified in the aesthetic makeup of *Widsith* must by no means be confused with the all-too-familiar cliché of the Middle Ages' lack of historical consciousness. On the contrary, though Niles does not actually spell this out, his notion of "temporal flattening" presupposes a view that grants early medieval English texts—or some of them, at least—a considerable potential for developing a complex sense of history. Such a view of Old English heroic-elegiac poetry has been promoted by Roberta Frank in a number of now classic articles; see, for instance, footnotes 16, 21, and 35 of this chapter. Tom Shippey, too, has recently argued vociferously for the sophistication of the *Beowulf*-poet's understanding of history. Drawing on Erich Auerbach's famous chapter from *Mimesis*, Shippey compares *Beowulf* to the *Odyssey*, echoing Auerbach's accusation that Homer lacks historical depth, of constructing his epic universe in the setting of a straightforward and uncomplicated present. Shippey states: "How different is the Old English poem, how very much in possession of a historical and political perspective that he deploys without the slightest hesitation or contradiction!" (Tom Shippey, "'The Fall of King Hæðcyn': Or, Mimesis 4a, the Chapter Auerbach Never Wrote," in *On the Aesthetics of Beowulf and Other Old English Poems*, ed. John M. Hill [Toronto: University of Toronto Press, 2010], 247–65, here 254; see also Erich Auerbach, *Mimesis: The Representation of Reality in Western Literature*, trans. Willard R. Trask [Princeton: Princeton University Press, 1953], 3–23). While the *Beowulf*-poet's complex understanding of history ought to be beyond reasonable doubt in the critical climate of the twenty-first century, Auerbach's perspective on Homer has met with considerable criticism. As Egbert J. Bakker explains: "we are now prepared to see more silence, more elliptic moments, and more 'unplumbed depth' in Homeric poetry than Auerbach granted" (*Pointing at the Past: From Formula to Performance in Homeric Poetics* [Cambridge, MA: Center for Hellenic Studies, Harvard University, 2005], 56).

to the Danish kings Hrothgar and Hrothulf, uncle and nephew, and appears to be giving an inkling of the murderous strife that according to *Beowulf* is destined to break out between them in the none too distant future. Because this brief moment provides us with a glimpse of a larger history—albeit a history merely alluded to rather than spelt out—we become aware of the potentially vast depth of history that, theoretically, could have been rendered accessible behind the poem's flattened canvas of great historical characters:

> Hroþwulf & Hroðgar heoldon lengest
> sibbe ætsomne, suhtorfædran,
> siþþan hy forwræcon Wicinga cynn
> & Ingeldes ord forbigdan,
> forheowan æt Heorote Heaðobeardna þrym.[14]
> (*Widsith*, ll. 45–9)

Hrothulf and Hrothgar, nephew and uncle, held peace together for a very long time, after they had driven off the Viking people and humiliated Ingeld's vanguard and cut down at Heorot the host of the Heathobards.

The poet-narrator's thumbnail sketch of an episode from the Scyldings' history provides a remarkable sense of historical specificity, a historical specificity that comes with a rather chilling tinge. This tinge is reinforced, as Roberta Frank has recently shown, by the special, conspicuously circumlocutious vocabulary the passage employs, as encapsulated in the rare *dvanda*-compound *suhtorfædran*, "brother's son, father's brother." The word can be found only twice in the whole Anglo-Saxon corpus, the other occurrence being in *Beowulf*, where it is used not only in the same context, but in a line which seems to echo that in *Widsith*, or vice versa. As Frank explains, in Old English and Old Norse poetry, words like *suhtorfædran* often fulfill a special structural function that gestures beyond their particular semantics:

> Pointed circumlocutions like these open cracks in the frame surrounding the immediate action of the story, letting past and future in; they are condensed allusions to a legend everyone knew. Taken innocently, the epithet *suhtergefæderan* [...] describes an everyday kinship relation; read suspiciously, it is a mocking reminder of a particular family's disintegration.[15]

---

14. All quotations from *Widsith* are taken from Malone, *Widsith*.
15. Roberta Frank, "*Beowulf* and the Intimacy of Large Parties," in *Dating Beowulf: Studies in Intimacy*, ed. Daniel C. Remein and Erica Weaver (Manchester: Manchester University Press, 2020), 54–72, here 64.

In *Widsith,* one might argue, the "crack" opened by the word is of an even greater significance, since, against the backdrop of the poem's flattened historical landscape, what the term seems to be letting in is history itself.

Widsith's passage about the Scylding-dynasty adds historical depth in yet another way. It achieves this effect by gesturing toward a very particular time period, that is, the time period during which Hrothgar and Hrothulf "heoldon lengest / sibbe ætsomne" (ll. 45b–46a), a time period destined to come to a terrible end. Because this narrative move is crucial to establishing a notion of the historically specific, it simultaneously serves to create an impression of temporal contrast with the vast majority of the other items on the list, most of which seem to exist in a temporal void. In structuralist terms, one might even say that the sense of historical depth evoked at the level of a single and very particular syntagma, that of Hrothgar and Hrothulf, only serves to reinforce the glaring absence of such historical depth at the paradigmatic level, that is, the list. The very move that appears to be carving out a space for an understanding of a more complex historical temporality thus also produces an oddly counterproductive effect. In structural and aesthetic terms, then, the poem's flattening of time and history, on the one hand, and its intimations of historical depth, on the other, are mutually dependent.

Moreover, the list's spatializing approach to temporality clearly constitutes an act of poetic empowerment, as the poem's flattened and spatialized temporality opens up the temporal itself to poetic appropriation. And this poetic appropriation of temporality, we realize, already takes place, or rather, is already exploited on the very level of the list. After all, as we have seen, the poem's list structure is not remotely as monotonous as some earlier criticism maintained. Nor is this a unidirectional list, let alone a teleological one; in fact, this list provides a narrative structure that permits the poet-narrator to reorder time according to his requirements, regardless of what we think we know of the general course that history has actually run.

At first glance, a phrase like "the list provides a narrative structure" may appear provocative or simply self-contradictory, since lists have frequently been seen as the direct opposite of narrative. But this, I would argue, is a particular characteristic of *Widsith*'s list-making, that is, that it embeds narrative elements in its list structure, a combination that ultimately draws the list into the orbit of narrative.[16] As Jan-Peer Hartmann has observed, such a combina-

---

16. Narratologists are becoming increasingly sensitive to the complex relations that exist between lists and more conventional narrative; see Eva von Contzen, "The Limits of Narration: Lists and Literary History," *Style* 50, no. 3 (2016): 241–60, here 246–7.

tion of a catalogue structure with narrative elements is by no means unusual for the "elegies" and the "wisdom poems" in the Exeter Book.[17]

As the poet-narrator zooms in on a chosen few specific events—either those he experiences himself and in which he is generously rewarded or those to which he only alludes from a distance, such as the reference to the House of the Scyldings—rather than only flattening time, he accelerates and condenses it. In other words: far from making the temporal irrelevant as a category, *Widsith*'s quasi-geographical notion of time, its spatial entanglement of multiple temporalities,[18] actually renders the temporal supremely adaptable to poetic and historical purposes lying far beyond a scope that would have been available to a mere chronicler, for instance. This aspect of the poetic list, its capacity for shaping, through creative realignments of historically specific references to time and space, not only alternative temporalities but the sense of a global modernism, is central to this inquiry. It is important, therefore, to scrutinize more closely those of *Widsith*'s structural elements that contribute to the unravelling of the ostensible flattening of time that, according to John D. Niles's important observation, can be identified as the list's immediate effect. And, as a closer look reveals, the text employs a whole variety of devices that render the supposedly straightforward surface of the poem even more complex.

First of all, there is the frame.[19] While the list as a whole is part of the poet-narrator's monologue, that monologue itself is preceded by a few lines spoken

---

17. Jan-Peer Hartmann, "The Structure of the Exeter Book: A Reading Based on Medieval Topics," *Leeds Studies in English* 47 (2016): 29–61, here 37–8.

18. By referring to "multiple temporalities," I am showing my conceptual indebtedness to Carolyn Dinshaw's groundbreaking work on the complexities of medieval temporalities. Developing her argument on the Middle Ages' capacity for constructing queer temporalities through the different forms of temporal experience that overlap and become entangled in Margery Kempe's autobiographical account, Dinshaw has drawn on a wide variety of theoretical inspirations, ranging from Ernst Bloch's "asynchronous temporalities" to Dipesh Chakrabarty's postcolonial attack on Western interpretations of world history (Carolyn Dinshaw, "Temporalities," in *Middle English*, ed. Paul Strohm [Oxford: Oxford University Press, 2007], 107–23, here 120). For a critique of the various notions of queer temporalities that have been developed in premodern studies, see Valerie Traub, "The New Unhistoricism in Queer Studies," *PMLA* 128 (2013): 21–39.

19. John D. Niles has suggested that this frame is governed by the perspective of a Christian narrator who stands in marked historical contrast to Widsith, the poet-narrator. While the degree of the frame's emphasis on Christianity is not entirely clear, Niles is undoubtedly right in stressing the difference in historical outlook between the frame and Widsith, the poet-narrator (John D. Niles, *God's Exiles and English Verse: On the Exeter Anthology of Old English Poetry* [Exeter: University of Exeter Press, 2019], 100). And what is certainly clear is that the poem's frame is given to a character of considerable wisdom (Eric Weiskott, *English Alliterative Verse: Poetic Tradition and Literary History* [Cambridge: Cambridge University Press, 2016], 57, and "The Paris Psalter and English Literary History," in *The Shapes of Early English Poetry:*

by an anonymous voice introducing the poem's principal speaker, Widsith, and establishing a setting in which the poet-narrator's performance approximates that of a poem within the poem:

> WIDSIÐ MAÐOLADe, wordhord onleac,
> se þe [monna] mæst mægþa ofer eorþan,
> folca, geondferde. Oft he [on] flette geþah
> mynnelicne maþþum. Hine from Myrgingum
> æþele on wocon. He mid Ealdhilde,
> fælre freoþuwebban, forman siþe
> Hreðcyninges ham gesohte
> eastan, of Ongle, Eormanrices,
> wraþes wærlogan. Ongon þa worn sprecan.
> (ll. 1–9)

Widsith spoke, he unlocked his word-hoard, he who among men most had traversed peoples and nations on earth. He often received desirable treasure in the hall. His ancestors originated from the Myrgings. With Ealhhild, the beloved peace-weaver, he first went out of the East, out of Angeln, to the home of the king of the Goths, Eormanric, the evil oath-breaker. He then began to speak many words.

Readers/listeners thus become privileged members of an imaginary audience, witnessing the poet-singer Widsith unlock his word-hoard. This emphasis on performance, together with the biographical/historical references to the singer's diplomatic role, that is, taking Ealhhild to her future husband Eormanric, initially seems to prepare us for a conventional narrative rather than a list as described above.[20] What we are at first led to expect then, is a report on the— doomed? fateful? triumphant?—expedition meant to unite one of legendary

---

Style, Form, History, ed. Irina Dumitrescu and Eric Weiskott [Kalamazoo, MI: Medieval Institute Publications, 2019], 107–34, here 113).

20. This expectation is reinforced by the general tendency in Old English heroic-elegiac verse to add to and expand the known legendary material by introducing new heroes and new stories into the story's gaps and lacunae. As Roberta Frank explains: "No-one had ever mentioned, for example, who took Ermanaric's bride-to-be, the legendary Svanhild, to the land of the Goths; it was *Widsith*. No story gave the name of Heoden's first court poet, the scop cast aside when his patron hired the golden-voiced Heorrenda; he was called Deor" ("Germanic Legend in Old English Literature," in *The Cambridge Companion to Old English Literature*, ed. Malcolm Godden and Michael Lapidge [Cambridge: Cambridge University Press, 1991], 88–106, here 98).

history's most famous Gothic kings with a bride who is linked genealogically to a specifically Anglo-Saxon context.

In a structurally similar manner, the poem comes to an end not with the words that conclude Widsith's poetic performance—words with a vaguely political bent celebrating strong rulers—but with the anonymous voice that, we must assume, already provided the brief introduction at the poem's beginning, and now brings the poem to a close by praising the relations between wandering poets and generous patrons. To put it differently: through the contrast with its narrative frame, the poet-narrator's temporally flattened list is marked as a special poetic performance looking back on historical events through a particular, aesthetically inflected lens. While seemingly preparing its readers/listeners for a fairly conventional heroic narrative by way of the frame's introduction, the poem changes tack via the list-like structure of Widsith's performance.

But the sequence of lists itself, too, betrays internal complexities, as we have seen. This complexity becomes especially evident if one switches one's focus from the mere content of the three thulas to the different ways in which the lists position the poet-narrator vis-à-vis that content. While each of the three lists adheres to a similar anaphoric pattern, the particular poetic formulae used to connect the items in the lists vary from one list to the other, with each individual list held together by its own special connecting phrase or formula. The first list is organized around the repetition of a formula structured 'X ruled Y,' for example, "Ætla weold Hunum" (l. 18), 'Attila ruled the Huns.' List number two employs the formula 'I was with X,' for example, "Mid Wenlum ic wæs" (l. 59), 'I was with the Wendlas.' And the third and final list, which is also the briefest, hinges on the systematic repetition of the phrase 'I sought X,' for example, "Hehca sohte ic" (l. 112), 'I sought Hehca.'

Even though these three lists appear to share a basic temporality—they are composed in the past tense and, with the possible exception of the first, look back to the poet-narrator's former travels—the different phrases or formulae that tie them together internally each betray subtle differences with respect to the temporalities they engender. Whereas the first list's anaphorically connecting formula, 'X ruled Y,' has an impersonal, indeed, a chronicle-like ring to it—or potentially even a gnomic one—the second, 'I was with,' focuses on the speaker's personal experience—although it does so in a rather neutral, matter-of-fact fashion emphasizing the speaker's role as witness rather than participant. And this is all the more significant, given that this second list/catalogue offers the greatest wealth of narrative and autobiographical experience, as Nicholas Howe has pointed out.[21] The final list's linking phrase—'I

---

21. Howe, *Old English Catalogue Poems*, 178.

sought X'—by contrast, casts the speaker as something close to an agent, a character actively seeking those famous Gothic heroes and thus infusing the experience with something like a mild form of the quest.

Through their different anaphoric internal links, the three lists each offer different perspectives on history and temporality. The first clearly assumes a distant, almost bird's-eye view on historical events, a view that seems to be most attuned to the nature of the list as genre, an itemization more than anything else. The second list's anaphoric formula, 'I was with,' by contrast, more explicitly aligns the spatial ('with') and the temporal ('was'). It achieves this feat by establishing the poet-narrator ('I') as the experiential node tying together the two dimensions. The third list takes this strategy one step further, not by simply maintaining, but by actually intensifying that link between the spatial and the temporal. Here, the twin notions of direction and movement are introduced into the list, thereby putting the poet-narrator into the position of one who actively shapes the very spatio-temporal complexities he previously appeared merely to be witnessing passively.[22]

Much as the three lists are evidently presented to us by the same voice/character, the poet-narrator Widsith, a distinct progression evolves from one list to the next as regards the ways in which they imagine not only the temporal, but also the nature and degree of the poetic control wielded by the poem's speaker. The poet-narrator visibly exercises the highest form of control when he finally subjects the temporal and the spatial to the imperatives of a quest-like movement that self-consciously leads him from one famous Gothic warrior to the next.

At the very end of his list-narrative, the poet-narrator's increasing confidence and sense of power is highlighted by a fleeting meditation on the practice of list-making itself:

Rædhere sohte ic & Rondhere, Rumstan & Gislhere,
Wiþergield & Freoþeric, Wudgan & Haman.
Ne weran þæt gesiþa þa sæmestan,

---

22. Nicholas Howe has tied the idea of the traveling scop to the question of religion. He suggests: "In a profound sense, the *Beowulf* poet demands of his listeners that they imitate the poetic fiction of the traveling scop. Like the speakers of *Widsith* or *The Fates of the Apostles*, they must traverse the geography of the past in order to understand the meaning of their religious history and their faith as Christians" (*Migration and Myth-Making in Anglo-Saxon England* [South Bend, IN: University of Notre Dame Press, 2001], 177). While it is not entirely clear that Widsith designs his historical landscape in the same way as the narrator of *Beowulf*—the Biblical peoples in *Widsith* might actually suggest a more active blurring of Pagan and Christian elements—it is certainly true that Widsith's narrative, especially in its final part, seems to invite its readers to follow the poet-narrator on his travels.

þeah þe ic hy á nihst nemnan sceolde.
Ful oft of þam heape hwinende fleag,
giellende, gar, on grome þeode;
wræccan þær weoldan wundnan golde,
werum & wifum, Wudgan & Haman.
(ll. 123–30)

Rædhere and Rondhere I visited, Rumstan and Giselhere, Withergield and Freotheric, Wudga and Hama. These were not the worst companions, even though I should name them last. Very often from that troop the whining, screaming spear flew against a hostile nation; there, with coiled gold, the adventurers [or: exiles] Wudga and Hama ruled over men and women.

Here, the poet-narrator names Wudga and Hama as the final figures on his list. As far as the list proper is concerned, this constitutes its end. However, the speaker now displays a pointed awareness of the fact that lists are anything but innocent. Commenting on his own politics and poetics of list-making, he acknowledges the possibility that placing Wudga and Hama at the very end could be (mis)understood as a derogatory move, which is why, in the spirit of "last but not least," he conspicuously hastens to dismiss such a notion. Yet by drawing attention to the two heroes' placement, the poet-narrator underlines his own role in the process of list-making, openly arrogating to himself the power to position the figures in his list, thereby firmly establishing his poetic authority over the ordering of the list. And as if to reinforce that authority, he chooses to linger over Wudga and Hama just a little longer, adding to their names the mere sprinkling of a conventional touch of heroic narrative—those whining, screaming spears—before he finally and ambivalently identifies these last two characters as *wræccan,* a word which can mean both "adventurer" and "exile," thereby aligning their fates to something resembling his own, as he describes it in ll. 52b–53a: "cnosle bidæled / freomægum feor" ('separated from family / remote from the free kinsmen'). As this final thrust reminds us one last time of the control the poet-narrator exerts over his lists, we are left in no doubt that even the apparently most random of poetic lists must always be the product of a carefully contrived artistry—as must be, therefore, the particular makeup of the spatio-temporal relations that results from such a contrived randomness.

Taking stock of the poem's structural characteristics as discussed so far, we encounter an interestingly paradoxical state of affairs. *Widsith*'s narrative lists appear to be doing both at the same time, flattening history so as to virtually erase the temporal from the historical, but also creating a sense of temporality, or possibly even of overlapping temporalities, that restores a poignant presence of the historical to the poem's landscape of a supposedly detemporalized history. As we have seen, the poem initially puts a lot of effort into creating that semblance of temporal and historical flattening: first, through its basic structure, the list; second, through its jumbling of historical characters from entirely different eras as though they were contemporaries and hence all accessible through a straightforward mode of travel within an equally straightforwardly unified notion of geographical space; and third, through the ways in which each of the individual nations and peoples in the first thula are linked to a single ruler only.

At the same time, however, we witness a number of effective counter-strategies that restore to the poem a sense both of historical difference and of complex temporality. There are those few, but all the more significant instances—partly already addressed above—when something akin to narrative interrupts the seemingly serene monotony of the lists. This happens especially in the central list with Widsith's autobiographical references to the gifts he receives from royal personages: the Burgundian Guthhere, the Langobardian Ælfwine, the Goth Eormanric, and his new wife, Ealhhild.[23] But this effect is also visible in the first list with its allusions to Offa and, immediately afterwards, to Hrothulf, Hrothgar, and Ingeld. The latter reference offers an especially ominous little window onto historical depth, as it appears obliquely to be reminding us of the calamitous future that awaits the royal house of Denmark. And there is the unobtrusive change of historical perspective engendered by the poet-narrator's twice substituting his central narrative formula for a new one: from merely noting the existence of his object in the simplest of terms, through pronouncing himself an actual witness of events, and, finally, to presenting himself as an active seeker, a traveler directing his own course through the list, the narrative, and, therefore, essentially through his very own version of spatialized time, that is, through history.

Fascinating though these observations may be, their end result is also slightly disconcerting. It raises some considerable questions, most prominently: how exactly do these two contradictory trajectories interact—the historical flattening, on the one hand, and the reinsertion of history, on the

---

23. As Emily Thornbury has noted, the gift-giving in *Widsith* need not necessarily be linked to the poet-narrator's poetic achievements. On the contrary, the emphasis is first and foremost on Widsith's participation in the aristocratic ritual of gift-exchange as such. Proud and loyal retainer that he is, Widsith hands on the gifts he has received in foreign lands to his own lord, Eadgils: "What seems to matter is the intimacy of gift-giving, rather than how the gifts were acquired" (*Becoming a Poet in Anglo-Saxon England* [Cambridge: Cambridge University Press, 2014], 15).

other? The answer to this question lies, I believe, in the notion of a "global modernism" that the poem self-consciously seeks to construct.

The notion of a "global modernism" that I wish to introduce into the discussion of *Widsith* here derives from recent debates on world literature and global modernisms/global modernity. At first glance, it may sound anachronistic to draw on such discussions, simply because they are the product of very contemporary concerns. In the space allotted to me here, I can give only a very condensed version of what I believe to be at stake, and I encourage readers who wish to gain a deeper understanding to further their knowledge by taking advantage of the scattered cues I provide.

The aspect of these debates that is particularly pertinent to my discussion is the question of how, in an era of apparent rapid globalization, a concept of history can be developed that does not impose upon the world a notion of modernity that simply reproduces the West's traditional image of itself. It was the postcolonial historian Dipesh Chakrabarty who famously criticized the basic tenets of a progress-oriented history as replicating under the guise of modernization theory an utterly Western notion of historical progress as the yardstick of a universal modernity. He has referred to this Eurocentric way of conceptualizing historical change as "historicism":

> Historicism is what made modernity or capitalism look not simply global but rather as something that became global *over time,* by originating in one place (Europe) and then spreading outside it. This "first in Europe, then elsewhere" structure of global historical time was historicist.[24]

Theorists of world literature sounded similar alarms. Gayatri Chakravorty Spivak, for instance, has advocated a complete excision of the term "global" from the conversation, since she considers the term to be contaminated by the ideology of a neoliberal global capitalism, representing the world as an undifferentiated geographical entity devoid of differences in wealth, power, and culture. This globality becomes perfectly exploitable by an economic system which is primarily interested in rapidly moving capital across the globe as well as utilizing all manner of resources wherever they might be available in whatever form. As an alternative to words and compounds containing elements such as "world-" or "global," Spivak has coined the term "planetarity" in order to highlight the importance of both cultural difference and of hier-

---

24. Dipesh Chakrabarty, *Provincializing Europe: Postcolonial Thought and Historical Difference* (Princeton, NJ: Princeton University Press, 2008), 7.

archies of wealth and power for any meaningful discussion of transcultural political relations or for perspectives that focus on relations across the planet.[25]

One way to deal with the kind of issue raised by both Spivak and Chakrabarty has been to supplant the specifically Western notion of "modernity" that underlies modernization theory and similar accounts of economic and technological progress with the notion of "multiple modernities," a concept introduced by Shmuel Eisenstadt[26] and adopted for the purposes of cultural history by Jack Goody,[27] for instance. In the context of the world literature debate, Susan Stanford Friedman, in particular, has advocated such an understanding of multiple modernities/multiple modernisms. She argues on the basis of what one might call a structural, rather than a historically specific definition of modernism: a "loosely configured set of conditions that share a core meaning of accelerated change but articulate differently on the global map of human history."[28] But a closer look at the list of historically relevant constellations that according to Friedman typically exemplify this concept quickly reveals a very familiar chronological succession of triumphs of civilization much as we would find in any conventional history of the global rise of Western modernity. The list concludes in a staccato of the kind of places which have always served to privilege a particular Western notion of progress, the "Tang Dynasty, for example, or the Abbasid Caliphate, Al-Andalus, the Songhay Empire, Renaissance Florence, Enlightenment Paris, colonial Calcutta, or imperial London."[29] It is especially through its final four items—though by no means only through them—that this list exerts a silent structural influence that is anything but innocent. Veiled by a rhetoric of apparent cultural equality, a strict chronological order paired with an increasing shortening of the temporal distances between the items on the list—items now either European or within the purview of European power and expansion, that is, "colonial Calcutta"—combine to create an implicit narrative of European ascendancy *against the explicitly stated wish of the list-maker herself.*[30] Not to mention the

---

25. Gayatri Chakravorty Spivak, *Death of a Discipline* (New York: Columbia University Press, 2003), 71–102.

26. Shmuel N. Eisenstadt, "Multiple Modernities," in *Multiple Modernities,* ed. Shmuel N. Eisenstadt (New Brunswick, NJ: Transaction Publishers, 2002), 1–29.

27. Jack Goody, *Renaissances: The One or the Many?* (Cambridge: Cambridge University Press, 2010), 11–12.

28. Susan Stanford Friedman, *Planetary Modernisms: Provocations on Modernity Across Time* (New York: Columbia University Press, 2015), 93.

29. Friedman, *Planetary Modernisms,* 5.

30. As Katherine C. Little explains, this is a typical ideological *modus operandi* of the aesthetics of the list: "The seductiveness of the list should also suggest the way in which it might be performing ideological work at odds with its explicit claims for decentering and dehierarchizing" ("The Politics of Lists," *Exemplaria* 31 [2019]: 117–28, here 125).

fact that because of their very familiarity, the places/historical constellations listed already imply that the criteria which governed their selection are, at the very least, fully compatible with those that have traditionally informed the myth of the "Rise of the West."

Friedman's approach has been modified, however, in one significant respect by David Damrosch. Damrosch temporalizes the concept of global modernism by introducing into the notion of "modernism" the idea of a relationality between a given modernism (or modernity) and a particular past—a past he calls "antiquity"—from which that modernism/modernity more or less self-consciously differentiates itself. Such a mode of relationality can result in the past serving as a model to be imitated, as an ideal forever lost, as a burden to be shed, as a challenge to be overcome, as a trauma that haunts, or else as a period of glory that ennobles its self-styled inheritors.

This is what Damrosch has proposed in a recent article on "Antiquity" in a volume which claims, in its very title, to be offering *A New Vocabulary for Global Modernism*.[31] While Damrosch appears to be accepting the basic premises of Friedman's perspective, his approach nevertheless shifts the debate's focus from the question of a mere "accelerated change" to that of a culture's more sophisticated forms of historical self-understanding. Thus, for Damrosch, a "global modernism" is not simply a question of the increased rapidity with which a process of social and cultural change takes place—usually a key component of conventional Western narratives of progress—but of the ways in which a culture imagines itself in a complex relationship with its own past; a notion of the past which, to borrow Friedman's phrase, may indeed "articulate [very] differently on the global map of human history."[32] Accepting Damrosch's shift in emphasis, it becomes easier, in purely theoretical terms, to identify global modernisms in particular cultural configurations where the kind of change we witness may well be significant, though not primarily in terms of accelerated social change but rather in terms of a culture's shifting historical self-understanding. While the two issues—accelerated social and cultural change, on the one hand, and an increase in the complexity with which a culture constructs its relation to what it perceives as its own past, on the other—will frequently occur together, they need not automatically be assumed to take place in unison. Nor does an increase in the complexity of a given culture's historical self-understanding necessarily have to take place within the framework of the kind of modernization that characterizes traditionally Eurocentric notions of progress.

---

31. David Damrosch, "Antiquity," in *A New Vocabulary for Global Modernism*, ed. Eric Hayot and Rebecca L. Walkowitz (New York: Columbia University Press, 2016), 43–58.

32. Friedman, *Planetary Modernisms*, 93.

How does Damrosch's approach to the concept of "global modernism" matter in the context of *Widsith*? A radical reading of Damrosch would suggest that his proposal to define a modernity/modernism through the way it establishes its specific relation to the past—to its relation to its very own idea of "antiquity"—matters because his concept refuses to impose a single unified perspective on history. Instead, it seeks to establish a prism through which to conceptualize the problem of the simultaneity of different temporalities and different historical narratives and that of their intersecting and interacting.

After all, in *Widsith*, the flattening of history that is the first impression the poem usually makes on readers—even though they may describe that impression in very different terms—is consistently deconstructed by a whole variety of more or less surreptitious strategies for recovering the historical. *Widsith* presents us, therefore, with a fictional world where the poet-narrator is shown to be capable of unfolding different relations with the past, relations that can be developed simultaneously. Through the dialogue between the syntagmatic and the paradigmatic, each and every item on the list theoretically possesses the power to create its own particular version of a deeper, fuller, and, above all, different history—a history that may even be embedded in cultural difference.

In fact, as recent work by Leonard Neidorf has shown, *Widsith*, like *Beowulf*, betrays a pointed interest in historical specificity and cultural diversity. Using the notion of the Romans as a wine-drinking and wine-producing people, both poems establish a sense of cultural uniqueness for the Romans, a certain idea of *Romanitas*.[33] As it says in *Widsith*:

Mid Creacum ic wæs & mid Finnum & mid Casere,
se þe winburga geweald ahte,
wiolane & wilna & wala rices.
   (*Widsith*, ll. 76–8)

I was with the Greeks and with the Finns and with Caesar who held power over the wine-cities, over riches and desirable things and the empire of the Romans.[34]

Neidorf's findings corroborate Roberta Frank's crucial observation that *Beowulf* is at pains to evoke an idea of subtle cultural differences between its

---

33. Leonard Neidorf, "*Beowulf* and the Anglo-Saxon Postcolonial Imagination: Wine, Wealth, and *Romanitas*," *Modern Philology* 117 (2019): 149–62, here 150; 158–9.

34. For a discussion of the not entirely unambiguous terms *winburga* and *wala rices*, see Neidorf, "Wine, Wealth, and *Romanitas*." Malone glosses *winburga* as 'wine-cities' and *wala rices* as 'Roman Empire,' *Widsith*, 44.

various migration-period nations.³⁵ Now we see this perspective extended to the Romans as a nation, envisioned both in *Widsith* and in *Beowulf* as possessing a distinct culture clearly setting them apart from other peoples. If, from a modern perspective, wine-drinking and wine-producing may not exactly constitute the absolute epitome of cultural peculiarity, within the highly conventional style of Old English heroic-elegiac poetry, the insistence on associating wine with Romans, and Romans exclusively, must be regarded as a very strategic statement of historical specificity.

Another of Damrosch's points is worth highlighting. Discussing the writings of Apuleius, Damrosch argues that what he refers to as the Hellenistic period (strictly speaking: the Second Sophistic) possessed a particularly privileged access to antiquity. He contends that:

> writers of earlier eras had almost always been playing the historical hand that had been dealt them. For Hellenistic [sic] writers, antiquity was becoming less of a given, more a matter of choice. [. . .] One of the most modern features of the Hellenistic age, then, is the unusual freedom that people had to choose between competing antiquities.³⁶

In a rather traditional vein, Damrosch then sees that sophisticated beauty of the Hellenistic relation to the past decisively diminished by the triumph of Christianity with its supposed emphasis on historical uniformity.³⁷ While this is neither the time nor the place to discuss the larger historical narrative Damrosch here appears to be drawing on, in purely structural terms, his idea of an ancient culture being capable of developing so sophisticated a take on the past as to being capable not only of imagining different versions of antiquity but of actually choosing between them, closely resembles what *Widsith* is doing. *Widsith* seems to be celebrating what Matei Calinescu, on whose authority Damrosch himself relies,³⁸ has identified as one of modernity's principal characteristics, that is, "the total freedom of individual artists to choose their ancestors at their own discretion,"—though ironically, in *Widsith*

---

35. Roberta Frank, "The *Beowulf* Poet's Sense of History," in *The Wisdom of Poetry: Essays in Early English Literature in Honor of Morton W. Bloomfield*, ed. Larry D. Benson and Siegfried Wenzel (Kalamazoo, MI: Medieval Institute Publications, 1982), 53–65, here 55.

36. Damrosch, "Antiquity," 55.

37. Damrosch, "Antiquity," 55. For a similarly skewered view of Christianity's intellectual impact on late antiquity, see Stephen Greenblatt, *The Swerve: How the World Became Modern* (New York: W. W. Norton & Company, 2011).

38. Damrosch, "Antiquity," 55.

this "total freedom" happens not in the context of an "antitraditionalism,"³⁹ but rather within the conceptual framework of something very much like a hyper-traditionalism.

Whether or not it has ever been possible for artists to choose their aesthetic ancestors in total freedom is less of a concern here than their laying claim to such a freedom. Just as "Apuleius's modernism arises amid the tectonic shifting of competing antiquities just beneath the surface of the present,"⁴⁰ *Widsith*'s modernism arises through the many competing and potentially deep histories lurking beneath the apparently flattened historical landscape of the poet-narrator's highly improbable present—and at least one of these potentially deep histories is embodied by the stereotype of wine-consuming *Romanitas*. And inasmuch as the poem grants us mere glimpses of those deep histories lurking beneath its seemingly flattened historical surface, *Widsith*'s perspective on Germanic legend betrays close affinities with that of *Beowulf*. As Roberta Frank remarks of the epic: "The legends themselves are present in the poem chiefly as mysterious dark matter, sensed by the shadows they cast and by their gravitational pull."⁴¹

To sum up, even as *Widsith* employs its lists to open up before our eyes the historical landscape of an almost excessively flattened temporality, the poem paradoxically uses that very same list-format for purposes diametrically opposed, that is, for bringing into view competing histories of varying depth, all of which are inserted into the lists through minimal changes of treatment. Perhaps most impressively, it is through the poet-narrator's three different temporal approaches to his lists, as encapsulated in his three different anaphoric formulae, that we are confronted with the fact that the writing of history is first and foremost a matter of perspective, and, more specifically, of an actively created perspective. The power of poetry, as celebrated in various instances within the poem, would thus lie in its capacity for shaping, juxtaposing, and entangling different perspectives on history without their cancelling each other out. And in *Widsith*, that particular power is encapsulated in the generic affordances of the list itself, a structure that operates on the basis of a tension between sequence and juxtaposition. If properly exploited, that tension contains the potential to establish relations beyond the received narratives of cultural and political history. Paradoxically, it is through superficially eliding the very temporality of history itself that the poem demonstrates the multiplicity of competing temporalities that are hidden beneath its temporally

---

39. Matei Calinescu, *Five Faces of Modernity: Modernism, Avant-Garde, Decadence, Kitsch, Postmodernism* (Durham: Duke University Press, 1987), 8.

40. Damrosch, "Antiquity," 54.

41. Frank, "Intimacy of Large Parties," 57.

flattened surface, and that are potentially involved in history as it is written. And the poem does so by placing side by side, in the manner of a list, different perspectives on temporality. As Widsith, the poet-narrator, travels through history in directions designed to unhinge the principles of a uniform historical chronology, he brings into poetic dialogue and poetic competition different times and different cultures, different "antiquities" in Damrosch's sense, as well as different perspectives on those antiquities. He thus performs this feat according to a fashion that, in the light of recent debates, can best be labelled as an instance of "global modernism."

CHAPTER 3

Listing Divine Names
A Study in Liturgical Form

KATHRYN MOGK WAGNER

> Omnipotens + Dominus + Christus + Messias + Sother + Emmanuel + Sabaoth + Adonay + Unigenitus + Via + Vita + Manus + Homo + Ousion + Salvator + Alpha + et OO + Fons + Origo + Spes + Fides + Charitas + Oza + Agnus + Ovis + Vitulus + Serpens + Aries + Leo + Vermis + Primus + Novissimus + Rex + Pater + Filius + Spiritus Sanctus + Ego sum + Qui sum + Creator + Eternus + Redemptor + Trinitas + Unitas + Clemens + Caput + Otheotocos + Tetragrammaton
>
> —*Horae Eboracenses*, 126

How shall we speak of one whose name is above every name? How can human language ever describe God, much less invoke his power and presence? The Bible makes gargantuan promises on behalf of God's name, at which every knee will bow and on which everyone who calls will be saved,[1] yet the name itself remains enigmatic, ambiguous, defended by substitutions and circumlocutions. The tensions at the heart of this naming—the desire to know and possess, straining against the inadequacy of language and incomprehensibility of divinity—often find expression in the form of the list, which multiplies names while confessing that none is enough. Yet as we shall see, this form not only reflects existing theological commitments, but also shapes belief and religious practice in powerful ways.

This chapter studies Christian lists of the names of God, observing how they were circulated, recombined, and repurposed in the Middle Ages. Following this flexible form across contexts, we will see that the same features that made the list of divine names an especially appropriate tool for instruc-

---

1. Philippians 2:10, Joel 2:32, Acts 2:21, Romans 10:13.

tion and devotion also made it susceptible to interpolations and reappropriations, and therefore an object of scrutiny and attempted control.

There are three main contexts in which lists of divine names appear: didactic or expository texts, where they communicate theological knowledge; liturgical texts, like hymns, tropes, sequences, and litanies, where they invoke God's presence and praise his attributes; and a category I call "pragmatic performatives," where they are believed to achieve effects. Such texts are "performative" because the words are held to perform actions rather than communicate knowledge, and "pragmatic" because the effects sought are secular benefits like healing, safe childbirth, and protection from bad luck and sudden death. This category thus includes some, but not all, of what we now consider prayer, and some, but not all, of what we might call "magic," avoiding distinctions that are anachronistic or exogenous to the textual tradition. In general, the boundaries between theology and ritual, praise and supplication, prayer and superstition are porous, and the list is perfectly suited to traverse them.

Three properties of the list as a textual form explain its attractions and its dangers for religious uses. First, lists are portable. As Caroline Levine points out, the iterability of forms allows them to endure across time and operate in various media and materials.[2] The list, in particular, accommodates wildly heterogeneous contents, and its form is recognizable and interpretable even when its contents are unintelligible to the reader, as in the case of foreign, invented, and nonsense words. Lists rarely stand alone, but are embedded within longer texts for various purposes. The literal portability of name lists is materialized in their use as textual amulets—scrolls, letters, and parchment carried by their users. Second, lists are asyntactic: their minimal structure requires the reader to intuit relationships between terms,[3] whether by constructing a sequential narrative, specifying all the items in a limited set, or extrapolating an abstract category from its particulars by logical induction. How readers interpret the bare items of the list—their relationship with one another and with the world—is thus dependent not only on the surrounding text, but also on readers' own contexts and purposes. Third, lists are capacious and amendable, a baggy, open-ended form that can always hold a few more items. There are exceptions: some lists of divine names bear a specific number that symbolically represents completion, like seventy-two in Kabbalah or ninety-nine

---

2. Caroline Levine, *Forms: Whole, Rhythm, Hierarchy, Network* (Princeton: Princeton University Press, 2015), 7.

3. Eva von Contzen, "Experience, Affect, and Literary Lists," *Partial Answers: Journal of Literature and the History of Ideas* 16, no. 2 (2018): 315–27, here 322.

in Islam.[4] Yet even if a list claims to be comprehensive and closed, it frequently isn't; many Christian lists that claim to enumerate seventy-two names in fact range between seventy and eighty.[5] Because the items of a list are paratactically apposed rather than hypotactically subordinated, words can be added or removed without changing anything else, making it easy for copyists to modify lists. As we shall see, the accumulative and redundant logic of divine names drove users to gather as many as possible, including poetic coinages, syncretistic borrowings, and nonlexical creations.

These properties—especially openness to expansion—make listing an attractive technique for the task of expressing ineffability, which lies at the heart of theology. If God cannot be comprehended but must be spoken about, names for him must, even as they speak, somehow confess their own inadequacy. The classic approach is apophaticism, which asserts by negation—God is immortal, invisible, infinite, perfect. Yet while negation may be the most obvious example, other communicative strategies also paradoxically combine saying and unsaying. Obvious metaphors (e.g., light, lamb) make clear their own figural character, especially when many contrasting or contradictory metaphors are juxtaposed. The use of a language foreign to the speaker (Adonai, Emmanuel) suggests that the untranslatable proper name bears a mysterious excess of significance over ordinary words. More broadly, any style of expression that evokes defamiliarizing strangeness or draws conspicuous attention to the process of signification implicitly confesses the inadequacy of language. The list is an excellent tool for this task of saying and unsaying, because lists' expansibility naturally suggests that the knowledge they convey is incomplete, exceeded by an unarticulated potentiality. Moreover, their asyntactic character allows them to incorporate multiple other strategies for naming within a single text. Thus, wherever they travel, lists of divine names invoke the theological mystery of God's knowable-yet-unknowable identity.

Beyond explaining why theologians might write lists, this chapter tells a story about how form itself makes a difference. Circulating without authors or standard texts, lists of divine names are shaped less by artistic choices than natural forces: originally distinct lists aggregate and old lists gather new names as surely as raindrops on a window run together; ever-present entropy degrades the intelligibility of names through accumulated errors in transmission; a desire for incantatory, arcane sacral language pulls like a centrifugal

---

4. Don C. Skemer, *Binding Words: Textual Amulets in the Middle Ages* (University Park: Pennsylvania State University Press, 2006), 111.

5. Valentina Izmirlieva, *All the Names of the Lord: Lists, Mysticism, and Magic* (Chicago/London: University of Chicago Press, 2008), 126.

force against a centripetal desire for fixed, accurate reference. Users' attraction to the incomprehensible, in particular, generated texts characterized by unusual emphasis on normally nonsignifying properties of words, like their order, number, sounds, or component syllables and letters. Such lists' poetic qualities appear as emergent properties, consistently reproduced by virtue of the underlying conditions of the transmission environment and the impersonal psychological and social forces that drive pragmatic usage.

Here theory and form are mutually reinforcing, even mutually constitutive. The theological justification for unintelligibility sets loose phenomena beyond its control: only under conditions in which perplexity and strangeness are ascribed positive value could certain textual mutations arise and endure, as scribes themselves prefer and propagate *lectiones difficiliores*. As texts seem to move with an unruly life of their own, they continue to serve theological purposes: the presence of bizarre images, foreign words, and incantatory sound-play in lists of divine names shaped list-users' perception of God, making something closely akin to apophatic mysticism available to ordinary Christians. The form of the list itself powerfully replicates this way of thinking, even when unaccompanied by theoretical reflection.

Unchecked, the desire for ineffability and drive toward alienation I observe at work in lists of divine names would tend toward total ignorance, expressed in meaningless strings of syllables. Ultimately, I am most interested not in this extreme, but in the tensive balance of opposing principles: knowable and unknowable, intelligible and incomprehensible. Those who set out to write liturgical texts based on divine name lists were collaborators with forces far older and more powerful than they, attempting to harness the energies of popular desire for orthodox worship. It is this interplay between the mysteries of sacred sounds and the meanings of communicative words that produces the peculiar poetry of lists of divine names.

TRACKING LISTS ACROSS CONTEXTS

I begin not with the earliest Christian lists, but with a central node in their network of transmission: Isidore's catalogue of names for God, which begins the seventh book of his *Etymologies* (c. 600–625). Isidore's encyclopedic text both collates existing lists and is repeatedly mined by later writers, exerting a major influence on subsequent treatments of divine names. His mode of composition highlights the capacious quality of the list, which allows it to aggregate eclectic materials that use a variety of tactics to approach ineffability.

Isidore's list begins with ten Hebrew names for God copied from a letter of Jerome to Marcella.[6] Although Jerome and Isidore both offer Latin translation and commentary for each name, the Hebrew names themselves—the very words by which God made himself known in Scripture—are essential. Amid many lords and many so-called gods, many powers who could be complimented with words like "exalted" or "strong," retaining titles in untranslated Hebrew emphasized that they were not common nouns but proper names of the one and only Hebrew God. For some Christian thinkers, such names seemed to be performative words of power, "nonreferential," "effective," and "automatic," permitting no deferral or distance between the sign and the thing represented.[7] Given pride of place at the very beginning of Isidore's book, the Hebrew names secure all the other names' reference to the God of Israel, guaranteeing as orthodox the more ambiguous descriptive and metaphorical terms that follow. Isidore's explicit citation and almost verbatim quotation of Jerome thus authorize the rest of his miscellany.

Contrast this reverent treatment with a second important source for Isidore, a list of names for God found in the *Decretum Gelasianum*, a text attributed to fourth-century Pope Damasus but likely originating in the sixth century.[8] Its names, primarily metaphors from concrete objects like *petra* (rock), *panis* (bread), and *agnus* (lamb), enact the cataphatic technique of juxtaposing diverse images to triangulate on the ineffable. Such words for God, drawn from lowly material things, would be nonsensical or offensive if taken literally, but when they are presented together, each is clearly one partial glimpse of truth to be contextualized among and corrected by others. The form of the list is thus key to cataphatic approaches to God. Such lists are also open-ended and flexible, inviting additions and modifications. Isidore's use of the list from the *Decretum Gelasianum* is accordingly different from his reproduction of Jerome's: instead of copying the list in its entirety, Isidore pulls its names and explanations into his own organizational scheme, including twenty-six of its twenty-eight items—eight with a verbally identical explanation, nine with a close paraphrase, and nine with a different explanation. The names end up paraphrased and scrambled, obeying the new logic of Isidore's organization.

---

6. Jerome, *Sancti Eusebii Hieronymi Epistulae. Pars I: Epistulae I–LXX*, ed. Isidorus Hilberg, CSEL vol. 54 (Leipzig: G. Freytag, 1910), letter 25, pp. 218–20.

7. Naomi Janowitz, "Theories of Divine Names in Origen and Pseudo-Dionysius," *History of Religions* 30, no. 4 (1991): 359–72, here 360–5.

8. Ernst von Dobschütz, *Das Decretum Gelasianum de Libris Recipiendis et non Recipiendis in Kritischem Text* (Leipzig: J. C. Hinrichs, 1912).

In the *Etymologies,* Jerome's list, definitively cataloguing the Hebrew names that securely identify the Hebrew God, rubs shoulders with the list from the *Decretum Gelasianum,* sparkling with a variety of suggestive metaphors, as well as scores of other sources. Isidore's encyclopedic ambition encompasses very different kinds of name, and the asyntactic quality of the list form allows him to stitch sources together paratactically, without coordinating them or explaining their relation. The accumulative and syncretistic logic of list-making thus wreaks havoc on theoretical distinctions.

For Isidore's purposes, divine names primarily communicate knowledge about God, but didactic lists like his were also taken up by the liturgy to become performative speech-acts, invoking the presence and power of the one named. Although many hymns and sequences incorporate lists of names (e.g. *Analecta Hymnica* 8.36, 46.61), the most widely circulated such list is undoubtedly "Alma chorus Domini" (*AH* 53.87), a sequence first attested in the tenth century and belonging to the first epoch of Parisian chant.[9] All but eight of its fifty-three names appear in Isidore and are likely drawn from him.

The sequence is an elegant composition. Explicit speech-acts of praise in the first and last lines form a frame that guides worshippers' use of the names within; the second and second-to-last lines, which consist entirely of Hebrew and Greek names, create an inner frame of sacred names whose foreign language links them to their scriptural origin. This double setting charges the list of ordinary Latin words that makes up the bulk of the sequence with sacrality and secures their reference to the true God. The items of the list are held together by only the most minimal syntax, but they are loosely organized into groups of related metaphors, like "splendor, sol, gloria, lux, et ymago" or the memorably strange "agnus, ovis, vitulus, serpens, aries, leo, vermis."

This portable text serves several liturgical roles: sometimes, a Pentecostal multiplication of tongues for the Wednesday of Whit week; sometimes, a meditation on naming for the Feast of the Holy Name; sometimes, a sequence for nuptial masses.[10] A portion of the same sequence was also used to trope the lesson from Isaiah for the Nativity of the Lord (*AH* 49.383). This trope is a wonderful example of the list's capacious quality: a scriptural list of four

---

9. David Hiley, "Rouen, Bibliothèque Municipale, MS 249 (A. 280) and the Early Paris Repertory of Ordinary of Mass Chants and Sequences," *Music & Letters* 70, no. 4 (1989): 467–82, here 473.

10. Hiley, "Rouen, Bibliothèque Municipale, MS 249 (A. 280)," 481; Erica Kihlman, "Understanding a Text: Presentation and Edition of a Sequence Commentary in Oxford, Bodleian Library, Auct. F.6.8," in *Sapientia et eloquentia: Meaning and Function in Liturgical Poetry, Music, Drama, and Biblical Commentary in the Middle Ages,* ed. Gunilla Iversen and Nicholas Bell (Turnhout: Brepols, 2009), 381–455, here 390; Richard Rastall, *Music in Early English Religious Drama,* vol. 2, *Minstrels Playing* (Cambridge: D. S. Brewer, 2001), 99.

divine names ("Admirabilis consiliarius, Deus fortis, Pater futuri saeculi, Princeps pacis") has been stretched like an accordion, with nine complementary names interspersed, including a line straight from "Alma chorus Domini": "Messias, Sother, Emmanuel, Sabaoth, Adonay." Such quotations show how elements from this widely known list could be disassembled and recombined in new contexts.

To see how "Alma chorus Domini" was understood by educated readers, we can turn to a late thirteenth-century sequence commentary titled *Tractatus trium cantorum*. Part of a program of reading instruction in Bodleian Library, Auct. F.6.8, the commentary glosses each item of the liturgical sequence, taking most of the glosses from Isidore and often repeating him verbatim, although a few alternative interpretations are also included.[11] For at least some users, this text shows, liturgical lists of divine names remained intimately connected with the didactic ones from which they were drawn; performative praise and intellectual exegesis exist in symbiotic relation. In fact, both feed into each other. When it comes to especially difficult Hebrew and Greek words, the *Tractatus trium cantorum* commentary not only explains their meanings in prose, but recapitulates its terms and translations in mnemonic verse. The incorporation of such poetry makes this commentary a written trope, expanding a shared liturgical text with inventive riffs and responses.

Outside this scholarly reception, "Alma chorus Domini" also led a lively life in popular and pragmatic contexts, where lists of divine names are one of the most common elements in charm texts.[12] It was a common resource, for example, for the "Letter to Charlemagne" or "Prayer of Charlemagne," a charm type that first appears in the thirteenth century.[13] Such charms purport to be a letter sent from Pope Leo III to Charlemagne, which provides its bearers pragmatic benefits such as protection from ill fortune and sudden death. The contents of this letter frame vary widely; sometimes it offers a prayer to the Cross, sometimes a visual symbol like the "mensura Christi," but often a list of divine names.

The lists in question, though not identical to any liturgical source, frequently share ordered strings with them. Eamon Duffy identifies the "Prayer of Charlemagne" name list by the opening "Omnipotens + Dominus + Christus,"[14] but the examples I have found are marked most consistently not

---

11. Kihlman, "Understanding a Text," 390.
12. Skemer, *Binding Words*, 107–15.
13. Rosanne Hebring, "The Cultural and Material Contexts of Heavenly Letter Charms in Medieval England," Ph.D. diss., Radboud University, 2017, 29.
14. Eamon Duffy, *The Stripping of the Altars: Traditional Religion in England c. 1400–c.1500*, 2nd ed. (New Haven and London: Yale University Press, 2005), 273–8.

by a shared incipit but by two groups of names within the text: "Messias, Sother, Emmanuel, Sabaoth, Adonay" and "agnus, ovis, vitulus, serpens, aries, leo, vermis." Besides these lines that exactly replicate "Alma chorus Domini," charm lists often share other names with the liturgical sequence. For example, a list of thirty-four names from a thirteenth-century medical collection has twenty-six names in common with "Alma chorus Domini," rearranged to bring the Hebrew names at the beginning and the Greek names at the end together.[15] Comparing the two lists, it is clear that some of the charm's "new" names are misreadings of the old, replacing "ovis" with "omnis" and "aries" with "avis." Countless examples show the connection, and their variation indicates that the liturgical text passed into pragmatic use multiple times independently.

What does this textual history have to tell us about naming God? It is striking that the excerpts of "Alma chorus Domini" most frequently selected for pragmatic use are its two weirdest lines: the foreign names that promise a reference to God's unique, untranslatable being and the animal images that test metaphor to the limits of propriety. These are the elements that seem most powerful, because least intelligible, most unlike ordinary communication. Both of these techniques for naming God—direct quotation of foreign tongues and cataphatic suggestion through metaphors—are alienated from straightforward meaning, embracing deliberate, disorienting strangeness to acknowledge that God is beyond human understanding. Thanks to the indiscriminate aggregation of the list, these techniques circulate together and constitute a single textual tradition.

One more example will underline how readily portable name lists moved between the categories we now think of as worship and superstition. The *Horae Eboracenses* printed in 1536 includes a prayer based on a list of God's names, a list that is recognizably a variant on the "Letter of Charlemagne" tradition.[16] Even as this text circulated as an amulet bringing material benefits to its bearer, it was also authorized for worship within an official liturgical volume on the very eve of the English Reformation. Divine names thus travel easily across the porous boundary between liturgical and pragmatic use, always belonging to the same world of devotion.

---

15. Lea Olsan, "Latin Charms of Medieval England: Verbal Healing in a Christian Oral Tradition," *Oral Tradition* 7, no. 1 (1992): 116–42, here 128–9.

16. Christopher Wordsworth, ed., *Horae Eboracenses: The Prymer or Hours of the Blessed Virgin Mary, According to the Use of the Illustrious Church of York, with Other Devotions as They Were Used by the Lay-Folk in the Northern Province in the XVth and XVIth Centuries* (Durham; London: Andrews & Co., Bernard Quaritch, 1920), 126.

VAGARIES OF TRANSMISSION

As lists travel, their inner logic drives them to accumulate and expand. In theory, God's names are infinite; in practice, too, it is exceptionally easy for a scribe or user to tack on extras. A charm in BL Sloane 2584 shows this process in action: a later hand has added eleven more names in the margin, four of which duplicate names already present in the first scribe's list.[17] In Bodleian Library, Additional B. 1, a sixteenth-century scribe working from a copy of Reginald Scot's *Discoverie of Witchcraft* (1584) has reconstructed a censored list of names; where Scot wrote "Omnipotens + Dominus + Christus + Messias + with 34 names more," the scribe supplies a list of ninety-two names recovered from an alternate source.[18] This list, clearly belonging to the "Prayer of Charlemagne" tradition, also duplicates itself; four of its names appear twice.

Such repetitions may seem to betray a remarkably careless reader, but in fact, redundancy is so endemic to pragmatic performatives that it is better accepted as part of their basic orientation toward the world. As Valentina Izmirlieva puts it, the "operative logic" of what she calls heteropraxis is "cumulative and redundant: more of the same is better, and everything goes as long as it does the trick."[19] Repetitions within a list may evidence careful attention to features other than meaning. For example, a list in a fifteenth-century amulet roll repeats "Adonay" twice in just fifteen names,[20] but it has a clear reason to do so: "Adonay" appears in both the sources it stitches together, the familiar opening line from "Alma chorus Domini" and a butchered version of Jerome's ten Hebrew names. The scribe chose to place his sources side by side, likely because he thought the number or order of the items, normally nonsignifying properties, might be essential to the list's efficacy.

If redundancy was permissible within lists, it was positively desirable between them, as compilers often sought out as many versions as possible. Within four consecutive pages of the Burnet Psalter, an English liturgical manuscript from the early fifteenth century, there are four lists of divine names, three of them framed as heavenly letters from Pope Leo, all close variants of the same "Prayer of Charlemagne" tradition.[21] Remixing materials in multiple representations is typical of pragmatic practice, especially as evi-

---

17. Olsan, "Latin Charms," 128–9.
18. Frank Klaassen and Christopher Phillips, "The Return of Stolen Goods: Reginald Scot, Religious Controversy, and Magic in Bodleian Library, Additional B. 1," *Magic, Ritual, and Witchcraft* 1, no. 2 (2006): 135–76.
19. Izmirlieva, *All the Names*, 103.
20. Skemer, *Binding Words*, 263.
21. *Burnet Psalter*, 15th century, AUL MS 25, *University of Aberdeen Special Collections*, https://www.abdn.ac.uk/burnet-psalter/, fols. 66v–68r.

denced in amulet rolls, which reconfigure their repertoire of powerful names, words, and symbols again and again in lists, diagrams, seals, and other visual arrangements.

While it is easiest to accumulate names by tacking additional items on to the end of a list, some writers were more artful in their expansions. The eleventh-century hymn "Deus pater piissime" (*AH* 15.2), for example, uses Jerome's ten Hebrew names as a scaffold on which to build 268 lines of poetry. Each Hebrew name begins a long stanza bound together by a single rhyme-sound, full of Greek and Latin names, discursive accounts of salvation history, and appeals to God for blessing through the power of his names. The poem nestles its descriptive language, which could apply to more than one deity, and its metaphorical titles, with their potential to deceive the literal-minded, within an authoritative list of proper names that single out the Hebrew God. The hymn tropes Jerome's text, interpolating new material that is at once exegesis and poetic invention to produce a new work dependent on the old. Although this compositional technique shapes additions into an orderly poetic structure, it exhibits the same accumulative impulse that drives pragmatic users to tack on names in the margins. Whether lists embrace their open-endedness or strive for completion, their natural tendency is toward expansion, because it is easy to add items and impossible ever to grasp God.

This anarchic transmission context, in which scribes and users edit materials freely, allows not only freedom but errors—and a body of texts prized precisely for their propensity to frustrate the intellect ensures them. The *mouvance* visible in these lists reveals much about medieval Latin Christians' comprehension of other languages and how they handled words they did not recognize.

For one striking example, consider the history of "homousyon." The Greek *homoousios*, meaning "of one being" or "consubstantial," is crucial to the Nicene Creed's confutation of Arianism. It gets transliterated into Latin as "homousyon," which Isidore lists as a name of God the Son and glosses correctly. In later transmission, however, scribes ignorant of Greek read it as two words: Latin *homo*, appropriate to Jesus who is fully man, and *usyon* or *syon*, presumably a Hebrew word related to Jerusalem. Izmirlieva proves that the Slavonic amuletic text "The Seventy-Two Names of God" must derive from a version attested in Provençal documents, because its phrase "cheloviak u sione" ("man out of Syon") could only result from Greek transmitted through Latin.[22]

A similar translingual misreading appears in the hymn "Fortis El et Eloi" (*AH* 47.324). It seems an erudite poem, condensing Jerome's ten Hebrew

---

22. Izmirlieva, *All the Names*, 128–9.

names and definitions into compact verse, except for one mistake: somewhere along the chain of transmission, Jerome's Hebrew *elion* (*excelsus*, "exalted") has been misidentified with the Greek *eleison* (*miserere*, "have mercy"). The mistake is understandable, because the primary context in which Latin Christians would encounter the word *eleison* was the Kyrie, whose simple Greek text was frequently troped with Greek and Hebrew divine names (e.g. *AH* 17.1012; 47.162; 47.26). In such Kyries, *eleison* could easily be read as one more appositive item in a list, rather than the verb tying all these nouns together into a sentence. This substitution betrays a professional liturgist, either hymn-writer or scribe, who is surprisingly confused about the meaning of a basic liturgical element—or, perhaps, cannot resist a multilingual play on words.

Unintelligible foreign words in general tend to be read as names, regardless of their meaning. Not only "eleison" but "Amen," "Benedicite," "Otheotocos," and Jesus's last words from the Cross—rendered in various transliterations like "Helilam'asabathani" or "Lamazabatham"—appear within lists of names for God. Acronyms like "AGLA" (Hebrew "atta gibbor leolam adonai," "thou art mighty forever lord") and "INRI" ("Iesus Nazarenus Rex Iudaeorum," the inscription on the Cross) become names as well.[23] The irresistible attraction of nominalization has a grammatical explanation. Every part of speech can be correctly treated as a noun when it is not used to refer to its signified but mentioned as a signifier. A speaker who does not understand a word cannot use it meaningfully, but there are no obstacles at all to mentioning it in this nominalized, contentless way. Similarly, a vocative name can slip into second-person address at almost any point without requiring syntactic support or disrupting grammatical coherence. A person handling an unfamiliar language often tends to read and write unknown words in ways that require minimal syntactic coordination—as interjected vocative names and as items in an appositive list. There is thus an almost inevitable connection between names, lists, and unintelligible words; readers confused by a foreign language naturally turn words into names and reduce complex syntactic texts to lists.

KALEIDOSCOPIC EFFECTS

If lists need not be organized according to the grammar of well-formed sentences, they are open to a variety of other organizing principles, from logical categories to playful sound-associations.

Isidore establishes one influential organization, classifying his terms as names for God, subdivided into Hebrew and Latin; names for the Son of God,

---

23. Skemer, *Binding Words*, 112.

subdivided into a general list and a special class of metaphors drawn from material things; names for the Holy Spirit; and names of the whole Trinity. Within these categories, terms are often informally grouped by conceptual similarities: all the animals, all the stones, and all words related to light and vision appear together. In Isidore's relatively discursive text, the items of the list are knit together by surrounding prose that loops back and looks forward to similar terms. Those who drew on Isidore often abstracted just the names from this connective tissue of sentences, but the relationships between them can still be inferred from their order. In later lists of names, conceptual clusters often travel together as fairly stable units. Links sometimes hold across as well as within clusters; for example, the "light" group often appears alongside names focusing on the relationship between the Son and the Father like "sapientia," "verbum," and "imago," likely following the Nicene Creed's use of "lumen de lumine" to express this trinitarian relation.

While many texts think in terms of these clusters, some appear intentionally to disrupt them. Consider, for example, "Christe Salvator" (*AH* 8.36), a twelfth-century sequence that consists primarily of a dense, paratactic list of divine names. Of its eighty-three items, seventy-four appear in Isidore, including several unusual names that suggest the composer consulted the *Etymologies* directly. Despite this similar content, the hymn's order is jumbled. For example, while all of Jerome's Hebrew names appear in its first ten lines, their sequence is repeatedly interrupted by Greek and Latin names like "alpha," "sol," and "vita," which help complete rhymes. These alterations unexpectedly juxtapose different languages, domains of experience, and techniques for naming.

The poetry of this type of liturgical list lies in how it frustrates rational typologies or familiar sequences, disarranging them to create new, more difficult patterns. The formal requirements of meter and rhyme disrupt smooth transferal from the source text. Writing such a hymn requires precise manipulation within a tightly bounded formal structure, an exercise not unlike a crossword puzzle or sudoku. In such games, written signs are almost wholly alienated from the world of reference to obey the alternative logic of the puzzle square, a self-contained system in which nonsignifying properties, like numbers of letters or syllables, come to the foreground of attention.

The kaleidoscopically broken and remade order of such lists invites meditative engagement. As the reader works to find meaningful connections and associations among the terms—that is, to supply her own syntax to the list's enigmatic parataxis—she becomes an active participant in the hymn as puzzle. Writers reordering terms could be confident that any possible arrangement would be richly suggestive, because just as God exceeds every theological definition, so too divine names are charged with a surplus of significance that cannot be contained by any particular order.

The way that a verbal puzzle or challenging poetic form calls attention to normally nonsignifying properties, like syllables and letters, sets words apart from ordinary speech; in a religious context, it may mark them as sacred. For those reading names from languages they do not know, letters and sounds are the words' most accessible surface, available for meditation without the help of a translator. Such attention to sounds indicates that the signifier itself is considered an appropriate object of devotion, because it attaches in a real way to its referent, God, and shares in some of his holiness and power.

Organizing techniques besides formal verse likewise bring sounds and letters to the foreground of attention. In Isidore's solar cluster, sense and sound associations interact; "oriens," meaning both "sunrise" and "origin," pivots the list from astrological images to the idea of beginnings and endings, "alpha" and "O." Other connections are purely puns: in a list praising Mary, the astrological image "sol" leads one compiler playfully to "sola," "unique."[24]

List-makers also enjoyed purely aural associations. For example, items within a list often appear in alliterative groups. "Via," "veritas," and "vita" naturally cluster together as the "way, truth, and life" of John 14:6, but they attract more *vs* into their orbit and inspire other alliterative units: "Tu via tu veritas / Iesse virga tu vocaris, te leonem legimus."[25] Some list-makers are led by rhyme: "fons mons pons," "flos ros."[26] In this free-associative atmosphere, aural and alphabetic associations interact with conceptual ones: "sapientia" prompts "mens" by similar meaning, but "mens" prompts "mons" by sonic affinity.[27] Semantic and sonic resonances are packed even more densely in the cluster "lex, rex, lux, dux," which rings changes on metaphors of governance and knowledge as it stacks up similar monosyllables.[28] This group has been attested in church decorations and manuscripts since the Carolingian Renaissance;[29] like other widespread plays on words, it is public poetry, repurposed in hymns, architectural ornaments, and amulets alike. The cluster's intense internal resonances hold it together, even as its asyntactic detachment from surrounding discourse makes it portable.

---

24. W. Sparrow Simpson, "On a Seventeenth Century Roll Containing Prayers and Magical Signs, Preserved in the British Museum," *Journal of the British Archaeological Association: First Series* 40, no. 3 (1884): 297–332, here 327.

25. *AH* 51.214, ll. 3–4.

26. Simpson, "Seventeenth Century Roll," 327.

27. *AH* 46.61, l. 5.

28. *AH* 46.51, l. 25.

29. Robert Favreau, "Rex, lex, lux, pax: Jeux de mots et jeux de lettres dans les inscriptions médiévales," *Bibliothèque de l'École des chartes* 161, no. 2 (2003): 625–35.

Repetition; rhythm; paronomasia; alliteration; rhyme: these forms of verbal play are all characteristically literary features. Yet they appear not only in the artful forms of liturgical song, but in scattered snatches of popular devotion and pragmatic lore, arising half by accident among the contingencies of textual transmission. To understand why, we must look more closely at the inner logic of pragmatic performatives.

SACRED NONSENSE

Utterances aiming to achieve effects by nonnatural means tend to fall into certain patterns of use. Studying charms in the classical world, H. S. Versnel observes a compulsive tendency among their transmitters "to produce rhyme, repetition, and variation," distorting both native languages and foreign borrowings into nonsense words with no recoverable referent, but pronounced aural patternings.[30] He regards this tendency as a "drive to alienation" central to the poetics of the charm. Along similar lines, Bronislaw Malinowski speaks of the "very considerable coefficient of weirdness" that sets magical formulae apart from ordinary speech among Pacific Islanders, including phonetic, rhythmic, and alliterative effects, repetitions, cadences, and sing-song or chanted performance.[31] In medieval pragmatic performative texts, the same drive toward nonsense is clearly at work. Estrangement produced by the elevation of sonic over semantic qualities is characteristic of pragmatic performatives across cultures; it appears to be essential to how such utterances work psychologically, if not theologically.

The most extreme version of this tendency results in wholly unintelligible invented words, in which the impulse to play with sound is entirely liberated from the demands of sense. Such words—known as *onomata barbara, voces magicae,* or *verba ignota*—are employed in magical practices from Ptolemaic Egypt to classical Rome to the Latin Middle Ages. Analyzing similar "gibberish" in Anglo-Saxon charms, Leslie Arnovick understands it as a "hieratic dialect" or "spirit code," semantically empty but full of illocutionary force.[32] The best word for this effect may be "sacrality"—if we remember that *sacer*

---

30. H. S. Versnel, "The Poetics of the Magical Charm: An Essay in the Power of Words," in *Magic and Ritual in the Ancient World*, ed. Paul Mirecki and Marvin Meyer (Leiden: Brill, 2002), 105–58, here 138.

31. Bronislaw Malinowski, *Coral Gardens and Their Magic*, vol. 2 (New York: American Book Company, 1935).

32. Leslie Arnovick, *Written Reliquaries: The Resonance of Orality in Medieval English Texts* (Amsterdam: Benjamins, 2006), 27–57.

means not only "holy" but "set apart," even "accursed." Unintelligible language seemed, to some, uniquely suited to the holy God, but it also appeared terribly dangerous. Unknown words call on unknown powers; what is other than human and outside the world may be divine, but it may also be merely supernatural.

Accordingly, many Christian authorities forbid the use of *verba ignota*, identifying unintelligible words with the invocation of demons. Augustine writes that superstition, typified by amulets and *caracteres*, must be idolatry or alliance with demons; signs can only cause effects by communicating with spirits.[33] Likewise, Thomas Aquinas warns that even *ignota nomina* that do not explicitly call on demons must be treated with the utmost caution and suspicion, lest they conceal something unlawful.[34] These prohibitions strive to check the natural tendency of incanted words to become distorted in transmission and the popular appeal of unintelligible utterances.

In the later Middle Ages, the use of unknown names reached its most systematic in learned ritual texts like the *Ars notoria* (attested from the thirteenth century, though probably written in the second half of the twelfth).[35] The *Ars notoria*, with other pseudo-Solomonic texts, aims to achieve by a prescribed ritual practice what Solomon received from God: miraculous infusion of knowledge apart from the usual means of study. Instead, the operator performs an elaborate ritual over months of fasting, including recitation of prescribed prayers and gazing at certain *notae* or diagrammatic figures. At the text's core are its lists of unknown words, supposedly drawn from Chaldean, Hebrew, Greek, and Arabic.[36]

The *Ars notoria* claimed to be a form of religious devotion that complemented more normative practices like the liturgical hours.[37] One way to defend such texts was to claim that their *verba ignota* are angelic names, invoking good spirits in an extension of recognized, legitimate devotions to angels.[38] Other ritual texts used the same gambit: the *Liber iuratus Honorii, Almandal,*

---

33. Augustine, *De Doctrina Christiana*, ed. R. P. H. Green (Oxford: Clarendon Press, 1995), 2.20–4.

34. Thomas, *Summa Theologiae: Latin Text and English Translation, Introductions, Notes, Appendices, and Glossaries* (Cambridge; New York: Blackfriars; McGraw-Hill, 1964), II.IIae.96.2.

35. Julien Véronèse, ed., *L'Ars notoria au Moyen Âge: Introduction et édition critique* (Florence: SISMEL Edizioni Del Galluzzo, 2007).

36. Véronèse, *L'Ars notoria*, A.8.

37. Frank Klaassen, *Transformations of Magic: Illicit Learned Magic in the Later Middle Ages and Renaissance* (University Park: Pennsylvania State University Press, 2013), 111.

38. Richard Kieckhefer, "Angel Magic and the Cult of Angels in the Later Middle Ages," in *Contesting Orthodoxy in Medieval and Early Modern Europe: Heresy, Magic and Witchcraft*, ed. Louise Nyholm Kallestrup and Raisa Maria Toivo (Basingstoke: Palgrave Macmillan, 2017), 71–110, here 85–92.

Liber Razielis, and *Liber Theysolius* all purport to operate by invoking angels.[39] Like other lists we have seen repurposed for various ends, though, these texts' unknown words depend for their interpretation on context and users' intentions. Even at their most innocuous, they closely resembled the "necromantic" texts that theologians like Aquinas warned against, and could call on evil rather than angelic powers with only slight emendation. The slippage is easy enough; some angels have fallen.

Linguistically, these texts' invented names bear traces of the reverence paid to Hebrew and Greek, but instead of venerating scriptural names as divinely revealed, they evoke a generalized Hebrewishness or Greekishness. The *Ars notoria* describes the significance of its prayers as *ex hebreo distorta* ("twisted out of the Hebrew");[40] it at once casts the glamor of ancient, exotic origins over the text and acknowledges that its sources have been transformed in becoming pragmatic ritual. A few of the *Ars notoria*'s names come directly from authorized lists, while others have clearly recognizable origins ("Patir" from Latin *pater,* "Agion" from Greek *agios,* "holy").[41] Mostly, though, they are a fantasia of sonic play: "Samac, Gezacarin, Zeamiot, Lezeator, Sannamai, Gezeel, Gezietiel."[42] Some of the non-biblical angelic names are borrowed from contemporary Jewish compilations, but the majority can trace no genealogical connection to Hebrew.[43] Nevertheless, invented words are often marked with the Hebrew suffixes "-el" and "-oth" or the Greek "-on," mimicking the look and sound of scriptural languages.

The nonsense names generated with such fecundity in ritual texts unconstrained by orthodoxy may seem to signify nothing, but in fact they isolate in its purest form an alternate kind of significance. It is true that they lack intelligible meaning, since such signs correspond to no defined idea and cannot be translated into another language. They also abandon normal ways of securing reference: unconnected to a historical act of naming, the mutually supporting interrelations of a linguistic system, or a broad community of use, an "unknown" name is attached to its object only by the unverifiable intent of the speaker. Each word, considered by itself, is empty. Yet together, pouring out in the jumbled, accumulative, incantatory rhythm of the list, they unmistakably signify mystery, otherworldliness, sacrality. Sonic qualities that we normally

---

39. Klaassen, *Transformations.*
40. Véronèse, *L' Ars notoria,* A.6.
41. Véronèse, *L' Ars notoria,* A.10, A.16.
42. Véronèse, *L' Ars notoria,* A.92.
43. Julien Véronèse, "Magic, Theurgy, and Spirituality in the Medieval Ritual of the *Ars Notoria,*" in *Invoking Angels: Theurgic Ideas and Practices, Thirteenth to Sixteenth Centuries,* ed. Claire Fanger (University Park: Pennsylvania State University Press, 2012), 37–78, here 53.

consider nonsignifying mark the text as foreign, ancient, and sacred. What matters for practitioners who seek to communicate with or command spirits is often not the specific syllables of a rite, but utterances alienated from understanding, which feel appropriate to what lies beyond ordinary experience.

Returning to approved Christian practice, we find that while liturgical texts authorized for public worship scrupulously avoid pure nonsense or *verba ignota*, the same alienation effect that produces incantatory nonsense in pragmatic performatives is also present in the metrical, aural, and alphabetic play that characterizes liturgical lists of divine names. Features modern readers recognize as literary, like alliteration and paronomasia, set the text apart from ordinary speech for sacred purposes. Observing the consistent tendencies of performative language, I am inclined to think that liturgy does not contain poetry as an accidental or optional embellishment to its religious project; rather, it inevitably produces poetry because it operates under both an impulse and a constraint. On the one hand, it must alienate language from ordinary speech in a way that satisfies a human hunger for sacrality; on the other, it must remain (at least in theory) intelligible and orthodox. You could almost say that poetry is what happens under the tension of those two demands: a language that remains legible to the intellect as it maximizes the sacral charge of ritual sounds.

THE SINGULAR NAME

As we have seen, the form of the list was dangerously open to addition, emendation, and error in transmission, and Christian authorities condemned the use of unauthorized names. Nevertheless, there was enormous popular enthusiasm for divine names, which seemed to provide both intimate access to God and practical help in times of need. One solution was to substitute for the capacious and ever-changing list a single name, the "name that is above all names" (Philippians 2:9): the Holy Name of Jesus. Devotion to the Holy Name flourished throughout Europe in the late fourteenth and fifteenth centuries, propagated by teachers like Richard Rolle, Bernardino of Siena, and Heinrich Suso.[44] The singular name discards the cataphatic technique of approaching ineffability through multiple approximations. Instead of the denial and deferral of many names, none exactly right, it promises intimate access to Christ. This promise ratifies and legitimates what many Christians had always felt

---

44. R. W. Pfaff, *New Liturgical Feasts in Later Medieval England* (Oxford: Clarendon Press, 1970), 62.

about divine names: that certain words, especially untranslated Hebrew and Greek, directly manifest the presence and power of God.

Yet even as Holy Name devotion operated by the same logic as incantations and textual amulets, it sought to supplant these practices. This movement is particularly clear in the career of Bernardino of Siena, who was both an ardent advocate of the Holy Name and a forceful opponent of other name devotions. In sermons against superstition and witchcraft, he called for the burning of *brevi*, that is, textual amulets, likely full of the name lists so often used as pragmatic performatives. Yet he promised precisely the same practical effects sought by users of *brevi*—healing, fortune, safety—through the Holy Name.[45] Bernardino aimed to replace hundreds of portable, amendable pieces of parchment owned and used by individuals with a single, central monogram upon which all eyes could gaze together.

Yet the singular name of Jesus could not escape the form of the list. The office of the Holy Name developed in the mid-fourteenth century and appearing in the Sarum, York, Hereford, and Aberdeen breviaries includes as one of its hymns our old friend "Alma chorus Domini."[46] As Duffy points out, this inclusion legitimates the old, strange, quasi-magical list and equates it to the solemn use of the name Jesus.[47] A devotion arguably designed to supplant the troublesome form of the list here reinscribes it as part of its own official cult.

Holy Name devotion also embraced the logic of the list in a more profound way, illustrated by a fifteenth-century hymn "De nomine Iesu" (*AH* 46.51). The most striking thing about this hymn is its length: 856 lines. In one sense, the poem is obsessed with singularity: the name of Jesus is its only subject. In another sense, it is an agent of proliferation: the only way to write 856 lines about one word is to fracture, multiply, and distort it to the limits of recognition. The hymn exemplifies the reification and alienation of language, which it accomplishes through the same troping technique that stretched Jerome's ten Hebrew names into a 286-line hymn. The hymn's conventional praises of Jesus's saving work appear within a structure defined by the written sign "Jesus." In lingering detail, the text expounds the number of syllables in the name, the number of letters, each letter, each individual pen-stroke, all rich with allegorical interpretations. Broken into discontinuous units, the letters cannot be read as a whole word. The first letter, "iota," is given in Greek, adding the peculiar charge of foreignness to the already disorienting effects of atomization.

---

45. Franco Mormando, *The Preacher's Demons: Bernardino of Siena and the Social Underworld of Early Renaissance Italy* (Chicago: University of Chicago Press, 1999), 103–5.

46. Pfaff, *New Liturgical Feasts*, 70–1.

47. Duffy, *Stripping*, 283.

While users of pragmatic performatives who clustered alliterating and assonating sounds likely obeyed instinct in gravitating toward these alienating effects, I think this hymn-writer knew exactly what he was doing when he brought into such insistently focal attention the properties of the linguistic signifier. He praises Jesus with fantastic puns that play on the homonymy between actions and grammatical terms: "Dativum remedii, / mortis ablativum" ("the dative [giver] of healing, the ablative [taker away] of death").[48] The poem's acute consciousness of the lowly letters and syllables that bear the sacred mystery resonates with the semiotics of the Incarnation: even as our thoughts are imprisoned and glorified in fallible, punning symbols, the eternal Word of the Father deigned to take on fallible, punished flesh. The hymn's systematic defamiliarization of the word "Jesus" turns it into a verbal sign that— like God's incarnate Word—matters less for its meaning than its presence.

This transformation goes hand in hand with the hymn's troping expansion. Prevented from reading a legible word, the worshipper may pause forever on the sign itself. The commentary's sheer quantity makes the poem open-ended, inviting inexhaustible interpretation. The technique is remarkably similar to the mystical cataphasis that produces lists of images for God: that which is unknown, incomprehensible, and unspeakable generates around it countless linguistic attempts and approaches, each falling short but revealing a facet of the mystery. But here, the locus of unintelligibility has shifted from God himself to his name, the letters I-E-S-U-S.

Devotion to the Holy Name thus continues and intensifies the logic of earlier lists of divine names. Even though "De nomine Iesu" claims singularity, it in fact offers a list of six discrete letters, each of which functions grammatically as a name and has no meaning but recursive self-reference. Though the six letters are fixed, they serve as a capacious form that can be filled with more and more interpretative matter, expanding without limit. Minute analysis of syllable and letter, like incantations' playful foregrounding of sonic qualities, draws attention to the signifier, producing the alienation effect key to a felt experience of sacrality.

How shall we name the unnameable God? Medieval Christians answered: by showing in our very language the limits of language, distorting and stretching words until they no longer mean anything we can understand, but strangely signify what we cannot. What lies beyond those limits may differ: a central silence surrounded by images and negations, an alterity evoked by whatever feels alien, a sign mysteriously one with the one it signifies. Each technique for naming found in the list a hospitable form, offering capacious

---

48. *AH* 46.51, ll. 87–8.

room to accumulate names and interpretations, a freedom from syntax that made it easy to handle unknown languages, and a rhythmic quality suitable for incantation—plus the flexibility to mix approaches and repurpose texts. Yet the list was not simply chosen because it suited theological arguments and satisfied devotional desires; it in turn shaped theory and practice, guiding users' behavior and resisting ecclesiastical control, an enduring testament to the power of form.

CHAPTER 4

Naming the Children of Jacob
The Shape of Negative Theology in the Benjamin Minor

SUZANNE CONKLIN AKBARI

The Middle English *Benjamin Minor*—a late fourteenth-century adaptation of a twelfth-century Latin work by Richard of St. Victor—yokes an explicit commitment to affective piety to a highly formal diagrammatic structure that provides a template for devotional practice. That structure emerges from the list of the children of the patriarch Jacob that appears in Genesis 35:23–26: each of these four verses names in order of birth the offspring from one of the four mothers—Jacob's two wives, Leah ("Lya") and Rachel, and the wives' handmaids, Zilpah ("Zelpha") and Bilhah ("Bala"). The family of Jacob is elaborately allegorized, with several of his children being expounded as emotional states: these include fear, sorrow, hope, love, joy, hate, and, finally, shame. The apparently simple list of children, and its corresponding list of emotional states, proves to be a dynamic machine of memory and devotion, a conceptual scaffolding that enables spiritual movement and—ultimately—the annihilation of apophatic fulfillment.

When we think of the visual stimuli that served the purposes of affective piety, we might first come up with images of the enfleshed Christ, the Virgin, or the saints. We expect images that invite empathetic engagement. The *Benjamin Minor*, by contrast, gives us diagrams—literal diagrams, in the case of several of the manuscripts, and an underlying diagrammatic structure that is implicit in the list of names, and the relationships of the people they name—and the affective states they represent—detailed in the prose. Linear forms, like number, are abstract, rational, and cold; here, however, they are in the service of a practice of contemplation that seeks to raise the devout soul to a state of ecstasy. The list of Jacob's offspring found in the *Benjamin Minor* can be read in the context of genealogical diagrams of the late Middle Ages, ranging from the ubiquitous Tree of Jesse, expressing in visual form the human lineage of Christ, to the historical genealogies laid out in overlapping timelines in universal histories by Peter of Poitiers (ca. 1130–1205) and Matthew Paris (ca. 1200–1259). Yet the familial list of the *Benjamin Minor* is, strikingly, bidirectional: it combines the upward flow of the Tree of Jesse, which culminates in the fruit of the Incarnation, with the "descending structure" of the historical genealogy, which conveys "the implicit metaphor of a stream—of blood, of wealth, of values—flowing from the same source situated on high, down to a group of individuals placed much lower."[1] The sequence of the list moves sequentially forward in time, from progenitor to descendent, in keeping with the conventional flow of the historical genealogy; but through devotional practice, the reader moves upward through the list, back toward the source of all things.

By using symbolic forms, especially the bidirectional sequence of the list, elaborately structured by the geometrical relationships that both link and cut across branches of genealogical trees, the *Benjamin Minor* generates an elaborate system for religious practice, one that assists the reader in the effort to grow spiritually, to have a fruitful devotional life, and to ultimately reach the ecstatic state of "rauesching of mynde" (*in mentis excessu*) that is embodied in the figure of Benjamin, youngest child of the patriarch Jacob. This chapter begins by sketching out the context of the *Benjamin Minor* in late medieval England and its place in the tradition of contemplative literature, before turning to a close examination of the work's structure and the organizational principle of the list of Jacob's offspring. The *Benjamin Minor* is at once a genealogical list and a highly structured treatise on contemplation, a work whose sequential mnemonic structure simultaneously offers up a dynamic, generative environment for spiritual growth.

I will then put the *Benjamin Minor* in the context of another insular devotional text that also refers to the genealogy of the family of Jacob, especially as presented in the form of the family tree: namely, the *Reule of Crysten Religioun* by the fifteenth-century writer Reginald Pecock. I will treat Pecock's *Reule* much more briefly than the *Benjamin Minor*, with the goal of illustrating the ways that, in both works, the family tree is used in a devotional context both

---

1. Christiane Klapisch-Zuber, "The Genesis of the Family Tree," *I Tatti Studies in the Italian Renaissance* 4 (1991): 105–29, here 112. On Peter of Poitiers' *Compendium historiae in genealogia Christi* and English royal genealogies, see Klapisch-Zuber, "Family Tree," 116–17.

to organize knowledge and to facilitate the process of the reader's intellectual and spiritual growth. As a simple list of words, the genealogical sequence appears to be whole, contained, and closed; as a list of names of living beings, however—and, implicitly, of the abstract qualities they represent—the genealogical sequence is also dynamic and generative, sometimes in very unexpected ways. The closed nature of the list thus emerges as the paradoxical site of reproduction and multiplication, yielding spiritual fruits.

CONTEMPLATIVE LITERATURE AND NEGATIVE THEOLOGY IN MEDIEVAL ENGLAND

The devotional literature of medieval England is heterogeneous, including a wide range of works informed by different theological perspectives. Among these is a strand described by modern scholars as "mysticism"; this is not an inaccurate term, but it is a somewhat anachronistic one, emerging from the late seventeenth-century effort to systematize various contemplative theologies in the context of the Counter-Reformation. Commentaries on figures such as Teresa of Avila and John of the Cross were at that time integrated into a set of practices that were united in the service of an explicitly mystical theology. Yet even though the codification of these practices was relatively late, the underlying concept of the "mystical" was there from the very outset of the tradition, in the fifth-century treatise by pseudo-Dionysius, the *De mystica theologia*.[2] This work of apophatic or "negative theology," like other works in the Dionysian corpus, elaborates the nature of God by defining that which He is not; and it outlines the means for the individual soul to meet the divine in Neoplatonic terms, identifying not only a processual chain of being but also a hierarchy through which the human comes into contact—in a highly mediated way—with the divine. Pseudo-Dionysius's works were translated from Greek into Latin several times, each time having a significant impact on the development of both philosophy and contemplative literature, beginning with Eriugena in the ninth century and continuing with Robert Grosseteste in the thirteenth century.

I will not attempt to give an account of the impact of pseudo-Dionysius's writings on medieval philosophy, which was significant; but I will address the impact of his work on the literature of contemplation, which was pro-

---

2. On the history of "mystical theology" and its key texts, see the useful overview by Nicholas Watson ("Introduction") in *The Cambridge Companion to Medieval English Mysticism*, ed. Samuel Fanous and Vincent Gillespie (Cambridge: Cambridge University Press, 2011), 1–28, esp. 4–7.

found. This is apparent, for example, in Bonaventure's *Itinerarium mentis in Deum* (dated in the prologue to 1259), where he writes, concerning the work of contemplation:

> If you want to know how these things may come about, ask grace, not learning; desire, not understanding; the groaning of prayer, not diligence in reading; the Bridegroom, not the teacher; God, not man; darkness, not clarity; not light, but the fire that wholly inflames and carries one into God.[3]

Both the apophatic quality of pseudo-Dionysius and the habit of speaking in paired opposites can be seen in Bonaventure's words: "darkness, not clarity; not light, but the fire." In addition, the effect of pseudo-Dionysius was felt in the work of the twelfth-century Victorines, the theologians attached to the Abbey of St. Victor, who taught in the schools and ultimately in the University of Paris. The Victorines developed a richly elaborated sense of the "mystical": that is, a systematic way of expounding the apparent paradoxes found in scripture into an intricate allegorical account oriented toward contemplative practice.[4] Among the most influential of these were two works by Richard of St. Victor, the *Benjamin Major* and the *Benjamin Minor*, both of these grounded in Psalm 67's reference to the last son of Jacob, "Benjamin adolescentulus in mentis excessu" ("the young Benjamin, lifted up in the mind"; Psalm 67:28). Both works are guides to contemplative practice, and the latter—the *Benjamin Minor*—does this through an elaborate exposition of the family of Jacob, naming each member in a sequential list.[5] Figure 4.1 shows the family of Jacob: the patriarch, who is both father and husband, stands at the top, with his two wives, Rachel and Leah ("Lya"), below. Each wife is accompanied by her handmaid, Zilpah and Bilhah (here "Zelfa" and "Bala"). The children of Jacob are shown below, each descending from their mother. This diagram comes from

---

3. Bonaventure, *The Mind's Road to God*, trans. George Boas (Indianapolis: Bobbs-Merrill, 1953), VII.6; quoted in the preface to Samuel Fanous and Vincent Gillespie, eds., *The Cambridge Companion to Medieval English Mysticism* (Cambridge: Cambridge University Press, 2011), ix–xiv, here xi.

4. On the use of "architectural... symbols" to support "mystical teaching," including "the ark of Noah, the ark of Moses, the temple of Solomon, and the City of Jerusalem," see Patrice Sicard, "Mystical Experience According to Hugh of Saint Victor: Principles, Foundations, and Types," in *A Companion to the Abbey of Saint Victor in Paris*, ed. Hugh Feiss and Juliet Mousseau (Leiden: Brill, 2018), 469–515, esp. 483–90, here 483; on the "tree in the center," see 500–1).

5. For an overview of the Victorines, see Brian McGuire, "c.1080–1215: Culture and History," in *The Cambridge Companion to Medieval English Mysticism*, ed. Samuel Fanous and Vincent Gillespie (Cambridge: Cambridge University Press, 2011), 29–47, esp. 38–9. A detailed study of the *Benjamin Minor* (82–133) and the *Benjamin Major* (134–78) can be found in Ritva Palmén, *Richard of St. Victor's Theory of the Imagination* (Leiden: Brill, 2014).

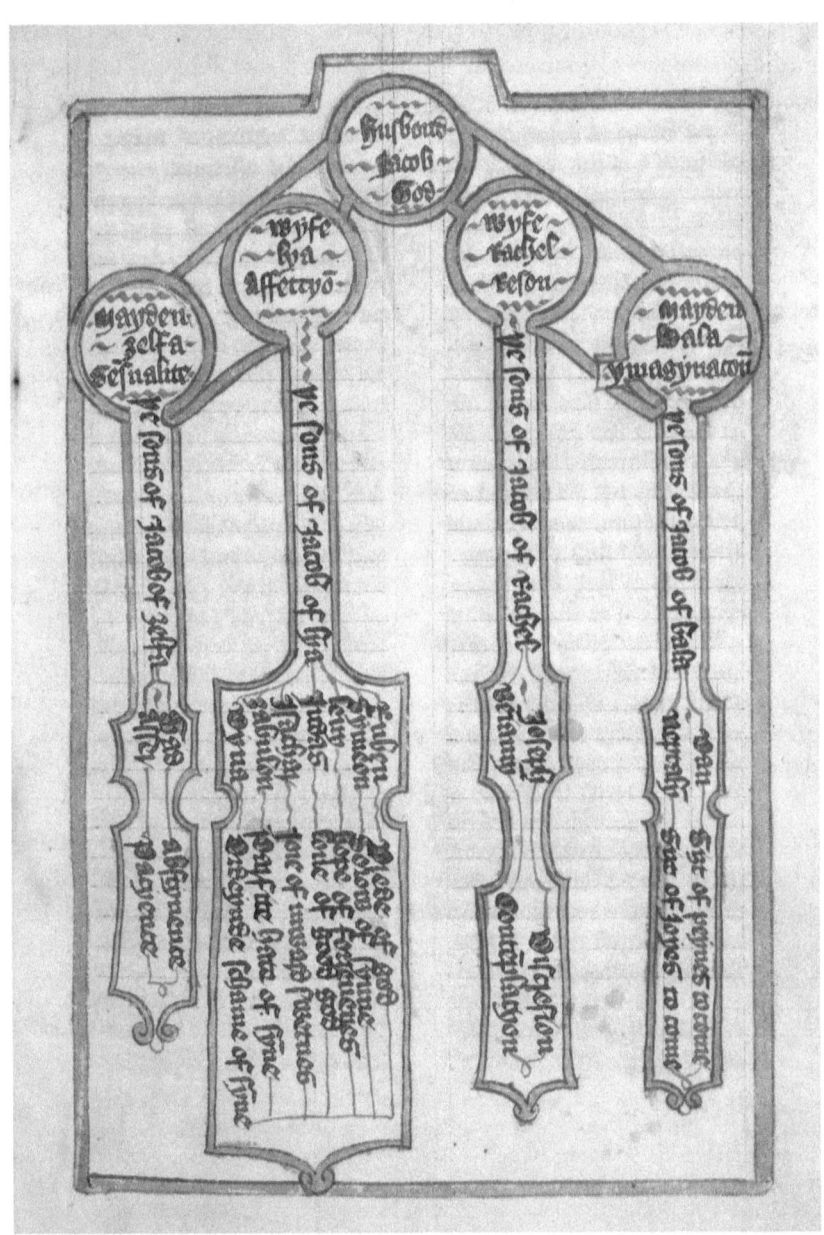

FIGURE 4.1. British Library, Harley MS 674, fol. 112r. By permission of the British Library.

British Library, Harley MS 674, fol. 112r, one of the manuscripts of the Middle English adaptation of Richard of St. Victor's Latin text, several of which include some version of this diagram. One of the manuscript diagrams also includes numbers to indicate the birth order of the children, which corresponds to the order in which they are described in the *Benjamin Minor*, as we will see in more detail below.

The late fourteenth-century Middle English adaptation of the *Benjamin Minor* is shorter than the Latin text; the version that is the focus of this chapter survives in six fifteenth-century manuscripts, and is found in compilations containing what is sometimes called "the Cloud group"—that is, a cluster of texts that travel with the late fourteenth-century *Cloud of Unknowing*, a deeply moving work that seeks to bring its reader to a deeper knowledge of God.[6] What these texts share is a common basis in negative theology, along with a richly affective discourse harnessed in the service of contemplation. While the *Cloud* is an original work, the others are adaptations of earlier Latin works: *Deonise Hid Divinite* is a short translation of pseudo-Dionysius's *De mystica theologia*, for example, while the *Benjamin Minor* (also called *A Tretyse of the Stodye of Wysdome that Men Clepen Beniamyn*) adapts Richard of St. Victor's twelfth-century work. The relationship of the texts in the *Cloud* group, especially in terms of their affective vocabulary, has been well studied by Cheryl Taylor, who highlights three aspects of the Middle English adaptations: 1) the emphasis on "affection"; 2) the enhancement of pronoun usage, to suggest the presence of a speaker and a listener; and 3) the abundance of binary oppositions, including paradoxes, along with associated vivid physical imagery.[7]

Let me return briefly to the first of the three points, "affection." The Middle English term *affectyon*, sometimes modernized as "love," is actually something a bit different—for example, as seen in Figure 4.1, Lya represents "affection," while one of her sons represents "love of good God," so clearly these are different things. Affection, in Middle English usage, refers to longing or yearning, here as a means to spiritual union. The use of the Middle English term *affectyon* in the *Benjamin Minor* follows Richard of St. Victor's use of the compa-

---

6. The edited text of the Middle English *Benjamin Minor* (under the title "A Tretyse of the Stodye of Wysdome that Men Clepen Beniamin") appears at pp. 11–46 in Phyllis Hodgson, ed., *Deonise Hid Diuinite and Other Treatises on Contemplative Prayer Related to The Cloud of Unknowing* (Oxford: Oxford University Press, 1955, rpt. 1958). The text appearing in Hodgson's edition is based on the early fifteenth-century British Library, Harley MS 674; five additional witnesses to this version date from the same century. In addition to the six manuscripts of this version, an additional five (also from the fifteenth century) are extant. A summary can be found at https://quod.lib.umich.edu/m/middle-english-dictionary/bibliography/BIB285?rid=hyp.386.19990513t124835.

7. Cheryl Taylor, "The *Cloud*-Author's Remaking of the pseudo-Dionysius' *Mystical Theology*," *Medium Aevum* 75, no. 2 (2006): 202–18, esp. 204–8.

rable Latin term, *affectio,* to describe Lya; the Middle English text elaborates the term, however, sharing with the other works in the *Cloud* group a special emphasis on affective engagement in the spiritual labor of the contemplative. The affective yearning of Lya gives rise, as we will see, to multiple emotional offspring—fear, sorrow, hope, love—while the rational power of Rachel gives birth to very different qualities.

THE *BENJAMIN MINOR*: BACKGROUND AND STRUCTURE

Having provided some background on the work, let us turn to the genealogical structure and the ways in which the basic diagrammatic relations seen in Figure 4.1 are further elaborated within the text. First, one is struck by the extent to which this genealogy privileges pairs: there are two wives, served by two handmaids; each handmaid has two children, as does one of the wives; only one of the women here—Lya—gives birth to a larger number of children. Beyond this, additional pairings emerge based on the allegorical meanings attributed to each of the children. In some cases, this pairing emphasizes an existing pair, as when the two sons of Rachel's handmaid, Dan and Neptalym, represent two aspects of "sight"—"sight of pains to come," and "sight of joys to come." In other cases, the pairing cuts across maternal genealogies, as when Gad is matched with Dan, and Asser with Neptalym. These pairings affirm the implicit claim to completeness provided by the list, with each additional couple providing a symmetry, either of resemblance or opposition, that further adds to the list's capaciousness.

Before unpacking the genealogical relations before us, it is worth putting this practice of pairing into context, particularly with regard to the maternal genealogies recounted here. The pairing of Rachel and Leah was used in medieval culture in two distinct (though interrelated) ways: 1) as the maternal figures in a foundational national genealogy, the people of Israel, who would themselves become a template for medieval conceptions of the nation; 2) as a complementary yet opposed pair of sisters, who are similar (because they are sisters) but are simultaneously diametrically opposed on some fundamental level. In this latter respect, Leah and Rachel were frequently coupled with other pairs of sisters, especially Martha and Mary. In each of these pairings, one sister represented the active life, one the contemplative.[8] We can see this well illustrated in the life of Hugh of Avalon, Bishop of Lincoln in the late

---

8. On Rachel and Leah in association with other pairings in Christian exegesis, especially Mary and Martha, see Giles Constable, *Three Studies in Medieval Religious and Social Thought:*

twelfth century, who, according to his biographer, would sometimes leave his episcopal duties to go on a retreat with his Carthusian brothers: his biographer writes, "Here . . . he could freely enjoy the embraces and feast fully on the beauty of his lovely Rachel, and get away completely from the dreariness of blear-eyed Leah."[9] Rachel and Leah were also expounded allegorically in a number of other ways, perhaps most importantly as Ecclesia and Synagoga: here, Rachel's beauty and desirability associated her with the Church, while the "blear-eyed" quality of Leah associated her with the blindness of the Jews.[10]

In the *Benjamin Minor*, however, the active and contemplative template is at the fore, elaborated by Richard of St. Victor in terms of affect (*affectio*), embodied in Leah, and reason (*ratio*), embodied in Rachel. Studies of the *Benjamin Minor*—whether the Latin original or the Middle English adaptation—tend to focus on the figure of Rachel and her offspring, especially her younger son, Benjamin, who represents contemplation itself. The work closes with a meditation on how Rachel is both fulfilled and consumed by giving birth to Benjamin, just as the devout soul is both fulfilled and consumed by the apophatic experience of the divine:

> No man may take soche grace wythoutyn greet study and brennyng desires comyng before. And that wote Rachel ful wel. And for-thi sche multyplieth hir study, and whetteth hir desires, iche desire on desire, so that at the laste, in greet habundaunce of brennyng desires and sorrow of the delaiing of hir desire, Beniamyn is borne, and his moder Rachel diyeth. For whi in what tyme that a soule is rauischid abouen himself by habundaunce of desires and a greet multytude of loue, so that it is enflawmyd with the liȝt of the Godheed, sekerly than dyȝth al mans reson.[11]

In this passage, we see the emergence of perfect contemplation in the moment that reason surrenders, in an ecstasy mediated through apophasis.

The Interpretation of Mary and Martha, the Ideal of the Imitation of Christ, the Orders of Society (Cambridge: Cambridge University Press, 1995), 10–11; 18–19.

9. Decima L. Douie and Hugh Farmer, eds. and trans., *The Life of St. Hugh of Lincoln* (Oxford: Clarendon, 1985), 2.44 (ch. 9). Quoted in McGuire, "c.1080–1215," 29–47, here 37.

10. On the opposition of Ecclesia and Synagoga, see Suzanne Conklin Akbari, *Idols in the East: European Representations of Islam and the Orient, 1100–1450* (Ithaca: Cornell University Press, 2009), 121–2. On the depiction of Synagoga with regard to the gaze, see Sara Lipton, *Dark Mirror: The Medieval Origins of Anti-Jewish Iconography* (New York: Metropolitan Books / Henry Holt and Company, 2014), 42–5; 61–3; 120–2.

11. Hodgson, *Benjamin Minor*, 45.

Yet while this aspect of the *Benjamin Minor* has been well analyzed by scholars such as Michelle Karnes and Ritva Palmén, the earlier parts of the text have been neglected, particularly with regard to the formal structures that cut across the lines of the diagram, complicating the austere simplicity of the list.[12] We can see clearly here in the diagram the orderly hierarchy of the family, as the patriarch Jacob sits at the top, with a pair of wives, and their pair of handmaids, followed by the rows of children arranged in vertical rows. Yet there is a second ordering sequence as well: that of birth order, which skips around. One of the manuscripts, Cambridge University Library MS Kk.vi.26, actually includes this sequential numbering of children. The birth order sequence is also deployed in the narrative, as we move from an account of the wives of Jacob to the series of offspring, each of which is allegorically expounded both in terms of the quality that appears in the diagram—for example, Ruben is "drede" (or fear) of God, while Symeon is "sorrow of sin"—and also in terms of a secondary quality. An interesting case appears with the sons of Zelfa, the handmaid of Lya: in the diagram and in the text, they are said to represent abstinence (Gad) and patience (Asser). Yet they are also said to have another allegorical signification, where Gad represents "happynes or selynes," while Asser represents "blissidheed," or the state of being blessed (27). A similar double level of meaning is associated with the sons of Rachel's handmaid, Bala: Dan and Neptalym represent "the sight of pains to come" and "the sight of joys to come," respectively; but they also represent "doom" (or judgement), in the case of Dan, and "likeness" (25). In each case, the additional quality is based on a scriptural reference, as each mother names her child based on her state of mind or the condition she experiences. For the author, however, each moment of naming provides another opportunity to expound the allegorical significance of the children of Jacob, and to provide the contemplative matrix for spiritual growth.

Beyond these, additional structures are created within the text based on interrelations that link the sons of Jacob across matrilineal lines. This takes place, for example, when lines are (figuratively) drawn connecting the two sons of Lya's handmaid, Gad and Asser, with the two sons of Rachel's handmaid, Dan and Neptalym. The text states that "thees foure sones of thes two maydens" can be understood allegorically as "the cite of our concyence" which is tempted from within, by "thou3tes," and from without, by "our fyue wittys." Dan—the son of Bala—protects us, however, by "deme" or judgement of those "yuel thou3tes," while Gad—the son of Zelfa—protects us from "fals delices by

---

12. Michelle Karnes, *Imagination, Meditation, and Cognition in the Middle Ages* (Chicago: University of Chicago Press, 2011), 28–31; Palmén, *Theory of the Imagination*, 82–133.

vse of abstinence." Each of them is supported by his full brother, Dan by Neptalym and Gad by Asser. A whole series of relations linking the four sons of Jacob is laid out, in a kind of matrix, so that they together form a fortification so that "the cytee walles"—that is, the united soul and body of the individual person—"ben not brokyn."[13]

Another set of parallel structures is established that links not the offspring of the handmaidens, but the offspring of the wives. This is carried out by a set of parallels that juxtapose the last child born to Lya—that is, Dinah ("Dyna")—with the last child born to Rachel, Benjamin. Readers tend to simply focus on the climactic function of Benjamin at the end of the narrative, but it is important to notice the ways in which the author highlights the birth of Dyna both as a new beginning—with a new chapter break, and a recapitulation of some of the material that opened the work—and a secondary ending, with her birth repeatedly described as being "last." Just before the first child born to the patriarch Jacob, Ruben, is introduced early in the text, the author pauses to explain how each of the children born to Lya represents a quality; each of them, he emphasizes, is "ordained" or ordered, so that it is in the right measure:

> Also the seuen children of Lya ben seuen vertewes, for vertewe is not ells bot an ordeynd and a mesurid felyng of a mans soule. Than is mans feling in soule ordeynd when it is that thing that it schuld be. Than is it mesurid when it is as moche as it schuld be. Thees felynges in a mans soule mowen be now ordeind and mesurid, and now vnordeind and vnmsurid. Bot when thei ben ordeynd and mesurid, than ben thei acomptyd amonges the sones of Jacob.[14]

This concept of "ordained"—orderly, measured—qualities in the soul returns late in the text, with the introduction of Dyna in a new chapter heading on "Ordeinde Schame" that includes a long account of how the shame related to sin depends upon and follows hatred of sin, just as Dyna is born after Zabulon. The account of how Dyna's quality of shame is "ordained" is then expanded

---

13. "Bot here it is to witen how that with thees foure sones of thees two maydens, the cite of our concyence is kept wonderfuly from alle temptaciouns. For alle temptacyon outher it riseth withinne by thou3t, or ells withouten by somme of oure fyue wittys. Bot withinne schal Dan deme and dampen yuel thou3tes by si3t of pyne, and withouten schal Gad put a3eyn fals delices by vse of abstinence. Dan wakith withinne, and Gad withouten. And also thees other two brethren helpen hem ful mochel. Neptalym makith pees withinne with Dan, and Asser biddeth Gad haue no drede of his enmyes. . . . Also Asser helpith his brother withouten, so that thorow hem bothe the cytee walls ben not brokyn. Gad holdeth out ese, and Asser pursueth disease" (Hodgson, *Benjamin Minor*, 29).

14. Hodgson, *Benjamin Minor*, 16.

into an account of how all the qualities of Lya's children are "ordained"—if they were unordained, says the author, "than ben thei vices," but if they are ordained, "than ben thei vertewes."[15]

Dyna's role as the last of Lya's children is emphasized by the author, who explains that "therfore it is that after hem alle, and last, is Dyna borne, for after a foule fal and a faylyng cometh sone schame. And thus after many fallynges and faylynges, and schame folowyng, a man lerneth by the proof that there is nothing / betyr than to be rewyld afer counsel, the whiche is the rediest getyng of discrecioun."[16] Joseph—who signifies discretion—follows Dyna, just as discretion follows shame. This allegoresis of Dinah is a fundamentally positive one, where she represents the shame that paves the way for discretion and, ultimately, the contemplation embodied in Benjamin that will ravish and consume the rational soul. Here, shame is instrumental, the gateway to salvation. This interpretation of Dinah is very unusual in the medieval exegetical tradition, which more often interpreted her story in negative terms, focusing particularly on an episode in Genesis that, interestingly, is entirely omitted from the *Benjamin Minor*. This is the story of Dinah's rape by Shechem and the subsequent revenge taken on him and his entire tribe by her brothers Simeon and Levi.[17]

---

15. Hodgson, *Benjamin Minor*, 38.

16. Hodgson, *Benjamin Minor*, 40–1.

17. An overview of the exegesis of Dinah can be found in Joy A. Schroeder, *Dinah's Lament: The Biblical Legacy of Sexual Violence in Christian Interpretation* (Minneapolis: Fortress Press, 2007), building on the work of Barbara J. Newman in "Flaws in the Golden Bowl: Gender and Spiritual Formation in the Twelfth Century," in *From Virile Woman to WomanChrist: Studies in Medieval Religion and Literature* (Philadelphia: University of Pennsylvania Press, 1995), 19–45. The three main interpretations of Dinah, according to Schroeder and Newman, are: 1) Dinah represents ordinary Christians, Shechem is heresy, and the brothers are the Church hierarchy. This shows up in: Bede, *In Genesim commentarium*, c. 34 (PL 91.261–2); Hrabanus Maurus, *Commentariorum in Genesim libri quatuor*, c. 34 (PL 107.615); Bruno d'Asti, *Expositio in Genesim*, c. 34 (PL 164.215–16); Peter Riga, *Aurora: Petri Rigae Biblia Versificata, A Verse Commentary on the Bible*, vol. 1, ed. Paul E. Beichner (South Bend, IN: University of Notre Dame Press, 1965), 67.1023–8. 2) Dinah as a figure for the vice of *curiositas*. The most famous instance is Bernard of Clairvaux, *S. Bernardi opera omnia*, vol. 3, *Liber de gradibus humilitatis et superbiae*, ed. Jean Leclercq, C. H. Talbot, and H. M. Rochais (Rome: Editiones Cistercienses, 1963), 13–59, here 13–15. 3) Schroeder and Newman also argue that Dinah was interpreted for female monastic audiences as a literal warning about the need for strict enclosure. I am very grateful to Tristan Sharp for the above summary, and for the following two supplemental interpretations based on his own research: 4) Dinah used as a warning to male monastics against entanglement in worldly affairs and *vagatio* (not the same as *curiositas*): see Peter Damian, *Die Briefe des Petrus Damiani*, vol. 3, *Die Briefe d. dt. Kaiserzeit*, ed. Kurt Reindel (München: Monumenta Germaniae Historica, 1993), 202; and Peter of Celle, *De disciplina claustrali*, in Petrus Cellensis, *L'école du cloître*, ed. and trans. Gérard de Martel (Paris: Éditions du Cerf, 1977), 146. The *Speculum novitii* sometimes attributed to the Cistercian Stephen of Sawley is arguably in this category as well. See Edmond Mikkers, "Un 'Speculum Novitii' inédit d'Étienne de Salley,"

The Dyna of the *Benjamin Minor* is anomalous, in part because of the omission of the rape and revenge narrative, and in part because of how elaborately her position among the siblings is articulated within the overall genealogical patterning of the text. Dyna stands out among the children of Lya as a kind of remainder: if we look at the list of the sons of Lya, we see that the six sons form pairs of conventional contraries in a way that is familiar in personification allegory, such as the evenly matched battles found in Prudentius's *Psychomachia* or the paired figures found in the Garden of Deduit in Guillaume de Lorris's opening section of the *Roman de la Rose*. Dread (or fear) is paired with hope, Ruben with Levy; sorrow is paired with joy, Symeon with Isachar; love is paired with hate, Judas with Zabulon. Shame is left over, leaving Dyna out of the paired sequence of the children of Lya; but this quality of being the remainder is precisely what generates the juxtaposition of Dyna, last-born of Lya, with Benjamin, last-born of Rachel. The list of siblings provides a sense of completeness, a sense that is amplified by the symmetrical pairings of the six sons of Lya: Dyna stands apart from these, being a kind of remainder or superfluity. Yet in serving as a counterpart to Benjamin, who himself stands apart from his older brothers, Dyna holds the promise of offering something more, of being not just that which is left over.

These two remainders or surplus children are further contrasted in the language of vision that is applied to each of them. Benjamin is seen to be ravished by the sight of the divine, while Dyna is said to be exposed bodily to the sight of others. Of Benjamin, the author says:

> Bot longe aftyr Joseph is Beniamin borne; for whi trewly bot ʒif it so be that we vse us besyly and longe in goostly trauayles, with the whiche we ben lernid to knowe oure-self, we mowen not be reisyd to the knowing and contemplacioun of God. He doth for nouʒt that liftyth up his iʒe to the siʒt of God, that is not ʒit able to see himself.... And wite it wel that he that desireth to se God, hym behoueth to clense his soule, the whiche is a mirour in the whiche alle thing is cleerly seen when it is clene. And when the mirour is foule, then maist thou see nothing cleerly therin. And riʒt so it is of thi soule. When it is foule, neither thou knowest thiself, ne God.[18]

Collectanea Ordinis Cisterciensium Reformatorum 8 (1946): 17–68, here 66. 5) Another Cistercian, Baldwin of Forde, focuses on Shechem's desire for Dinah as an instance of disordered love: see Baldwin of Forde, *Opera* (Turnhout: Brepols, 1991), 331. This seems to be related to Abelard's *Planctus Dinae*, in which Dinah and Shechem are portrayed as tragic lovers separated by her no-good family. On the *Planctus*, see Gilbert Dahan, "La Matière biblique dans le *Planctus* de Dina de Pierre Abélard," in *Hortus troporum: Florilegium in honorem Gunillae Iverson*, ed. Alexander Andrée and Erika Kihlman (Stockholm: Stockhoms Universitet, 2008), 255–67.

18. Hodgson, *Benjamin Minor*, 42–3.

And of Dyna, he says:

> Bot whatso thou be that wenyst that thou haste getyn Dyna, think whether thee wolde schame as moche and a foule thou3t were in thin herte, as thee wold and thou were mad stonde nakid bifore the kyng and alle the rewme. And sekirly ellys wite thou ri3t wel that thou hast not getyn 3it ordeinde schame in thi felyng, 3if it so be that thou haue lesse schame with thi foule herte than with thi foule body; and 3if thou more schame with thi foule body in the si3t of men than with thi foule herte in the si3te of the kyng of heuen and of all his aungelles and holy seyntes in heuen.[19]

Like Leah and Rachel, Dinah and Benjamin are both similitudes and opposites: they are both described as coming "last," and both are defined in terms of vision. Yet they differ not only in their maternal descent, but in terms of the visual experience: Benjamin is the one who sees, while Dinah is the one who is seen, as she undergoes the salvific experience of shame. This shame, however, is a fruitful one—or at least, it was perceived that way by medieval readers. This is vividly illustrated in another manuscript of the *Benjamin Minor*, this one in the Houghton Library at Harvard (MS Richardson 22, ca. 1425).[20] It includes a version of the diagram we have seen already in the Harley manuscript, but not a very interesting one. What *is* striking about this manuscript, however, is its fascinating decorative program. The opening page is ornamented, followed by a series of ordinary pages featuring only decorated capitals. Then the diagrammatic list of the children of Jacob appears (Figure 4.2), not nearly as ornate a schematic as in the Harley manuscript (Figure 4.1); then, suddenly, on the page immediately after the diagram, which expounds its content, we have a wonderful profusion of ornament, at least as lavish—perhaps a little more so—than the opening page (Figure 4.3). It seems as though the text has begun again, with an abundance of efflorescence. We then go back into the usual page format, until we suddenly get another flowering, smaller than the others. This is the section on Dyna, which returns to the theme of "ordained" virtues that appeared on the earlier ornate page, after the diagram. The decorative program here, in other words, brings out more fully the internal logic of the text, highlighting the importance of the Dyna narrative to the overall structure of the work, and bubbling forth in exuberant color detail at moments where the diagrammatic intensity of the

---

19. Hodgson, *Benjamin Minor*, 37.
20. A description of Harvard University, Houghton Library, MS Richardson 22 can be found online at: https://curiosity.lib.harvard.edu/medieval-renaissance-manuscripts/catalog/34-990098807420203941.

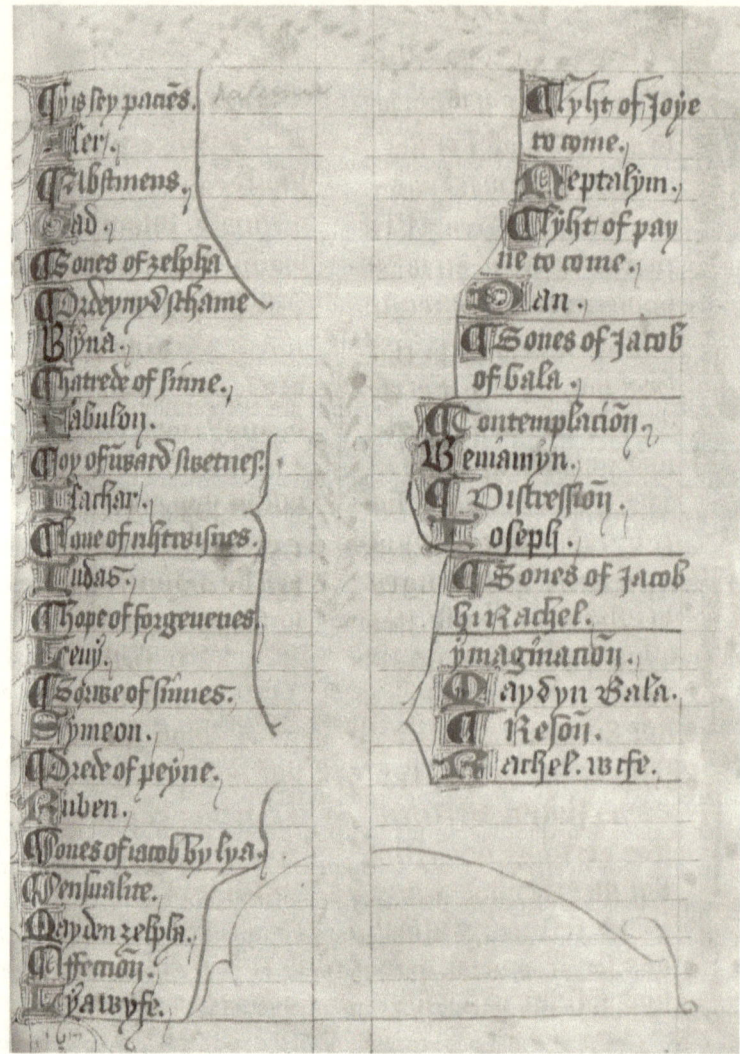

FIGURE 4.2. Harvard University, Houghton Library, MS Richardson 22, fol. 54r.

allegory is at its highest. In the genealogical diagram, the red and blue capitals pick out the names of the children of Jacob; only two are picked out in black letters instead—Benjamin and Dyna, the last-born children of the wives of Jacob (Figure 4.2).

The last lines of the text, too, provide a visual, formal counterpart to the prose narrative. The final folio concludes with the end of the *Benjamin Minor* in the left column and some shorter prayers on the right. The last vestiges of

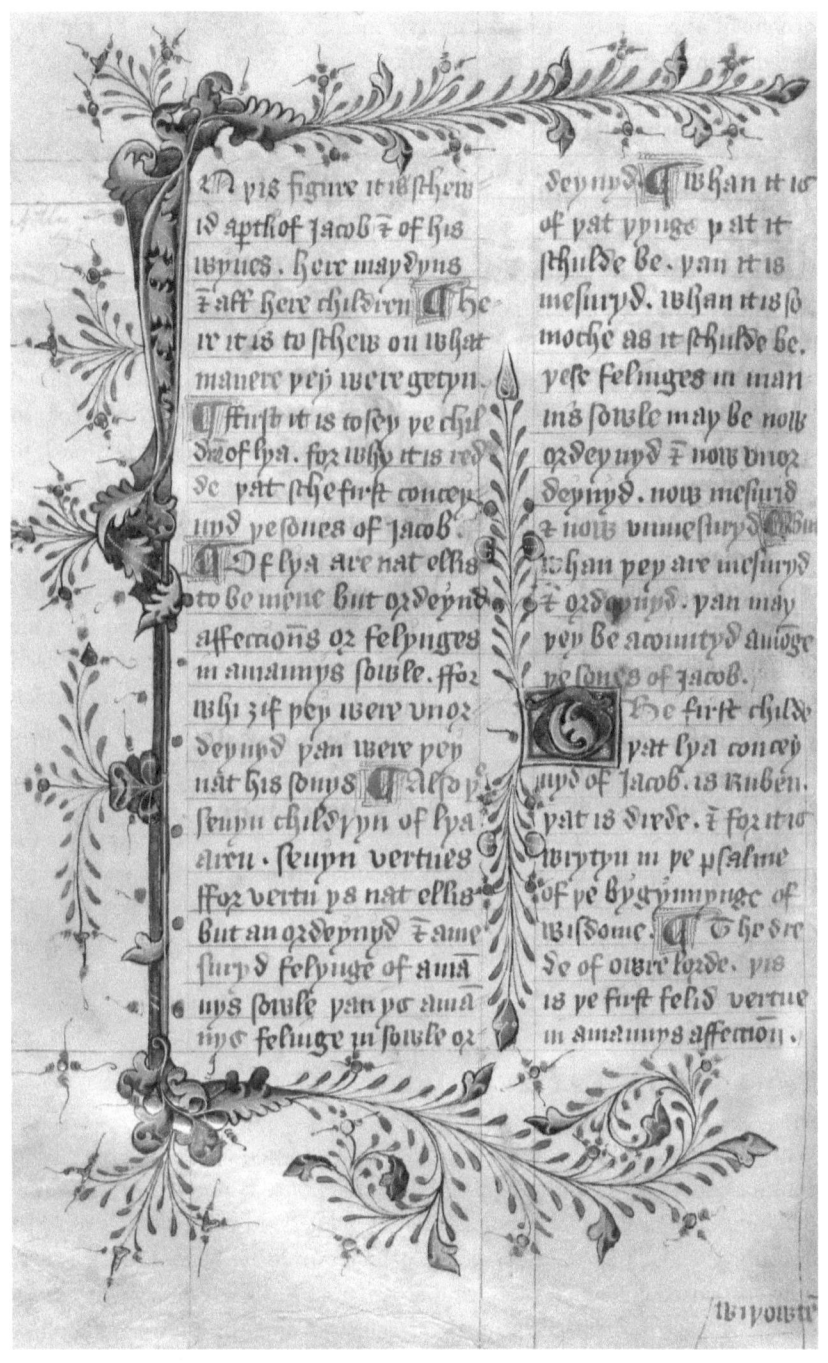

FIGURE 4.3. Harvard University, Houghton Library, MS Richardson 22, fol. 54v.

ornament appear here, with two capitals marking out two lines of Latin, followed by three lines of English translation:

> So that it be fulfillid in the that that is iwretyn in the psalme.
> Ibi beniamyn adolescentulus in mentis excessu.
> That is / There ys beniamyn the ȝonge childe in rauisschinge of mynde.[21]

By closing with the biblical passage, the *Benjamin Minor* makes a kind of circle. The work as a whole is an elaborate exposition of this very biblical passage (Psalm 67:28), which itself becomes the climax of the text. The reader is brought face to face with the fact of Benjamin's ecstatic contemplation, raised up step by step through the genealogical hierarchy of the family of Jacob. In other words, the genealogical ladder flows in two directions: downward, in the fecund reproduction of the family tree; and upward, as the individual soul in contemplation is raised up, step by step, to the sight of God. The list of the names of the children of Jacob makes up the rungs of that ladder.

The literary form of the Middle English *Benjamin Minor* is thus both linear and cyclical, ordered by the list of Jacob's children, which proceed from the patriarch and yet also lead back to him. In this way, the reader is interpellated into a spiritual journey which is as much affective as intellective, and which uses an elaborately intertwined and symmetrical formal structure to enable the soul's ascent. The *Benjamin Minor* serves as a handbook that seeks to provide the reader with the directions needed in order to become the soul that is united with God, inhabiting in turn the roles of Lya (in its affection), Zelfa (in its sensuality), Bala (through the faculty of imagination), and Rachel (through the faculty of reason). Through enacting each of these receptive roles, the soul seeks to bear the offspring of Jacob, hoping to achieve that perfect, fecund moment of utter annihilation.

REGINALD PECOCK'S FAMILY TREES

While the Houghton manuscript (Figures 4.2 and 4.3) appears to have been commissioned for a community of female religious, as noted on fol. 51v, the *Benjamin Minor* also circulated among lay readers, in compilations of short devotional texts. It appears, for example, in Westminster School MS 3, a carefully composed collection of items that Amanda Moss has described as typical of "the fashion for devotional miscellanies and common-profit books

---

21. Harvard University, Houghton Library, MS Richardson 22, fol. 68v.

circulating among London merchant families from the early fifteenth century onwards."[22] This audience is the same reading community targeted by the fifteenth-century writer and bishop Reginald Pecock in the pedagogical program outlined and carried out in his major works; the mode of spiritual education, however, especially with regard to the role of reason and the way in which knowledge is acquired, is substantially different in Pecock's work from what we have seen in the *Benjamin Minor*.[23] The genealogy of the family tree, in both cases, plays a key role in structuring the acquisition of knowledge and spiritual growth: the *Benjamin Minor* and Pecock's devotional works, however, differ sharply with regard to how that takes place. In the *Benjamin Minor*, knowledge is achieved through divinely inspired illumination, as the soul is drawn upward through affective engagement, yoked to the faculties of the mind; in Pecock's works, knowledge—including spiritual knowledge—is achieved primarily through human intellectual effort, with little attention to affect. In both cases, the polyvalent metaphor of the tree, including the family tree, illuminates late medieval attitudes toward knowledge: it is, on the one hand, infinitely generative and all-consuming, and, on the other hand, limited and in need of careful husbandry.

Although his writings are generally didactic and programmatic, Pecock sometimes adds color to his texts by including vivid descriptions and figurative language to illustrate his rational arguments. A good example of this appears in Pecock's *Reule of Crysten Religioun* (c. 1443), where the prologue includes an elaborate description of how the mournful narrator of the work found himself unexpectedly visited by "a multitude of persoonys ful comely and faire"—that is, personifications in the form of beautiful women.[24] This passage recalls similar scenes in some of the most famous dream visions of the Middle Ages, including Boethius's *Consolation of Philosophy* and Alanus de Insulis's *Plaint of Nature*. Mishtooni Bose has also suggested that this scene may owe something to the opening of Christine de Pizan's *Cité des dames*.[25]

---

22. Amanda Moss, "A Merchant's Tales: A London Fifteenth-Century Household Miscellany," *Yearbook of English Studies* 33 (2003): 156–69, here 158.

23. On Pecock's educational program, see Kirsty Campbell, *The Call to Read: Reginald Pecock's Books and Textual Communities* (South Bend, IN: University of Notre Dame Press, 2010).

24. Reginald Pecock, *The Reule of Crysten Religioun, now first edited from Pierpont Morgan ms. 519*, ed. William Cabell Greet (London: Oxford University Press, 1927 [for 1926]; rpt. New York: Kraus Reprint, 1971), 31. An overview of Pecock's works and their chronology can be found in James Simpson, "Reginald Pecock and John Fortescue," in *A Companion to Middle English Prose*, ed. A. S. G. Edwards (Cambridge: D. S. Brewer, 2004), 271–87, see esp. 272–7.

25. Mishtooni Bose, "Vernacular Opinions," in *Uncertain Knowledge: Scepticism, Relativism, and Doubt in the Middle Ages*, ed. Dallas G. Denery II, Kantik Ghosh, and Nicolette Zeeman (Turnhout: Brepols, 2014), 239–59.

Pecock's scene differs from its Boethian model—and resembles Christine's—in the presence of multiple personifications instead of just one. Another key difference, however, that separates Pecock's text from all of the others is that these personifications are explicitly said to be generative.

Pecock uses biblical genealogies twice in the *Reule,* first in an allusion to the fallen angels or "sons of God" who mated with "the daughters of man" to produce giants, recounted in Genesis, chapter 6 ("gigantes autem erant super terram in diebus illis . . . ingressi sunt filii Dei ad filias hominum illaeque genuerunt"; "There were giants in the earth in those days . . . the sons of God came in unto the daughters of men, and they bare children to them" [Genesis 6:4]), and second in an allusion to the wives and children of Jacob. In the first case, Pecock opens the *Reule* by stating that clerks are "sones of God" who, like the fallen angels, seek out not spouses like themselves, but instead "the doughtris of men." These daughters, in Pecock's allegory, are "worldly trouthis, oolde rehercellis, strange stories, fablis of poetis, newe invenciouns." In other words, these daughters represent figurative writing that does not refer to a higher truth, enabling intellectual ascent through the exercise of reason, but which serves instead only to titillate the imaginative faculty of the mind. The progeny of these "doughtris of men," like that spawned by the fallen angels of Genesis, are said to be "giauntis manye and stronge"; allegorically, they are the "manye grete volumes and bookis" that are "myghti and famose," like the monstrous offspring of Genesis ("isti sunt potentes a saeculo viri famosi"; "these ones became mighty men which were of old, men of renown" [Genesis 6:4]).[26]

This first genealogical reference in Pecock's *Reule* is followed by a second one that refers to the sons of Jacob who would father the Tribes of Israel. The personified truths who address Pecock's narrator go on to suggest an alternative genealogy that should take place: they say that clerks, the "sones of God," should direct their affections not toward the unworthy "doughtris of men" or literary fictions, but rather toward the personified "treuthis" themselves. Because of that unnatural union, say the "treuthis," "we doughtris of god lacken oure religiose and goostlie progenye" (33). They invite Pecock's narrator to remedy the omission: "But thou man to whom this grace is youen to haue oure profre . . . forsake not the yifte which is to thee presentid" (34). After fathering the longed-for "goostlie progenye," begotten by "sones of God" (clerks) upon the "doughtris of God" (the "treuthis"), the narrator has another task before him: namely, to take up with the "daughters of men." Pecock writes, "After whanne thou art with vs and oure progenye thus plenteuousely bigoon,

---

26. Pecock, *Reule,* 32–3.

we wole fuche saaf that thou in secundarie maner attende to the doughtris of men, but oonly as to oure seruantis and not our ladies." The offspring of this secondary union will be "children of good werkis," receiving "her herytage and her right names" not from the low-born handmaidens who physically give birth to them, but from the "treuthis" who stand in the legal position of mother: "thei schulen be to vs children of purchace legal and leful and no bastard braunchis."[27]

This family tree, including both wives and handmaidens who bear additional children, is based on the lineage of Jacob described in Genesis 29 and 30, just as we saw in the *Benjamin Minor*. Like the sons of Noah, the progeny of Jacob multiply and fill the earth. While Jacob's sons are literally the fathers of the Tribes of Israel, for Pecock, they represent not only the chosen people of the New Covenant of Christ, but the virtues and vices encountered and expressed by the individual soul. Just as we saw in the *Benjamin Minor*, the progeny of Jacob's wives is clearly set apart from the progeny of the two handmaidens. The projected children begotten by the "sones of God" upon the "doughtris of men"—that is, the offspring who are generated by the union of clerics and allegorical figures—will be included within the legitimate family structure in which the "doughtris of God," the "treuthis" who address Pecock's narrator, function as matriarchs, in the same way that the offspring of the two handmaidens are included within the family tree structured by the two wives of Jacob, Rachel and Lya. For Pecock, only through this properly ordered family relationship can figurative writing be confined to its proper place both within the discursive realm, and within the operation of the individual soul.

It is striking, in this passage, to observe the level of interpretive ability that Pecock expects his reader to possess. These include not only familiarity with the operation of allegorical language, but also the ability to correlate the text with appropriate biblical analogues as well as the interpretive traditions associated with those analogues. In other words, this text requires a sophisticated and knowledgeable reader, one who is ready to participate in the process of their own education. In his wide range of writings, Pecock expects very different levels of interpretive ability from his readers: in the *Donet* (c. 1443-9) and the *Folower to the Donet* (c. 1453-4), he expects a relatively uneducated reader, while in the *Reule* (c. 1443) and the *Repressor* (c. 1449), he expects a more sophisticated one. Pecock himself remarks that the dialogue form of the *Donet* is meant to make the book easier to understand, and that the doctrine contained in it is "a fore taast, a fore assaie, and a fore general and a confuse

---

27. Pecock, *Reule*, 35-6.

knowing of the ful draught and of the ful feeding" found in the more substantial (and difficult) *Reule of Cristen Religioun*.[28] In the latter book, Pecock's *Reule*, the reader is expected to know how to feed himself.

I will not discuss Pecock's use of figurative language in any more detail, though it is rich and elaborate. For our purposes, what is useful to note in Pecock is his use of the family tree of Jacob as a template for mapping out how the individual soul might approach God. Unlike the author of the *Benjamin Minor*, who uses the family tree to account for and to improve the state of the individual soul, Pecock is deeply concerned not only with the individual but also with the welfare of the community. In this context, one might compare the genealogical structures produced within the mendicant orders during the fifteenth century, which feature not only significant Dominican and Franciscan figures but also allegorical figures such as Obedience, Poverty, and Chastity, all of whom serve as guides on the path to spiritual salvation even as they are also presented as roots, trunk, and branches of a figurative tree.[29] Pecock's use of the family tree in the context of the spiritual formation of the community thus appears as a secular counterpart to similar practices within the mendicant orders.

While the systematic approach to theological doctrine and practice found in Pecock's works is distinctive, he can also be seen as one in a long genealogy of devotional writers who use highly schematic, even diagrammatic materials to spell out how the worshiper should approach God. This genealogy includes not only the anonymous author of the *Benjamin Minor* but also the thirteenth-century scientist and theologian Robert Grosseteste. In his *Chastel d'amur*, Grosseteste uses spatial optical metaphors to describe the Incarnation, explaining how the single colorless white ray of light is refracted into the full spectrum as it passes through the "castle of love" that is the body of the Virgin, in the moment when she conceives the Word made flesh. In his *Templum Dei*, the architectural allegory is more universal than that of the *Chastel d'amur*: there, only the body of Mary was the allegorized edifice; in the *Templum Dei*, each one of us. Finally, the spatial organization of knowledge is also fundamental to Grosseteste's *Tabula* (ca. 1230): this is an unprecedented cross-

---

28. Reginald Pecock, *The Donet, now first edited from MS. Bodl. 916 and collated with The poore mennis myrrour (British Museum, Addl. 37788)*, ed. Elsie Vaughan Hitchcock (Oxford: Oxford University Press, 1921), 2.

29. Christian Nikolaus Opitz, "Genealogical Representations of Monastic Communities in Late Medieval Art," in *Meanings of Community Across Medieval Eurasia: Comparative Approaches*, ed. Eirik Hovden, Christina Lutter, and Walter Pohl (Leiden: Brill, 2016), 183–202, see esp. 191–8.

indexing system organized by logographs that functions as a kind of machine for the synthesis of scriptural and natural information.[30]

Like Grosseteste, Pecock uses tables to facilitate the reader's understanding and retention of lists pertaining to the Christian religion. Although none of the few surviving manuscripts of Pecock's works contains diagrams, it is easy to imagine an enthusiastic reader including them in the margin or adding them to his own copy of Pecock's text, much as at least one reader of the *Benjamin Minor* did in adding numbers to the listing of Jacob's children in order to facilitate the Christian exegesis of the family tree of Israel (Cambridge University Library MS Kk.vi.26). It is unsurprising that Pecock's tables are largely unstudied, since diagrams and tables in medieval texts have until recently tended to be ignored by textual scholars, who consider them to be images, and by art historians, who consider them to be text. In a sense, the fact that Pecock's tables exist only in textual form, rather than as drawn diagrams, is totally appropriate to the learning process he lays out: Pecock continually invites the reader to participate in the process of acquiring knowledge. The reader is not to be a passive recipient but an active gardener, working with the author in the cultivation of truth. The tables function in just this way: although Pecock does not hesitate to defend the structure of his tables, arguing that they represent the best-reasoned and most efficient means of conveying doctrine and preserving it in memory, he acknowledges explicitly that a better composition of the tables might well be possible, and encourages his readers to try to do so.[31]

---

30. On Grosseteste's *Chastel d'amur*, see Suzanne Conklin Akbari, *Seeing through the Veil: Optical Theory and Medieval Allegory* (Toronto: University of Toronto Press, 2004), 43. For a comparative study of the *Chastel*, the *Templum Dei*, and the *Tabula*, focusing on architectural allegory, see Suzanne Conklin Akbari, "Diagramming Devotion: The Place of Grosseteste in English Affective Piety" [forthcoming]. For the text of Grosseteste's *Tabula* (completed ca. 1230), see Philipp W. Rosemann, ed., *Tabula magistri Roberti Lincolniensis episcopi cum addicione fratris Ade de Marisco*, in *Roberti Grosseteste Expositio in epistolam sancti Pauli ad Galatas; Glossarum in sancti Pauli epistolas fragmenta; Tabula*, ed. James McEvoy, Richard C. Dales, and Philipp W. Rosemann (Turnhout: Brepols, 1995).

31. In his *Folower to the Donet*, for example, Pecock remarks that "y myghte haue disposid the v e poynt of the ii e table and the v e poynt to the iiij e table. . . . Also y myght haue smyte awey the viij e poynt of the first table" (224–5). Yet Pecock does not reserve the possibility of revising the composition of the tables only to himself; on the contrary, even though Pecock has done his best to compose his materials in the manner most conducive to understanding and retaining in memory, "y wole that men chese whiche of these disposicions [that is, arrangements of the tables] schulen to hem plese; for litil fors it is, as anentis the mater and the trouth of vertuose lyuyng, whethir the oon or the othir be holde. . . . Y wole therfore lete men chese and take these bothe weies, as foryeuen to hem of me, vndir choice" (226). Here, the reader is explicitly invited to participate fully in the cultivation of his own garden—that is, the fruitful garden of his soul. While this terrain will never return to a state of Edenic, prelapsarian grace, it can be a paradise that bears fruits, and that sends up flowering branches

What the authors of these texts have in common is a deep commitment to the generative nature of the reading process. For Grosseteste, in his *Tabula*, the reader manipulates the logographs across the nine *distinctiones* or subject headings in order to cross-reference a range of passages—secular and sacred, written in Latin, Greek, and Arabic—to generate new knowledge, which is at once the product of human ingenuity and divinely revealed to mankind through the ladder of intellectual ascent. For Pecock, the reader is even more explicitly in charge of their own salvation, working with his tables in order to assimilate—and teach—Christian theological truths. Yet for Pecock, intellectual knowledge of those truths is not enough: those truths are also, allegorically, the wives of the rightly guided clerks, who—like the wives of Jacob—are both the wellspring of a maternal genealogy of virtues and also the matriarchal heads of a large progeny, which includes the offspring of their handmaids. There is a generative process at work in the acquisition of knowledge. This same genealogy, as we have seen, underlies the *Benjamin Minor*, where the family of Jacob is both a structure that makes intelligible the relationship of the various faculties of the mind and affects of the soul, and also a kind of ladder by means of which the worshipper can ascend. The list of names, in the *Benjamin Minor*, makes up the rungs of that ladder of ascent. Dinah—and in particular, the shame of Dinah—marks the threshold of this mystical ascent, where the various affects of the spirit that inhabits the body give way to the purely incorporeal features of the eternal soul—discretion and contemplation—that are embodied as the sons of Rachel. For the devout reader who studies this genealogy, the children of Jacob are both a manifestation of the divine and the pathway that leads to sweet and eternal annihilation. The names of his children, lovingly listed—and even numbered—in the manuscript diagrams of the Middle English *Benjamin Minor*, are the waypoints in this journey to God.

---

of truths to nourish not only the individual soul, but also those who participate in his community of fellow gardeners. Reginald Pecock, *The Folewer to the Donet, now first edited from Brit. Mus. Roy. Ms. 17D. ix*, ed. Elsie Vaughan Hitchcock (Oxford: Oxford University Press, 1924, rpt. New York: Kraus Reprints, 1971).

CHAPTER 5

Out of Eden and Back Again
Following the Flow of Concepts, Categories, and Lists in the Four Rivers of Paradise

MARTHA RUST

In the midst of its second Creation story, Genesis takes what biblical scholar Susan Brayford calls "an unexpected geographic detour" and describes the river that flows out of Eden and the four rivers into which it divides.[1]

> Now a river flows out from Edem ['Εδεμ] to water the garden; from there it separates into four heads. The name for the one is Pheisōn. This one surrounds all the land of Hueilat, where there is gold; but the gold of that land is good; and there is coal there and the light green stone. And the name for the second river is Gēōn; this one surrounds all the land of Aithiopia. And the third river is Tigris; this one goes opposite the Assuriōs. Now the fourth river, this one is Euphratēs.[2]

To geographers down the centuries this passage has presented numerous riddles, beginning with the identity of the river Phison and the land it surrounds. Isidore of Seville (c. 560–636) identifies it as the Ganges, "going out from Paradise and continuing on to the regions of India" (XIII.xxi.8) while French religious scholar Rashi (Shelomoh b. Izhaq [1040/1–1105]) maintains, through an

---

1. Susan Brayford, *Genesis* (Leiden: Brill, 2007), 229.
2. Genesis 2.10–14; trans. of Septuagint by Brayford, *Genesis*, 37.

etymological association between Phison (Hebrew *pîšôn*) and flax (*pištān*), which he associates in turn with Egypt, that it is the Nile.[3] Among modern scholars, Philip S. Alexander nominates the Karkheh river in present-day Iran as the biblical Phison; Old Testament scholar Yehuda T. Radday lists twenty problems in the passage—lettered a through t—including the enigma of the river Phison, which, he notes, appears nowhere else in the Bible or in "extra-Biblical texts." For her part, Brayford asserts that the Phison "is completely unknown, as is the land . . . it is said to surround." More important than the river's location, she argues, is its connection to the Garden of Eden as "the ultimate source of life-sustaining water."[4] The flow out of the Garden is what makes this "geographic detour" important in the context of the study of lists as well. From that point of view, Paradise, its rivers, and the lands they run through take their places on a cognitive rather than a geographic map, which shows the place of lists in processes of thought that partake of the geographical characteristics of a river that feature in this biblical passage: whence it flows, where it goes, and the regions it thereby defines.

We may see the outlines of this map by considering the passage as if from an aeriel view. From this perspective its list of the four rivers that flow out of Eden stands out as the territory's most prominent feature thanks primarily to its numbering, which confirms that all four have been accounted for even as it gives the list internal coherence:

The name for the one is Pheisōn. . . .
And the name for the second river is Gēōn. . . .
And the third river is Tigris. . . .
Now the fourth river, this one is Euphratēs.

In addition, the repetition of "name" in the list's first two lines points out that the items enumerated here are just that, names. In order to associate these names with actual bodies of flowing water, we must see where they go, which the passage displays in another list:

This one surrounds all the land of Hueilat . . .
This one surrounds all the land of Aithiopia . . .
This one goes opposite the Assuriōs.

---

3. See Philip S. Alexander, "Early Jewish Geography," in *The Anchor Bible Dictionary*, vol. 4, ed. David Noel Freedman (New York: Doubleday, 1992), 977–88, here 980; and Yehuda T. Radday, "The Four Rivers of Paradise," *Hebrew Studies* 23 (1982): 23–32, here 23.

4. Brayford, *Genesis*, 229.

In this process of describing the rivers, the passage produces another list of names—this time of "lands"—each associated with a verb for a pattern a river may make in its course: winding or straight. A straight course connects lands—the Tigris connects Eden and the Assuriōs—while a winding pattern may define a land: the Geon defines the region of Aithiopia, and the Phison defines Huelat. An interesting shift occurs when the passage proceeds to describing the land of Huelat in the form of a third list: "Pheisōn surrounds all the land of Hueilat, where there is gold . . . coal . . . and the light green stone." Here the surrounding and defining action of the river Phison operates on a metaphorical as well as a descriptive level, for its encircling course circumscribes both a physical territory and a category of things, minerals. In doing so it brings the whole passage into view as delineating a cognitive topography in which lists serve a flow of thought by collecting its products, thereby producing those products as the objects of further thinking. In their treatments of the four rivers and their Edenic source, we can see theologians as well as poets and visual artists working with its pattern of collecting and flowing as a means of thinking with and through fluid concepts. For first-century theologian Philo of Alexandria (c. 20 BCE–c. 40 CE), the geographical details Genesis supplies about the rivers provided a flexible set of constraints for theorizing about the nature of the principal virtues. For artists and writers giving expression to the affective piety of the late Middle Ages, the four rivers and their Edenic source served as a heuristic device for thinking about Christ's wounds.

In his *Allegorical Interpretations of Genesis 2, 3*, Philo asserts that in the four rivers, God's "purpose" was "to indicate the particular virtues": specifically, "prudence, self-mastery, courage, justice."[5] In support of this assertion, Philo takes a close look at certain key words in the passage describing them in Genesis, beginning with the word "river." "River," he reasons, stands for "generic virtue, goodness," and as this river flows through the garden, it "waters the particular virtues." Next Philo turns to the word "heads" (ἀρχὰς): specifically, the heads that the river—generic virtue—"separates" into upon leaving the garden. Philo explains that in using the word "heads," the biblical text does not refer to "locality" as one might assume; instead, it refers to "sovereignty," since "each of the virtues is in very deed a sovereign and a queen." What about the process of separation, which led to the formation of these sovereign heads? According to Philo, the words "is separated" are "equivalent to 'has boundaries to define it.'"[6] "River," generic goodness; "heads," sover-

---

5. Philo of Alexandria, *Allegorical Interpretations of Genesis 2, 3*, trans. F. H. Colson and G. H. Whitaker (Cambridge, MA: Harvard University Press, 1929), 189. These are the cardinal virtues, which have their origins in Plato's *Republic*, book 4.

6. Philo, *Allegorical Interpretations of Genesis*, 188–9.

eignty; "is separated," bounding and defining: putting the allegorical meanings of these words together, we come to understand that all of the particular virtues derive from generic virtue, but that each is sovereign, with boundaries that make it distinct from the other virtues. Evoking a river's capacity to define a territory, Philo goes on to specify the categories of action these sovereign virtues define: "Prudence, concerned with things to be done, sets boundaries round them; courage round things to be endured; self-mastery round things to be chosen; justice round things to be awarded."[7] Thanks to the system of rivers that signifies the particular virtues and their relation to generic virtue, Philo's interpretation of this passage in Genesis gives us a clear picture of the particular virtues at once deriving from generic goodness and remaining connected to that source, continuing to partake of generic virtue.

At the same time, Philo's allegorical reading of the rivers as virtues may be read as a meta-allegory of the linked thought processes described above, each of which is served by a list: first, the process of deriving subconcepts from concepts; and, second, the process of associating a concept with a category of attributes, in this case, four categories of action. By mapping the relationship between generic virtue and particular virtues onto four rivers that flow out of one, Philo visualizes the process of deriving subconcepts from a main concept as a matter of thought flowing into distinct channels. The persistent connection between main idea and subconcepts also provides a mental diagram of a key property of a list: that it is governed by a principle, what Stephen Barney defines as the "object, the 'what' [that] a list explicates," what a list is "of."[8] In that diagram, we see the principle of a list—virtue—enforcing an ongoing connection between the products of a division of thought into separate channels: here, four particular virtues. In turn those "products" are given verbal forms by a list's lexical items—its "contents"—which serve at once as labels for each newly distinguished, still "fluid" channel of thought and as objects for thinking "about," objects for that same thought stream to flow around and about, depositing defining attributes: in this case, categories of actions associated with each virtue.

In the next part of his exegesis, Philo models the usefulness of such categories for defining concepts. Returning to the biblical passage, "a river flows out from Edem to water the garden; from there it separates into four heads," we are reminded that the text does not say specifically that the River of Eden separates into four rivers; instead, it separates into four heads. The Greek word

---

7. Philo, *Allegorical Interpretations of Genesis*, 189; 191.

8. Stephen A. Barney, "Chaucer's Lists," in *The Wisdom of Poetry: Essays in Early English Literature in Honor of Morton W. Bloomfield*, ed. Larry D. Benson and Siegfried Wenzel (Kalamazoo, MI: Medieval Institute Publications, 1982), 189–223, here 191.

that is translated as "heads" is *archas* (ἀρχὰς), meaning both "beginnings" and "leaders," hence Philo's "sovereign virtues." Each of the four heads is thus literally the beginning of a river and figuratively a governing virtue; in its subsequent course, each separate river of virtue defines and puts boundaries around the domain of action it governs.

For our meta-allegory, it is particularly interesting that Philo has us envision the virtues' sovereignty in consistently encircling terms. In the passage I have just quoted, he notes that each virtue sets boundaries "round" the domain it governs; later, he notes that the river Pheisōn—or Prudence—"encompasseth all of the land of Evilat" and again that it "encircles in its roundel the land of Evilat."[9] Similarly the river Gēōn—courage—both "encompasses" and "encircles" while the Tigris—self-mastery—is said to have a "sphere" of action.[10] Only the Euphrates—or justice—is not figured as a circle since, as Philo explains, following Plato, Justice appears "when the three parts of the soul are in harmony."[11] As noted above, Philo stresses that the river heads are not to be understood as "localities," and certainly a concept—like prudence, or justice—cannot be said to have a precise location. Indeed, just as the names Pishon, Geon, Tigris, and Euphrates name rivers without indicating anything about their physical properties, the words "prudence," "justice," "temperance," and "courage" function solely as names of concepts, which are themselves, according to linguists and cognitive scientists, prelinguistic. Unlocatable though they may be, Philo's description nevertheless invites us to locate the virtues in a mental "flow" chart, consisting of lines that loop back on themselves to create concept-laden circles.[12]

Although those circles define each of the virtues' territories as concepts, it is the contents of the circles that define the virtues, and those contents are members of categories: as Philo put it, the categories of things to be done, things to be endured, and things to be chosen. Since members of categories substantiate concepts, we may picture each of Philo's circles as two fused concentric circles (see Figure 5.1): the outer one defining a concept as distinct from other concepts, the inner bounding the members of a category that concretize the concept. Philo does not enumerate members of the categories of things to be done, things to be endured, and so on and so forth, but, not one to pass over any possibly interpretable detail, he does describe Prudence in terms

---

9. Philo, *Allegorical Interpretations of Genesis*, 191.
10. Philo, *Allegorical Interpretations of Genesis*, 191; 195.
11. Philo, *Allegorical Interpretations of Genesis*, 195.
12. The treatment of concepts and categories is grounded in the classical theory of the lexical concept and in the representational theory of mind as articulated by Susan E. Cary in *The Origins of Concepts* and by Eric Margolis and Stephen Laurence in their "Concepts" entry for the *Stanford Encyclopedia of Philosophy*.

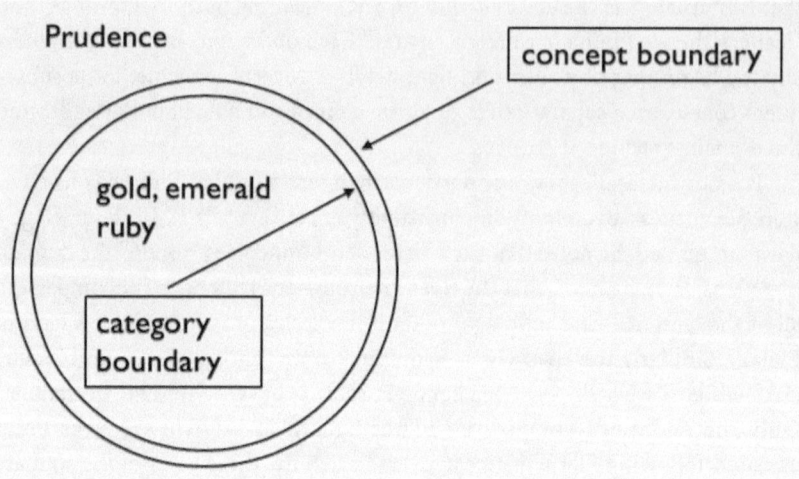

FIGURE 5.1. Diagram of concept, category, and category members.

of the category of minerals: specifically, those minerals that Genesis locates in the land of Evilat, gold, ruby, and emerald. In Philo's reading, each of these minerals is a kind of person who occupies "the place where prudence dwells": the ruby is "the man who is prudent"; the emerald, "the man who exercises prudence"; and gold, the man "whose is the treasure, even prudence gleaming like gold, tried by the fire, and precious."[13] Truly these mineral people serve their sovereign queen well by exemplifying her in their actions. In terms of our meta-allegory, this list of the constituents of a category populates the otherwise empty circle representing prudence—the place in our mental map "where prudence dwells"—thereby fleshing out our understanding of this concept.

Having defined the virtues in terms of the rivers flowing out of Paradise and the geographic territories around and toward which they flow, Philo proceeds to consider them in relation to two more domains, producing two additional lists: one of domains in the human body; the other, aspects of human psychology. Thus the "place and abode" of reason is the head and therefore the "sphere" of prudence; the site of "high spirit" is the breast, and therefore the realm of courage; and since the abdomen is the site of lust, it is the domain of self-mastery.[14] In associating the virtues with these additional domains, Philo drops his river conceit entirely, yet he would seem to have a river in mind—specifically, a river-based heuristic—for the features of a river—its directional

---

13. Philo, *Allegorical Interpretations of Genesis*, 191.
14. Philo, *Allegorical Interpretations of Genesis*, 193.

flow and its capacity to define multiple territories in a course that links them all—are reflected in Philo's inventive thinking, boldly carving out new territories for the virtues and rendering their connections fully visualizable all the while. Indeed, with the addition of anatomical regions and psychological faculties, our mental diagram has become a full-fledged four-column table, in which each of the rivers governs a column populated by items from lists that by turns name and concretize concepts and categories.

Picturing this table, we find that Philo's explication of the passage in Genesis renders each particular virtue as the principle—in Philo's terminology, a "head" or "sovereign queen" of members of a category—prudence is the principle of things to be done, courage of things to be endured—even as it is also the head of an associative stream of thought, each of which encompasses a body part, which encompasses in turn a psychological faculty. All of this streaming had its beginning, though, in generic virtue, which "takes its start" as Philo says, "in Eden, the Wisdom of God, which is full of joy."[15] It takes it start, in other words, from the ultimate "principle." That divine wisdom also gave rise to the life of Christ, and for artists and writers of the late Middle Ages, the four rivers and their Edenic source served as a mental chart for thinking about his Passion and about how to convey its redemptive power in images and texts. In a set of Latin prayers on the image of the Crucifixion, the rivers become Christ's wounds, which flow toward the devout Christian; in a pair of anonymous Middle English works, the wounds have become wells, while in a poem by John Lydgate (c. 1370–c. 1451), the wounds as wells rejoin the river of Paradise, which now flows back to Eden, returning a faithful Christian to Paradise. In each of these works, the worshipper gets a provisional hold on the concept of Christ's sacrifice on the level of the listed detail.

Beginning around 1420, the set of prayers in Latin appears frequently in Books of Hours, where it is usually accompanied by a series of images, beginning with an image of the Crucifixion, showing the Virgin Mary and the apostle John on either side of the Cross.[16] In contemporary scholarship the

---

15. Philo, *Allegorical Interpretations of Genesis*, 189.

16. The sequence of prayers is edited by Clemens Blume and Guido M. Dreves under the title "De Vulneribus Christi," *Analecta Hymnica Medii Aevi* vol. 31, no. 68 (Leipzig: O. R. Reisland, 1898), 87–9. All quotations from this prayer cycle are from this Latin edition, and from the English translation by J. Moyes, "How English Catholics Prayed in the Fourteenth Century," *The Dublin Review* 123 (1898): 391–400.

Blume and Dreves list twenty-eight mostly fifteenth-century manuscript witnesses of the prayer, giving no indication of which have images; Flora Lewis, "From Image to Illustration: The Place of Devotional Images in the Book of Hours," in *Iconographie médiévale: Image, texte, contexte*, ed. Gaston Duchet-Suchaux (Paris: CNRS, 1990), 29–48, here 44, adds nine more with images, to which may be further added, also with images, Berkeley, Bancroft Library MSS 135 and 138; New York, General Theological Seminary Special Collections Library

collection of prayers goes by the name *Omnibus consideratis,* after its opening lines, but its manuscript witnesses often give it the rubric "Ad imaginem dominum nostrum *ihus* christi," which aptly describes it, for together the prayers address the image of the Crucifixion by dividing it into its component parts and devoting a prayer to each. Accordingly, the cycle includes a prayer to the wood of the Cross, to the head or the crown thorns, to the two most important witnesses to the Crucifixion, Mary and the apostle John, and, most important for our purposes, to each of the five wounds, which are likened to the river flowing out of Eden and the four into which it divides. Before considering the cycle's treatment of the wounds, a brief analysis of the mode of list production it exemplifies will be useful.

Unlike Philo's list of particular virtues, which was predicated on a process of division already represented in his text, the flow of one river dividing into four, the list of image parts that structures this set of prayers imposes a division upon a still tableau, one representing the culminating scene in a narrative. By cutting that image into pieces, the prayer cycle produces a series of details—etymologically cut-out pieces—each of which becomes an object of thought, more specifically, an object of adoration.[17] Since the Cross is the essential material instrument in the Passion narrative, it is fitting that its wood is the first detail the set of prayers addresses: "Oh triumphant wood of the Cross, through which we, by sin seduced, are brought back to the joys of heaven" (394) ("Triumphale lignum crucis, / Tu seductos nos reducis / Ad superna gaudia" [87]). In framing the wood as leading worshippers back to heavenly joys, the prayer may allude to the legend that the wood of the Cross came from the Tree of the Knowledge of Good and Evil; accordingly, Christ's suffering on it became its redeeming fruit.[18] The wood of the Cross is rightfully the "leader" in the context of the properties of the list form as well, for given the centrality of the Cross in the image of the Crucifixion, the list that structures this set of prayers is a list "of" the details of the Cross. In other words,

---

Western MSS 11 and 12; Oxford, Queen's College Library MS 349; and San Marino, Huntington Library MSS HM 1086 and HM 1144. Lewis provides a history of the images but does not note their representations of water (43–4). Both Lewis (45) and Nigel Morgan, "An SS Collar in the Devotional Context of the Shield of the Five Wounds," *The Lancastrian Court,* ed. Jenny Stratford (Donington: Shaun Tyas, 2003), 147–62, here 156, date the prayers' earliest appearances to the 1420s, first in England and then in Flanders.

17. The *Oxford English Dictionary* explains that "detail" is formed from the prefix "de," meaning, in this case "down to the bottom, completely," and the French verb *tailler,* "to cut in pieces." See Barney, "Chaucer's Lists," 191, on lists items as details "cut off" from principles.

18. See Jacobus de Voragine, *The Golden Legend: Readings on the Saints,* trans. William Granger Ryan, with an introduction by Eamon Duffy (Princeton: Princeton University Press, 2012), 209. Other legends held that the cross of the Crucifixion was made of four different kinds of wood (palm, cedar, cyprus, and olive), on which see Voragine, *Golden Legend,* 278.

the Cross is its "principle," or, recurring to the prayer cycle's title, it is a list of the details that pertain *to the image—Ad imaginem—*of the *Crux-*ifixion.

That image in its not-yet-cut-up form is the subject of the cycle's opening prayer, which figures Christ as the Garden of Paradise and his blood as its here-unnamed four rivers. It reads as follows:

> Omnibus consideratis
> Paradisus voluptatis
> Es, Iesu piissime;
> In te fons paternitatis
> Omnes fructus suavitatis
> Plantavit plenissime
> Passionis tuae fructus
> Et cruoris tui fluctus
> Defluens largissime
> Finem fecit nostri luctus,
> Per hunc infernus destructus
> Gemit amarissime. (87)

> When we have considered all things, Thou, O most loving Jesus, art the Garden of Paradise. In Thee, the Father of all has most copiously planted the fruits of every kind of sweetness. The fruits of Thy passion, and the rivers of Thy blood, flow forth abundantly and sweep away our sorrows, and the power of hell thus broken groans must bitterly. (393–4)

In its brief figuration of Christ as the Garden of Paradise, this opening prayer portends a typological reading of the image of the Crucifixion, exemplifying, as translator J. Moyes puts it, medieval Christians' "passion for synthesis and symbolism by which [they] dearly loved to group and to grasp under one idea the sublime harmonies of God's actions in the old dispensation and in the new."[19]

That passion is most clearly on display in the cycle's five prayers to Christ's wounds and the images that accompany these prayers in many manuscripts, which together map each wound onto one of the rivers in Genesis 2: the wounds of the hands are associated with the rivers Phison and Geon, the wounds of the feet with the Euphrates and the Tigris, and the side wound with the river of Paradise before it divides into these four. The paintings depict each wounded body part surrounded by some kind of representation of water

---

19. Moyes, "How English Catholics Prayed," 392.

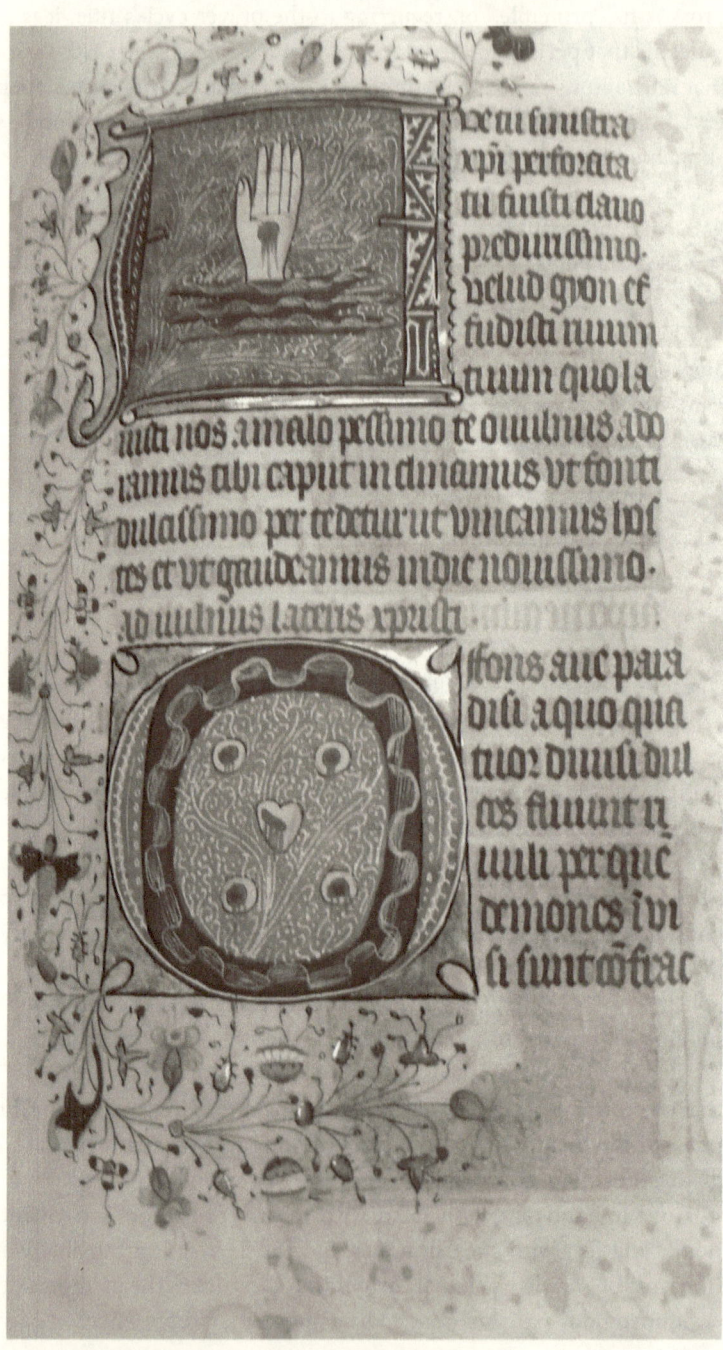

FIGURE 5.2. HM 1086, f. 97, The Huntington Library, San Marino, California.

while the side wound is often depicted along with small representations of the other four with a circle of blue running around them all (Figures 5.2 and 5.3).[20] The circular form of this image of all five wounds is especially suited to be the content of an historiated initial for the prayer it accompanies since that initial letter is O. The prayer begins "O fons ave paradisi, / A quo quattuor divisi / Dulces currunt rivuli" (87) ("Hail, O fountain of Paradise, out of which flow forth the sweet rivers parted into four" [394]). While these prayers do bring out certain parallels—Moyes's "harmonies"—between Creation and the Crucifixion—one "old," the other "new"—their evocations of the physical properties of rivers and wounds invite worshippers to look beyond those analogies to envision a commingling of the two from the beginning, in which the original watery rivers are now and always were, as the opening prayer puts it, "the rivers of Thy blood."[21] At the same time, the river motif in these prayers sketches the flow of thought that supports this vision: a movement from concept (the wisdom of God at the Creation) to category (the events of the Passion), to details of that category, that is, the list of details represented in the image of the Crucifixion that structure the prayer cycle. Recalling the associative stream we saw in Philo's thinking about the rivers in Genesis, each of these categories suggests a further category; here, the thinking flows on to the individual worshipper with book in hand, to the category of appropriate responses to Christ's sacrifice. In turn, those responses, actionable items at the most concrete level of the flow of thought, imply a turn in the flow of Christ's blood, initiating, on a narrative level, the return of the worshipper to Paradise and, on a conceptual level, a turn in attention from listed detail—a wound—to overarching concept, God's wisdom.

In the prayer to the wound of the right hand, the encircling potential of a river also functions as a redeeming property of Christ's blood. It reads as follows:

Salve, vulnus dextrae manus,
Velut Phison rivus planus
Miseris scaturiens,
Quod Iudaeus inhumanus,

---

20. Some scholars have seen the type of depiction of the wounded hands that we see in Figure 5.2 as a hand emerging from a cloud, but in the context of the prayers' central metaphor, the parallel lines drawn on the blue "clouds" would seem to indicate ripples or waves (i.e., a river), while its placement in the upper portion of the image frame would indicate a heavenly source.

21. For an overview of types of typology and their methodologies—e.g., using analogy, parallels, symbols—see Francis M. Young, *Biblical Exegesis and the Formation of Christian Culture* (Cambridge: Cambridge University Press, 199), 192–201.

Inhonestus et insanus
Fodit Deum nesciens.
Te adoro, te honoro,
Te inquiro, te imploro
Ut miser iam moriens,
Ut in contritorum choro,
In quo sperans iam laboro,
Nunquam sim deficiens. (87)

Hail! wound of the right hand, like to the river Phison, whose plain bubbled forth with waters for the parched. Thou, whom the cruel, wicked and furious Jew, knowing not his God, didst pierce; I, in wretchedness and death, adore Thee. I worship Thee, I seek Thee, and implore Thee that I may never cease to be of the number of the penitent, amongst whom I labour in hope. (394)

In the logic of its parallels, this prayer suggests that just as the river Phison gave life to the parched inhabitants of its plain, the river of blood that flows from the wound in Christ's right hand redeems the person who is alone "in wretchedness and death." In the logic of its flow, the prayer also figures the worshipper as being defined by the river of blood from the right hand just as Philo saw the river Phison defining Evilat as "the place where prudence dwells." In beseeching the wound/river that he never cease to labor in hope among the number of the penitent—"ut in contritorum choro"—the prayer's speaker envisions that stream as having already enlisted him in the circle of the penitent, given that the Latin *chorus* connotes both a "multitude" and "a dance in a ring."[22]

Each of the subsequent four prayers to the wounds describes a different category of devotional response to Christ's Passion, but they all figure the blood as flowing both towards the devout, as they do in the images, and into them, thus defining the response to the Crucifixion as a matter of partaking of Christ's sacrifice. In this way, these prayers to the rivers recall the Eucharist, even as they locate that sacrament's origins in the waters that flowed from Paradise at the beginning of time. Of all the images in the prayer cycle, the central depiction of all five wounds enclosed in a letter O (Figure 5.2) offers perhaps the most compelling illustration of the idea that the Eucharistic blood of Christ springs first from the Garden of Eden since the five wounds in these images would seem to well up from the waters of Paradise flowing around them. With respect to our study of the flow of thought from concept to cate-

---

22. Charlton T. Lewis and Charles Short, *A Latin Dictionary* (Oxford: Clarendon Press, 1933), s.v. "chorus," sense 1.

gory to categorical attributes, this image also recalls Philo's reading of the river Pheisōn, how it encircled and thus both defined Prudence as a conceptual territory and enclosed its category of prudent things to be done. Analogously, in this image the letter O, a graphic circle, bounds the concept of the Wisdom of God, which, as Philo said, "takes its start" in Eden; the encircling river of Paradise positioned just inside the "O" at once bounds a category of that wisdom, Christ's sacrificial blood, and defines the green territory or "ground" for members of that category, given here as a visual list of his wounds.

A group of fifteenth-century Middle English poems on the wounds of Christ reconfigures the components of the Latin *Omnibus consideratis*—the rivers of Paradise, the wounds, the Eucharist, and the prospect of a return to Paradise—and recalls Philo's analysis of Genesis 2 as well by producing new lists along the way. While the names of the four rivers do not appear in these works, Philo's metaphor of the rivers' "heads" as the beginnings of the four virtues finds an analogue in figurations of Christ's wounds as fountains—in Middle English, "welles"—from which a variety of graces flow.[23] In this way, a treatise on the Passion in British Library, Arundel MS 286 (produced in the first half of the fifteenth century) uses the fountains in a verse in Isaiah, "You shall draw waters with joy out of the saviour's fountains [de fontibus]" (12:3), as a vehicle for the wounds of Christ, which it figures as the wells of three pairs of gifts:

> ye schul drawe waters in ioye of the welles of oure saueoure þat is to mene
> 3e schul drawe out witt and wisdome loue and deuocioun pacience and contemplacioun of þe woundes of Crist þat ben welles of oure saueoure.[24]

Immediately following upon the scriptural passage, the writer's "þat is to mene" forecasts a metaphorical gloss, in which the wells of the old dispensation will stand for the wounds of the Savior. But here again, the properties of water take precedence, for as the writer continues with "3e schul drawe out" the enumerated gifts from the wounds of Christ, the implied cognitive move is not a metaphorical substitution but rather an associative stream, in which a certain flow of thought extends to encompass a new category, in this case of spiritual gifts.[25] The vessel into which one would draw these gifts would, like

---

23. For Middle English "welle" as "fountain," see the *Middle English Dictionary*, entry "welle," sense 2c. The most exhaustive treatment of the wounds in Middle English literature is still Douglas Gray, "The Five Wounds of Our Lord," *Notes and Queries* n.s. 10 [208] (1963): 50–1, 828–9, 127–34, 163–8. See also Eamon Duffy, *The Stripping of the Altars: Traditional Religion in England c. 1400–c. 1500*, 2nd ed. (New Haven and London: Yale University Press, 2005), 218–25.

24. Qtd. in Gray, "The Five Wounds," 133.

25. *Oxford English Dictionary*, s.v. "draw," phrasal verbs, "draw out," sense 1.

the encircling river Phison, define the boundary of the category and make a mental space for a list of its members, in this case, "witt and wisdom loue and deuocioun pacience and contemplacioun."

A vessel containing gifts derived from Christ's blood brings us into Eucharistic territory, which is made explicit in another fifteenth-century Middle English poem—this one in text and image—that also associates the wounds with gifts: the wound in the right hand is the well of mercy, the wound in the left hand, of grace; the wound in the side is the well of life; the wound in the right foot is the well of pity, the wound in the left foot, of comfort.[26] In its witness in Princeton University Library, Special Collections, Taylor MS 17, each of the wound/wells is venerated in a uniform composition of image and text, each of which occupies a page. The page for the right-hand wound (Figure 5.3) may serve as an example. Its image component consists of the hand topped with a bejeweled crown and showing a stream of red issuing from the center of the palm. Both hand and crown are set on a rectangular ground of blue within a red frame. The text component consists of the first two lines of the stanza set in a scroll that appears to float above the plane of the upper portion of the image's blue ground. The four remaining lines of the stanza are inscribed below the frame of the image. In addition, each wound has a label in the form of an identifying second scroll placed in the lower portion of the image frame. Together these labels compose a structuring list that runs through the (visual) center of the poem. In appearing to render each well as the font of a concept, this poem resonates with Philo's interpretation of the river of Paradise and the four rivers into which it divided. It recalls *Omnibus consideratis* as well in that it links images of wounds to prayers to wounds, both of which associate blood with water, whether in the form of flowing rivers or of gushing wells. A detail in the image for the poem's first stanza in Taylor MS 17 (Figure 5.4) also blends blood and Eucharistic wine, an idea that was latent in the treatise in Arundel MS 286, for in this image, we see a shield featuring a cross in front of which a bleeding heart is suspended over a chalice, a composition that pictures the real presence of Christ's blood in the sacramental wine. This image may also allude to the specific motif in *Omnibus consideratis* of the rivers of Paradise, for on either side of the Cross it depicts

---

26. *New Index of Middle English Verse*, 1011. The poem survives in two late fifteenth-century manuscripts, Bodleian Library, Douce MS 1, which is dated to 1460; and Princeton University Library, Special Collections, Taylor MS 17, a near twin of Douce MS 1, dated to around 1500; and in one early print witness, STC 14550, of 1523. Taylor MS 17 and Douce MS 1 have nearly identical images; the images in the early print witness is clearly based on those in the manuscripts. Taylor MS 17 is completely digitized at https://catalog.princeton.edu/catalog/11364120. It is edited from Douce MS 1 with emendations from STC 14550 in Gray, "The Five Wounds," 50–1.

FIGURE 5.3. Princeton University Library, Special Collections, Taylor MS 17, f. 9v. Courtesy of Princeton University Library.

each wounded hand and foot ringed with small circles of blue, replicating the bracelets of water in the images of the hands and feet in witnesses to *Omnibus consideratis*.[27] In view of this detail, the blue grounds of the other images also call to mind the poetic and pictorial tradition "upstream" from this poem, in

---

27. Morgan, "An SS Collar," 151–7 discusses this image in the course of his history of the Shield of the Five Wounds image.

FIGURE 5.4. Princeton University Library, Special Collections, Taylor MS 17, f. 9. Courtesy of Princeton University Library.

which the sacrificial blood, present in the Eucharistic wine, springs from the river of Paradise. While this poem thus exemplifies a continuity in variation with respect to the themes and images we have been considering, it also marks a reversal in the hitherto-standard direction of flow we have so far seen from concepts to categories to details. That reversal too is evident on the poem's opening page, in the form of its title. Appearing above the shield with the wounds, cross, bleeding heart, and chalice, it reads "Of the fyue woundes of oure lorde." This is a poem, this title suggests, that wells "up" from the details of the Passion—that is, from the wounds, as a group of five individual physical injuries—rather than flowing "down" through concepts and categories. Where Philo understood the principle virtues as preexisting the four rivers of Paradise—asserting that it was God's "purpose" to indicate them in the rivers—and where *Omnibus consideratis* and the treatise in Arundel MS 286 also nested their treatments of the wounds within scriptural precedent, this poem enumerates concepts that exist in the details, in the very molecules of the liquid springing from the wells. That is, according to this work in text and image, the wounds do not indicate mercy, grace, life, pity, and comfort; instead, these salvific gifts are infused with Christ's blood as it flows from his body. In this regard, the labels for each wound function to prevent a separation of the liquid gifts into symbol and sign, in which, for instance, the right hand wound would be understood as a symbol of mercy. Instead, the labels lend a virtual reality to each of the welling gifts. In this way, the image/text list of wounds/gifts realizes the Eucharistic implications of *Omnibus consideratis* and the treatise in Arundel MS 286 by presenting a kind of virtual transubstantiation, a real presence of the enumerated divine gifts in and as Christ's blood rather than a series of re-presented concepts associated with them.

While the poem "Of the fyue woundes of oure lorde" does not draw any explicit connections between the wells of Christ's wounds and the rivers of Paradise, it does invite readers and viewers to experience a sense of intimacy with the wounds and prompts a desire for even more intimacy with the Savior. This desire finds its most vivid expression in the lines appearing above the side wound image, "Wel of lyfe that euer shal laste, / My herte in the make thou stedfaste": that is, "Well of everlasting life, / Make your presence in my heart steadfast."[28] John Lydgate's poem "As a Mydsomer Rose" suggests a means for holding that well in one's heart by at once surfacing the rivers of Paradise and having them converge into yet another figure for the wounds, a rose.[29] The poem is a work in fifteen eight-line stanzas that meditates on the transitory nature of all worldly things, which, as its refrain teaches, "stant on chaung, like a mydsomyr roose." In its concluding stanzas, the poem argues that only devotion to the roses of Christ promises stability. Those roses were "portrayed in the sheeld, / Splayed in the baneer at Ierusalem" in the form of Christ's wounds on the Cross, and again, the poem goes on, when the "sonne was clips [eclipsed] and dirk in euery rem," which is when "Crist Ihesu five

---

28. Gray, "The Five Wounds," 50.

29. *NIMEV* 1865. The poem survives in eight fifteenth-century manuscript copies; I quote from the witness in British Library, Harley MS 2255 (c. 1460–c. 1483) as edited by Henry Noble MacCracken, in Lydgate, "As a Mydsomer Rose," in *John Lydgate: The Minor Poems, Vol. II: Secular Poems*, EETS o.s. 192 (London: K. Paul, Trench, Trübner, 1934), 780–5.

wellys lyst vncloose, / Toward Paradys, callyd the rede strem."[30] With its possible senses of "unfold" and "release," Lydgate's "vncloose" allows a vision of the roses' petals unfolding and at the same time transforming into five wells which then converge into a single red stream leading to Paradise, reversing the out-of-Paradise direction of the flow of the rivers Phison, Geon, Tigris, and Euphrates.

With Lydgate's envisioned return to Paradise, we may return this analysis to its well as well, to our aerial view of the passage in Genesis on the river flowing through the garden of Eden and the four rivers into which it divides. Brayford remarks that whatever rivers were originally indicated, they "likely signify the four ends of the earth."[31] The image of Christ crucified indicates four directions as well, as do the hand and foot wounds in images depicting all five wounds in the prayer cycle *Omnis consideratis* and in the poem "Of the Five Wounds." A layering of the wounds onto the rivers of Paradise would yield an image of the original rivers circulating in Christ's body as his blood. In view of the geographical reach of those four rivers flowing in the four cardinal directions, these images and the prayers that go with them invite readers and viewers to see Christ's wounds as streams of redemption irrigating the far reaches of the planet. That idea finds graphic realization in the mid-thirteenth-century Ebstorf Map, which pictures the body of Christ as the extent of the world, his head to the east, his wounded hands to the north and south, and his feet to the west.[32] Interestingly, the four rivers of Paradise are set apart, appearing within a framed space in the upper portion of the map, which also depicts Adam and Eve being tempted by the serpent. Flowing down from the head of God as Christ at the top of the map, we see only the Ganges and the Nile. In the context of our study of the place of lists in the flow from concepts to categories, the flow of those rivers, which soon divide into more, encircling lands in their course, look a lot like God thinking, or it is specifically Christ thinking, generating the concepts and categories and concrete details that exist in the human world, defined at its watery circular boundary as a product of the flow of his creative thought.

---

30. Lydgate, "As a Mydsomer Rose," 115–16; 118–19. Luke 23:45, "And the sun was darkened" [Et obscuratus est sol] is sometimes, as here, interpreted as referring to an eclipse of the sun (*The Vulgate Bible: Douay-Rheims translation,* http://www.drbo.org/).

31. Brayford, *Genesis,* 229.

32. For an introduction to the Ebstorf Map, see P. D. A. Harvey, *Medieval Maps* (Toronto: University of Toronto Press, 1991), 30–2 and figures 13, 21, and 23. See also David S. Areford, "The Passion Measured: A Late-Medieval Diagram of the Body of Christ," in *The Broken Body: Passion Devotion in Late-Medieval Culture,* ed. A. A. MacDonald, H. N. B. Ridderbos, and R. M. Schlusemann (Groningen: Egbert Forsten, 1998), 211–38, here 233.

CHAPTER 6

Epic Lists

The Matter of Troy and the Catalogue Form in Middle English Literature

EVA VON CONTZEN

In the third book of Geoffrey Chaucer's *House of Fame*, the dreamer visits the palace of Fama, the goddess of fame. Inside her impressive throne hall, there are pillars along the sides carrying statues of famous people. Prominent among them are ancient and medieval authors of epics. Chaucer repeatedly stresses the fame the poets have achieved through their works, and fittingly he *enumerates* the poets and their works: one of the key forms of epic poetry, the catalogue, becomes the means to catalogue, on a meta-level, literary achievement. 'Being on the list,' for Chaucer, is a sign of having achieved the status of poetic authority. However, this authority is far from stable: Chaucer uses the potential of the list form to create a seemingly objective truth while at the same time undermining it. Chaucer's approach to the catalogue form can be seen as a particularly playful example of a strategy that increasingly gains momentum in epic catalogues in the Middle English Troy tradition: the catalogues become sites of scepticism towards established truths, questioning the Trojan War, the claims of epic, and poetry itself.

This article was written as part of the research conducted in the project "Lists in Literature and Culture" (LISTLIT), funded by the European Research Council Starting Grant 2016 no. 715021.

CATALOGUING EPIC POETS IN THE *HOUSE OF FAME*

In his list of epic poets in the *House of Fame*, Chaucer sketches, in the first part, the history of the Trojan epic tradition: first Statius with the *Thebaid* and the unfinished *Achilleid*, then "gret Omer" (l. 1466), followed by "Dares and Tytus" (l. 1467), then Lollius, Guido delle Colonne, and "Englyssh Gaufride" (l. 1470). The medieval Homer was based on the prose accounts of the fourth-century *Ephemeris belli Troiani* attributed to Dictys Cretensis (the Cretan), and the sixth-century *De excidio Troiae historia*, attributed to Dares Phrygius (the Phrygian)—Chaucer's "Dares and Tytus."[1] The list continues with Virgil, Ovid, Lucan, and ends with Claudian, author of *De raptu Proserpinae*.[2] Chaucer makes unequivocally clear that he is writing in full awareness of the canon of classical epic. Yet the way in which this canon is presented is far from straightforward, and at least two of the names mentioned in the list have given rise to debate. The first is Lollius. Chaucer names him twice as the source of his *Troilus and Criseyde* (1.394; 5.1653), even though his source is clearly Boccaccio's *Filostrato* (who does not get a mention). Perhaps then, 'Lollius' is Chaucer's name for Boccaccio. Or Chaucer may (unwittingly) have followed a tradition based on a misreading of a line in Horace's epistles, according to which 'Lollius' was another author of Homeric material. Or Chaucer may have known about the misreading and used it in full awareness of the mistake.[3] Alternatively, he may have invented the figure of Lollius from scratch to inscribe himself into the tradition of poets writing about the Trojan War. The matter remains unresolved, as does the second issue: the identity of "English Gaufride." He is commonly identified as Geoffrey of Monmouth, author of the *Historia Regum Britanniae* (1136), who begins his account with Brutus,

---

1. Dares's account was the more influential one in the West, judging from the number of surviving manuscripts, and for obvious reasons: via Aeneas and the foundation of Rome, many European countries, including England—via Aeneas's great-grandson Brutus—claimed their ancestry from the Trojan line. See, e.g., Kordula Wolf, *Troja—Metamorphosen eines Mythos: Französische, englische und italienische Überlieferungen des 12. Jahrhunderts im Vergleich* (Berlin: Akademie Verlag, 2009), on the French, English, and Italian claims of the Trojan ancestry. The genealogical tables on pp. 68, 70, 73, and 78 are particularly useful.

2. All quotations from Chaucer refer to *The Riverside Chaucer*, ed. Larry D. Benson (Oxford: Oxford University Press, 1987). On Chaucer's ordering principles in the poem, see Lara Ruffolo, "Literary Authority and the Lists of Chaucer's *House of Fame*: Destruction and Definition through Proliferation," *The Chaucer Review* 27, no. 4 (1993): 325–41, here 333–5.

3. The passage in Horace is *Epist.* 1.2.1–2. For detailed accounts of the different possibilities, see Bella Millett, "Chaucer, Lollius, and the Medieval Theory of Authorship," *Studies in the Age of Chaucer* 1 (1984): 93–103; R. A. Pratt, "A Note on Chaucer's Lollius," *Modern Language Notes* 65 (1950): 183–7; Richard Waswo, "The Narrator of *Troilus and Criseyde*," *English Literary History* 50 (1983): 1–25.

great-grandson of Aeneas and the legendary founder of Britain. Helen Cooper has shed doubt on this identification. The adjective 'English' is the problem, given that Geoffrey was Welsh. Why label him 'English' if the more fitting adjective, 'British,' would have fit the meter just as well? Was Chaucer taking a stand in an argument which mobilized Geoffrey of Monmouth's *Historia* to justify fourteenth-century colonial adventures?[4] What is more, Cooper points out that even if 'English' was meant to refer not to nationality but to language—"the only meaning for the word used elsewhere in Chaucer"[5]—it would be problematic: "There is only one Geoffrey who is English both by nationality and by choice of language and who has also written on the history of Troy, and this is Chaucer himself."[6] The argument is analogous to the case of Lollius: perhaps Chaucer, as the author of a Trojan poem himself, plays an elaborate joke on the audience by turning himself into one of the great poets his dreamer admires in the hall. Both these arguments, however, would ideally require a late date of composition for the *House of Fame*, that is, at a time when Chaucer was working on or had completed *Troilus and Criseyde*. Based on its metre, *House of Fame* is conventionally counted among Chaucer's earlier works and would therefore predate *Troilus and Criseyde*.[7]

Simon Meecham-Jones has cautioned us not to take the possible identification of "English Gaufride" with Chaucer himself too literally. Rather, the phrase

> provides a characteristic Chaucerian stratagem of figuration in which the image invokes a primary meaning that is (to some degree) destabilized, for the observant reader, by the possible presence of a secondary meaning that comments ironically on the first.[8]

---

4. See Simon Meecham-Jones, "'Englyssh Gaufride' and British Chaucer? Chaucerian Allusions to the Condition of Wales in the *House of Fame*," *The Chaucer Review* 44, no. 1 (2009): 1–24, in detail. He argues that the *Historia* "provided the crucial grappling hook that made possible the textual boarding and appropriation of insular traditions by the historians, lawyers, and mythographers of the Angevin ascendancy" (19).

5. Helen Cooper, "The Four Last Things in Dante and Chaucer: Ugolino in the House of Rumour," *New Medieval Literatures* 3 (1999): 39–66, here 58.

6. Cooper, "Four Last Things," 59.

7. Cooper makes a case for a later date of composition; see "Four Last Things," 59. She draws on A. J. Minnis, who has likewise argued for a later date; see *Oxford Guides to Chaucer: The Shorter Poems* (Oxford: Oxford University Press, 1995), 170–1. On the difficulty of dating Chaucer's works, in particular the *House of Fame*, see also Kathryn L. Lynch, "Dating Chaucer," *The Chaucer Review* 42 (2007): 1–22.

8. Meecham-Jones, "'Englyssh Gaufride' and British Chaucer?"

Against the backdrop of destabilizing meaning, Chaucer's list of poets invites further questions. Virgil, for one, is described as bearing up "the fame of Pius Eneas" (l. 1485). At the beginning of the *House of Fame*, the dreamer-narrator has already encountered the story of the *Aeneid*, in particular the tragedy of Dido—albeit not in Virgil's but in Ovid's interpretation of events. In the Ovidian account, however, "Chaucer's Aeneas is not a model of *pietas*, but a traitor."[9] Authorship and authority are unstable: both Virgil and Ovid are named as sources if the reader wishes to learn more (ll. 377–80), even though their accounts offer two very different versions—which cannot both be true—of the events. In addition, Chaucer claims to be the sole author of a lament by Dido ("Non other auctour allege I," l. 314), thus further complicating the question of authorship and narrative truth. Truth is also at the center of the debate in the case of Homer, who is accused of lying and siding with the Greeks (ll. 1477–80).

At the heart of Chaucer's review of epic poets, then, we find a deep scepticism towards literary and narrative authority.[10] Claims of authorship are refuted or undermined repeatedly, and various truths stand side by side without any attempt at a reconciliation. That Chaucer uses the form of the *list* in this context is hardly a coincidence.[11] Taking his cue from Dante, Chaucer at one point addresses his own mind: "O Thought, that wrot al that I mette / And in the tresorye hyt shette / Of my brayn" (ll. 523–5).[12] In the thesaurus of his mind, he finds the details of his dream vision. As Stephen Barney has argued, the metaphor of the thesaurus "implies the paradigmatic nature of the material: one can select anything from the jumble of objects in the treasure room."[13] From the perspective of the arts of memory, the metaphorical storeroom of memory would not be randomly organized; based on visual props, it would be perfectly organized. Chaucer evidently plays with the clash of different principles of order and disorder and the effects of both a visual and a spatial dimension in the *House of Fame*.[14] The list form thus invites

---

9. Cooper, "Four Last Things," 54.

10. Scepticism, in the words of Helen Cooper, "is indeed the very point of the poem" ("Four Last Things," 54). Note that my use of the term 'scepticism' follows Cooper's looser sense, that is, in terms of a suspicion against seemingly established and fixed truths, and not Sheila Delaney's philosophical *terminus technicus* (*Chaucer's House of Fame: The Poetics of Skeptical Fideism* [Chicago/London: University of Chicago Press, 1972]).

11. In the words of Lara Ruffolo, "Through his lists Chaucer invites us to play the game of literature, to join in the multiplication of authorities and works" ("Literary Authority," 326).

12. See Dante, *Inf.* II, ll. 7–9.

13. Barney, "Chaucer's Lists," 200.

14. See T. S. Miller, "Forms of Perspective and Chaucer's Dream Spaces: Memory and the Catalogue in *The House of Fame*," *Style* 48, no. 4 (2014): 479–95. On the arts of memory in

an exploitation of plenitude and completeness, of encyclopedic amplification and striving for perfection. Yet, Barney points out, Chaucer is aware "that the appearance of plenitude is specious, that abundance cannot substitute for perfection, that lists need imply no order or end."[15]

The speciousness and unstable truths which the list form enables are by no means unique or restricted to Chaucer's deployment of enumerations. In fact, there may well be an additional dimension to Chaucer's list of epic poets that plays on the very notion of the list, or rather, one of its prominent types—the epic catalogue.[16] By cataloguing the epic poets, Chaucer uses a formal device that is central to the genre of epic. Its centrality notwithstanding, the epic catalogue is a fraught device: it grinds narrative progression to a halt and opens up a different (cognitive and metaphorical) space, one of ordering and enumerating, which can be a challenge for the audience.[17]

Catalogues feature prominently in all of the poets' works included in Chaucer's list, even (and especially so) in Dares's and Dictys's prose accounts, which were the source of most of the later medieval redactions. Many of these catalogues are lists of names, of heroes and warriors, contingents and fatalities. There are catalogues in the anonymous *Seege or Batayle of Troye* (early fourteenth century), in the *Laud Troy Book* (ca. 1400), in the *'Gest Hystoriale' of the Destruction of Troy* (second half of the fourteenth century), and in John Lydgate's *Troy Book* (1412–20). With the exception of the *Seege*, which was influenced by Dares as well as by Benoît de Sainte-Maure's hugely influential *Le Roman de Troie* (1160s), all of these texts go back to Guido delle Colonne's *Historia destructionis Troiae* (1287).[18]

---

medieval culture, see Mary Carruthers, *The Book of Memory: A Study of Memory in Medieval Culture*, 2nd ed. (New York: Cambridge University Press, 2008).

15. Barney, "Chaucer's Lists," 221.

16. All catalogues are lists, but not all lists are catalogues. Throughout this chapter, I use the term 'list' as the hypernym which comprises the full range of enumerative forms. The catalogue is thus a subtype of the list, and the epic catalogue an even more special form.

17. The Ancient Greek verb *katalegein* comprises four related sets of meanings: 1. "recount, tell at length and in order," "repeat, recite"; 2. "reckon up, tell in full tale," "reckon, count as," "conclude by enumeration"; 3. "enumerate, draw up a list"; 4. (*later*) "select" (Liddell-Scott s.v.). To catalogue something, then, means both to enumerate and to narrate. The range of meanings suggests the close interdependence of the two activities, an interdependence that is retained in the German lexical pair *aufzählen* and *erzählen*, both of which are derivatives of the verb *zählen*, 'to count': an enumeration of something may become a narrative, and a narrative can easily be reduced to a list of events.

18. See Friedrich Brie, "Zwei mittelenglische Prosaromane: *The Sege of Thebes* und *The Sege of Troy*," *Archiv für das Studium der neueren Sprachen und Literaturen* 130 (1913): 40–52, 269–85; George A. Panton and David Donaldson, eds., *Guido delle Colonne: The 'Gest Hystoriale' of the Destruction of Troy* (London: Trübner, 1869–74); J. Ernst Wülfing, ed., *The Laud Troy Book*

The story about the Trojan War and the ultimate Fall of Troy functioned as a powerful source for moral guidance on topics such as heroism, the transmission of power, and rulership, but also, on a smaller scale, good conduct and counsel. These issues became of particular importance to aristocratic classes from the twelfth century onwards, and gained momentum in the late fourteenth and early fifteenth centuries. It was then that the Troy material increasingly acquired the meaning of a *speculum principis* rather than that of a *speculum historiae* and offered a foil for fantasizing about imperialistic thought.[19] Towards the end of the Middle Ages, the emerging and more pressing discourses on nation and nationhood made the Trojan stories especially fecund, as they allowed for one's inscription into and thus participation in a particular historical legacy.[20] At the same time, in parallel to the genealogical and politically instrumental uses of the Trojan material, there was also a tradition following Guido delle Colonne that offered a more sceptical view on the Fall of Troy. In this counterperspective, heroism becomes problematic: rather than noble fights, it is the rulers' inability to fight nobly, and their diplomatic failures in their counsels and negotiations, that leads to their ultimate downfall.[21]

Against the backdrop of these developments, a close analysis of the catalogues in the Middle English tradition of the Trojan War shows that the catalogues are increasingly characterized by a scepticism towards established and fixed truths. Their scepticism targets the war and its justification, the genre of epic, and narrative poetry itself. In that the catalogues function as sites of contention and poetic instability, they point to and reverberate with Chaucer's suspicion of authority, truth, and fame.

(London: Kegan Paul, Trench, Trübner, 1902–3); Henry Bergen, ed., *Lydgate's Troy Book*, 4 vols. (London: Kegan Paul, Trench, Trübner, 1906–35).

19. Władysław Witalisz, "Epic or Romance: Authorial Concept of Genre in Middle English Visions of Troy," *Studia Anglica Posnaniensia* 38 (2002): 519–26; Sylvia Federico, *New Troy: Fantasies of Empire in the Late Middle Ages* (Minneapolis: University of Minnesota Press, 2003); Geraldine Heng, *Empire of Magic: Medieval Romance and the Politics of Cultural Fantasy* (New York: Columbia University Press, 2003). See also Francis Ingledew, "The Book of Troy and the Genealogical Construction of History: The Case of Geoffrey of Monmouth's *Historia regum Britanniae*," *Speculum* 69, no. 3 (1994): 665–704, on the genealogical information the Troy material offered for aristocratic circles.

20. See Wolfram R. Keller, *Selves and Nations: The Troy Story from Sicily to England in the Middle Ages* (Heidelberg: Winter, 2008), for a comprehensive study on the implications between selves and nations as fostered and complicated by the Trojan story.

21. I am indebted here to James Simpson, "The Other Book of Troy: Guido delle Colonne's *Historia destructionis Troiae* in Fourteenth- and Fifteenth-Century England," *Speculum* 73, no. 2 (1998): 397–423, and Alex Mueller, *Translating Troy: Provincial Politics in Alliterative Romance* (Columbus: The Ohio State University Press, 2013).

ANON., *THE SEEGE OR BATAYLE OF TROY*

The anonymous romance *The Seege or Batayle of Troy* (early fourteenth century; henceforth: *Seege*) is extant in four manuscripts.[22] The poem has not received much attention from scholars to date because it had been disqualified early on as a crude example of popular romance style with little to appreciate.[23] Based on Dares and Benoît, it begins with the Argonauts, recounts the Trojan War, focusing on the battles, and ends with the Fall of Troy, the reunion of Menelaus and Helen, and the Greeks looting the city. The rhymed couplet format accounts for its swift manner of narration and condensation of the plot, which makes the story suitable (and appealing) for oral delivery. Mary Elizabeth Barnicle fittingly calls it a "minstrel romance."[24] While the overall plot, as is to be expected, remains stable, there are a number of changes and additions that 'romanticize' the material.[25] Most notable perhaps is the inclusion of the Judgement of Paris in three of the four versions (Lincoln Inn's, Egerton, and Arundel)—more than 120 lines are devoted to Paris's fateful decision to resolve the three goddesses' dispute by choosing Venus.

Despite the changes in form and function, all four manuscript witnesses have the Catalogue of Ships firmly included as part of the story. The Catalogue of Ships holds a prominent position in the *Iliad* (2.488–759) and features in almost all later accounts of the Trojan War. The catalogue lists the contingents of ships that have followed Agamemnon's call to set out for Troy. For each contingent, the number of the ships is given as well as their leaders and the region or settlement from where they are coming. There are twenty-nine contingents in total, and forty-four names of leaders (plus two that are absent).[26] The Catalogue of Ships is often regarded as the epitome of the epic catalogue.

---

22. BL Egerton MS 2862, BL Harley MS 525, Lincoln's Inn MS 150, BL Arundel MS 22. Barnicle's edition is based on all four manuscripts (Mary Elizabeth Barnicle, ed., *The Seege or Batayle of Troye: A Middle English Metrical Romance. Edited from MSS. Lincoln's Inn 150, Egerton 2862, Arundel XXII with Harley 525 Included in the Appendix* [London: Oxford University Press, 1927]).

23. See the overview in Nicola F. McDonald, "*The Seege of Troye*: 'ffor wham was wakened al this wo'?," in *The Spirit of Medieval English Popular Romance*, ed. Ad Putter and Jane Gilbert (Harlow: Longman, 2000), 181–99, here 181.

24. Barnicle, *Seege*, xxxiii. Only the version in Harley MS 525 suggests that it was meant to be read rather than sung.

25. It is telling that the Egerton MS contains seven metrical romances in total—the Trojan material has become fully infused in the romance hotchpotch.

26. As starting points for research into Homeric catalogues, see Benjamin Sammons, *The Art and Rhetoric of the Homeric Catalogue* (Oxford: Oxford University Press, 2010); Edzard Visser, *Homers Katalog der Schiffe* (Stuttgart: Teubner, 1997); Christiane Reitz and Simone Finkmann, eds., *Structures of Epic Poetry*, 3 vols. (Berlin: De Gruyter, 2019).

Even though one would be hard-pressed to call the *Seege* an epic with respect to its form and narrative style, the catalogue form has evidently become a *sine qua non* as far as the material is concerned: the matter of Troy carries with it the catalogue inherited from the Homeric tradition, and it carries it through even into literary forms that are only loosely connected to the epic other than by way of the story they tell.

The romance form in the *Seege* takes advantage of the verbal repetitions in the catalogue: the information about how many fleets and contingents each leader brings with him becomes a kind of refrain that makes the passage particularly attractive for oral delivery. In three of the four manuscripts, the phrase "(and) an ost stout and good / To passe over Te salte flood" rounds off each new contingent in a number of cases and thus effectively punctuates the enumeration.[27] The catalogue itself (ll. 847–981) is somewhat unusual: while it occurs at the point in the narrative where one would expect it—after Menelaus and Agamemnon call their Greek allies for help—the first entries are in fact hybrids that are borrowed from another catalogue tradition, namely, the catalogue of hero portraits (*Heldenschau*). The catalogue of heroes—brief descriptive vignettes of the protagonists of the Trojan War including the women—goes back to Dares (Books 12 and 13). Following the tradition of the Catalogue of Ships, one would expect the leaders' names, their ethnic and/or geographical origin, and the number of their ships. Yet in the *Seege*, we also have brief descriptions of their character traits and outward appearance in a few cases. Menelaus, for instance, is introduced as follows:

> Þe kyng of grece, wiþ-oute les,
> A litel, mene mon he wes;
> His hed was red, his berd al-so—
> Þeo hendeste kny3t þat my3te go—
> And was stalworþe and hardy among
> And him was loþ to soffre wrong.
> (Lincoln's Inn MS, ll. 848–53)

The poet continues to say that Menelaus assembles 500 ships (l. 856) and has them stocked up well with provisions and strong men (ll. 857–63). Its conventionality notwithstanding, the technique here is one of compression that makes use of two originally distinct catalogues and merges them into one.

---

27. The passages are ll. 868–9, 878–9, 882–3, 891–2, 896–97, and 908–9. See also Barnicle, *Seege*, xxxi.

C. R. B. Combellack has referred to such a catalogue as "composite," and notes the very same procedure, though with greater fidelity and closeness to the sources, with respect to *The Sege of Troye*.[28] *The Sege of Troye* is a mid-fifteenth-century prose account extant in one manuscript (Bodleian, Rawlinson Misc. D 82) that is heavily indebted to John Lydgate's *Troy Book*.[29] As Combellack was able to show by means of a meticulous comparison, the catalogue of this prose text draws on both the list of portraits and Lydgate's Catalogue of Ships and merges them into one. A very similar practice, though not as refined and less consistent, appears to be behind the *Seege* as well. This is striking given the much earlier provenance of *Seege*. Evidently, Combellack's claim that the composite catalogue in the prose version is "unique, a catalogue *sui generis*"[30] requires qualification. As to the rationale behind the composite technique, one could surmise an inherent force of attraction in the form of the catalogue, which led the poet to merge the two passages. While the composite catalogue contains a greater density of information, it reduces the overall number of catalogues, and thus potential obstructions to the plot, in the poem.

The *Seege* is also noteworthy in that it shows that the appreciation of the catalogue, or rather, the task of copying it, was by no means shared by all. Harley MS 525 bears witness to this. Throughout the text, the scribe has shortened and condensed the material: he cuts descriptions and condenses battle scenes, thereby avoiding repetitions. In the Catalogue of Ships, "he starts out courageously," as Barnicle puts it,[31] only omitting the refrains, up to line 900, but then drastically cuts fifty-six lines and enumerates only thirteen out of the twenty-six warriors in total. Even though the scribe seems to have proceeded with some "point and purpose," the incantation-like effect of the long, repetitive, and almost musical catalogue in the other versions of the *Seege* is lost in the Harley version.[32] Curiously, the scribe cuts the number of warriors and the poem as a whole exactly in half. Perhaps he was taking his cue from a phrase in the Arundel MS. In this version, when the Catalogue of Ships is completed, the poet pauses—briefly inviting his audience to fill their cups and pray to God—and remarks that now half of the story has been told:

---

28. C. R. B. Combellack, "The Composite Catalogue of *The Sege of Troye*," *Speculum* 26, no. 4 (1951): 624–34.
29. See the editions by Nathaniel E. Griffin, "*The Sege of Troye*," *PMLA* 22, no. 1 (1907): 157–200, and Brie, "Prosaromane."
30. Combellack, "Composite Catalogue," 624.
31. Barnicle, *Seege*, xlviii.
32. Barnicle, *Seege*, xlix.

> Tho gunne þay to-gederis dryue
> xii^e shippis .l. *and* fyue.
> Her ys þe haluyndell of our geste;
> God saue vs, mest and lest.
> ffyl þe cuppe *and* mak ous glad,
> ffor þe maker þus so bad.
> (Arundel MS, ll. 978–83)

In the Lincoln's Inn MS, the end of the catalogue is also marked by an appeal to the audience: "Herkeneþ now to my spelle / And more of þis y wol ȝou telle" (ll. 980–1). This suggests that the catalogue was regarded as a natural pause from the story—that is, the narrative progression—to which the poet returns at this point and continues with the events. He could expect his audience to react differently: perhaps they may have joined in with the refrain, or clapped along, or used the repetitiveness to divert and start talking—in any case, a call to focus their attention back to the story was in order. Here, we can detect an awareness of the catalogue's narrative alterity in form, which is handled differently in the two versions. Behind both the blend of several catalogues and their abbreviating or cutting, there is an understanding of how narrative time and the unfolding of the narrative can become more effective. Perhaps the poets did not trust the unwieldiness of the catalogue form and therefore decided to streamline it.

On the level of the plot, the division of the poem into two parts in the Harley version may carry further weight: Nicola McDonald has shown how the treatment of the women and their objectification in particular guides the narrative in the Harley version. In that the romance puts in dialogue the different heroes' relationships to the women they capture and desire, it invites a contrastive reading that harks back to yet another epic catalogue—that of Apollonius in the first book of the *Argonautica*. Apollonius's catalogue also falls into two halves that juxtapose two different kinds of heroism, one exemplified by Orpheus the musician and poet, the other by Heracles the fighter (1.23–233). A similar approach, if not in technique but in effect, may be at stake in the *Seege*, too: the Catalogue of Ships with its numbers and air of record-keeping becomes a site for reflecting on the past (e.g., the Argonauts and the Judgement of Paris, and the two abductions of women under dubious circumstances), and for looking ahead to the future (i.e., the disastrous outcome of these irascible desires). The catalogue expresses a strong sense of pessimism as to the events to come, offering a skeptical view on the Trojan War and its aftermath.

JOHN CLERK OF WHALLEY, 'GEST HYSTORIALE' OF THE DESTRUCTION OF TROY

In the *'Gest Hystoriale' of the Destruction of Troy* (henceforth: *Gest*), the sceptical perspective toward the Trojan War becomes even further pronounced in and through its catalogues. The *Gest* survives in one manuscript (Glasgow UL, Hunter MS 388, V.2.8) and is composed in alliterative verse. Its authorship was unknown until Thorlac Turville-Petre discovered that the initials of the Prologue and Books 1 to 20 spell out the poet's name: "Maistur Iohannes Clerk de Whalele," that is, John Clerk of Whalley.[33] Whalley in Lancashire was home to a large Cistercian abbey.[34] The poem relies heavily on Guido delle Colonne and, like Guido, takes an overall historiographic approach to the Trojan material.[35] The poet stresses the eyewitness account of the events, and, as David Benson has shown, only somewhat streamlines his source by omitting overtly moralizing and other rather decorative passages.[36] More recently, James Simpson and Alex Mueller have revisited the *Gest* and argued that its subtle changes in content and form display a political agenda that goes against the otherwise dominant line of reading the Trojan story as a source for legitimizing aristocratic power. Rather, the *Gest* is much more ambivalent and presents a perspective on the Fall of Troy that is, in Mueller's words, "damnatory."[37] The *Gest*, he argues, thus emphasizes the Trojans' culpability and the 'destruction' also from within as the Trojan leaders fail to negotiate and use diplomacy. Simpson describes this line of tradition as "resolutely antiimperialistic" because it expresses "a sense of historical sequence generated by

---

33. Thorlac Turville-Petre, "The Author of *The Destruction of Troy*," *Medium Aevum* 57, no. 2 (1988): 264–9.

34. See Edward Wilson, "John Clerk, Author of *The Destruction of Troy*," *Notes and Queries* 235 (1990): 391–6, for further evidence of John Clerk of Whalley.

35. For the poet's source, his technique of translation, and style, see Hermann Brandes, "Die mittelenglische *Destruction of Troy* und ihre Quelle," *Englische Studien* 8 (1885): 398–410; David Lawton, "*The Destruction of Troy* as Translation from Latin Prose: Aspects of Form and Style," *Studia Neophilologica* 52 (1980): 259–70; John Finlayson, "Guido de Columnis' *Historia destructionis Troiae*, the *'Gest Hystorial' of the Destruction of Troy*, and Lydgate's *Troy Book*: Translation and the Design of History," *Anglia* 113, no. 2 (1995): 141–62, and, by the same author, "Alliterative Narrative Poetry: The Control of the Medium," *Traditio* 44 (1988): 419–51. On romancing the Trojan material in the *Gest*, see Alex Mueller, "Linking Letters: Translating Ancient History into Medieval Romance," *Literature Compass* 4, no. 4 (2007): 1017–29, with particular emphasis on the question of fiction and history in the Prologue.

36. David Benson, *The History of Troy in Middle English Literature: Guido delle Colonne's Historia Destructionis Troiae in Medieval England* (Woodbridge: D. S. Brewer, 1980), 47.

37. Mueller, *Translating Troy*, 69.

poor decisions and unfolding toward a catastrophe beyond the power of any king to control."[38] We will see to what extent the catalogues contribute to this impression.

Following Guido, the *Gest* begins with the story of Jason and Medea and follows up the events after the Trojan War with the Orestes story (Book 33), Odysseus's travels (Book 34), and Pyrrhus (Book 35).[39] Almost all of the catalogues are based on Guido delle Colonne: they include the catalogue of hero portraits (*Heldenschau*; ll. 3732–858) and the Catalogue of Ships (Book 9), as well as the Greek and Trojan divisions respectively (Book 15 and 19). Crucial for our present purposes is Clerk's final catalogue. Following Guido delle Colonne, Clerk closes his version with the statistics of "who dight hom to dethe with dynttes of hond" (l. 14,005). There are a number of subtle changes to be noted here. Already in Guido, the names form alliterative clusters; the structure is highly repetitive, almost incantational:

> Hector uero interfecit regem Archilogum, regem Prothesilaum, regem Humerum, regem Patroclum, regem Orchimenum, regem Pallamonem, regem Pheypum, regem Prothenorem, regem Dorium.[40]

Clerk, however, does not take advantage of the oral-aural effect the alliterations invite. Instead, he turns the simple statistical list of first names, punctuated by the qualification of their status as *rex* (*regem*), into an exercise in the use of synonyms for 'killing':

> Thies, honerable Ector auntrid to Sle,
> Er the doghty was ded, all of du kynges.
> Achilagon, a choise kyng, he choppit to dethe.
> Protheselon, in prese, he put out of lyue.
> Myrion the mighty, he martrid with hond.
> Protroculun, Prothenor, the prise knight slaght;
> Othemen, also, abill of person:
> Polexenun, Paralanun, Polibeton, also:
> Kyng Philip, þat bold britnet with strokes.
> Tedynur, in the toile he tyrnit to ground.
> Durion of his dynttes drepit was there.
>   (ll. 14,006–16)

---

38. Simpson, "The Other Book," 422.
39. I refer to and quote from the edition by Panton and Donaldson, *Guido delle Colonne*.
40. Nathaniel E. Griffin, ed., *Guido delle Colonne*: Historia destructionis Troiae (Cambridge, MA: Medieval Academy of America, 1936), 274.

Clerk not only adds the occasional detail to the victims ("Achilagon, a choise kyng"; "Myrion the mighty") where Guido only mentions their names, but he also varies the terms to describe—in this case—Hector's fatalities: "sle"; "choppit to dethe"; "put out of lyue"; "martrid with hond"; "slight"; "britnet with strokes"; "tyrnit to ground"; "of his dynttes drepit." With the exception of 'slay,' which is used twice (ll. 14,006; 14,011), there are seven different expressions for the act of killing someone. The same principle can be observed also for the remainder of the list. What led the poet to rewrite the list to this effect? That he was weary of the catalogue form seems unlikely, given that overall the catalogues are translated faithfully and were evidently taken as an important feature of the material. It seems, rather, that the changes are very much strategic, and in line with Clerk's overall critical outlook on the Trojan story. The final 'kill list' is that of Pyrrhus:

> Pyrrus, the pert kyng, put vnto dethe
> Pantasilia the prise qwene, pertest of ladies;
> Kyng Priam, with pyne, Polexena his doghter:
> Thies worthy to wale, as werdes hom demyt,
> Were martrid in maner, as I mynt haue.
> (ll. 14,038–42)

This passage does not correspond to Guido, who ends on Diomede's killings (another four names). Clerk chooses to close with an outrageous example: a warrior killing two women. The deaths of the two women, who frame Priam's death, can almost be read as a miniature stand-in for the Trojan War as a whole: Priam, King of Troy, epitomizing his city, the downfall of which is brought about by women who become entangled in the masculine game of warfare. That they choose to die, as was their fate, is Clerk's final comment before he laconically marks the end of his work by adding "now the proses is plainly put to an end: / He bring vs to the blisse, þat bled for our Syn" (ll. 14,043–44). The ending of the *Gest*, then, is a demonstration of the outrageousness of the events: the semantic variation on bringing about someone's death brings to the fore the brutality of the war. It is essentially a killing feast, and not only that: its very purpose, or driving force, is men's failure to curb their desires, to be moderate, and to govern wisely. Through the linguistic changes in the catalogue, Clerk gives voice to his skepticism towards the Trojan War and its many fatalities. He questions the justification of fame that is implicit in the statistics of fatalities as a price too high to pay. The final comment on fate's influence sits uneasily with the foregoing list—in the absence of any divine influence on the events, was it not men's very own decision to act against every good counsel? The diction in Clerk's final lines suggests a different approach altogether: *martrid* is linked up with the *blisse* of Christ, to whom the poet turns. If Polyxena's death was a kind of martyrdom, who is to blame then for their disregard of the true belief? I would not overstress this point—Clerk clearly does not offer any systematic approach for a typological reading—but he hints at its possibilities. The final list and its transformation make that abundantly clear, and give further weight to the claims made by Mueller and Simpson that the *Gest* presents us with a decidedly anti-imperialistic, negative reading of the Trojan story.

ANON., *LAUD TROY BOOK*

The *Laud Troy Book* further problematizes the catalogue form—though not by using it as a vehicle for critique but by assuming a sceptical view on the effectiveness of the device itself. The poem receives its name from its unique source, the Laud Manuscript (Bodleian, Laud Misc. 595). Authorship, provenance, and origin remain unresolved; it appears to have been written between the late fourteenth and early fifteenth century. David Benson calls it "a serious work of history" and a "Hector romance" due to its unmistakable focus on Hector for some parts of the narrative.[41] It is a rather large work of more than 18,500 lines in four-stress couplets. Its form, not least due to the many dramatic speeches, strongly suggests oral delivery: the audience is frequently addressed. The preface to the story proper already features a noteworthy list of great romances and their heroes:

> Many speken of men that romaunces rede
> That were sumtyme doughti in dede,
> The while that god hem lyff lente,
> That now ben dede and hennes wente:
> Off Bevis, Gy, and of Gauwayn,
> Off kyng Richard, & of Owayn,
> Off Tristram, and of Percyuale,
> Off Rouland Ris, and Aglauale,
> Off Archeroun, and of Octouian,
> Off Charles, & of Cassibaldan,
> Off Hauelok, Horne, & of Wade;—
> In Romaunces that of hem ben made

---

41. Benson, *History of Troy,* 67.

That gestoures often dos of hem gestes
At Mangeres and at grete ffestes.
Here dedis ben in remembraunce
In many fair Romaunce.[42]
(ll. 11–23)

The Trojan heroes, first and foremost Hector, are both set in line and set apart from the protagonists of romances. The poet enumerates examples from the "matter of Britain" (Gawain, Owen, Tristram), the "matter of France" (Roland, Charlemagne), and the "matter of England" (Bevis, Havelock, Horn), thus giving his audience a sense of his repertoire and drawing attention to the context in which he places his Troy version. It will feature as a "matter of Rome" example of a popular romance to be enjoyed in a minstrel context. More than in any of the other versions discussed so far, the Trojan material is appropriated here into the genre of romance, defined in terms of the stories it tells as well as the method and manner of delivery. By way of those that have already been sung about, the poet announces that he will go back to an earlier hero, Hector, "for ther was neuere man that myght stand / A strong stroke of Ectores hand" (ll. 57–8) except for Achilles. The *Laud Troy Book* thus reduces the Trojan story—or condenses it, rather—from the start to a conflict between the two heroes.

The prominent list at the very beginning of the *Laud Troy Book* notwithstanding, the poet is evidently not a great lover of the catalogue form. At the point in the narrative where Dares has the portrait of the leaders, the poet announces that "gret tarrying it is to telle / That Dares makes vpon his spelle" (ll. 3317–18). He then offers a summary of Dares's description of all the kings and their appearance and concludes that overall it was a congregation never before seen (ll. 3320–6). There are two brief lists of all the Greek kings that come together for battle (ll. 6665–72; 7551–61) and an enumeration of all the Greek leaders led by Pyrrhus in his father's armor (ll. 16,649–57). The Catalogue of Ships is likewise much reduced, with the result that it is no longer visible or discernible as a catalogue. The *Laud Troy Book* provides two numbers instead: there were sixty-eight dukes and more than 1,800,000 men under their command. However, the poet attempts to replicate the *effect* of the catalogue by means of two techniques: first, exaggerations and hyperbole. Phrases such as "Off men of Armes . . . / To-gedre at ones sene was neuere on o day" (ll. 3343–4); "ne neuere" (ll. 3346; 3347); "As longe as erthe sene schal be, / Ne so fele shippus to-gedur y-set" (ll. 3348–9) stress the hugeness of the assembly

---

42. All quotations are from the edition by Wülfing, *Laud Troy Book*.

that cannot be described adequately. The second technique is a combination of lamentation and apostrophe: the poet addresses Paris and Hector directly and laments the loss of several other key figures in a series of exclamations (ll. 3352–80).

Overall, then, the *Laud Troy Book* bears witness to the rejection or stark condensation of catalogues and thus to a different approach to this formal element. One reason is clearly to be sought in the strong, even programmatic indebtedness to the romance tradition. As a result, the catalogue form becomes suspicious. The *Laud Troy Book* does not even attempt to retell history but is framed as a romance from the very beginning. Its approach is not a faithful recollection of 'factual' material but a heroic story that lives up to the audience's expectations of other great romance heroes. As such, the Catalogue of Ships and similar statistic-like passages are redundant and therefore replaced, while the effect of grandeur and enormity is retained by means of alternative narrative strategies.

JOHN LYDGATE'S *TROY BOOK*

With John Lydgate's *Troy Book*, we come full circle to Chaucer and his scepticism towards authority and authorial truth. Both in form and outlook, Lydgate's take on authority, fame, and the unreliability of poetic, linguistic, and historical truth equal Chaucer's in the *House of Fame*.[43] If the *Laud Troy Book* was already extensive in its scope, John Lydgate's *Troy Book* is massive. Based (once more) on Guido delle Colonne, the story is spread out over 30,000 lines in five books. The work was commissioned by Henry V in 1412, that is, before he became king, and Lydgate completed the task in 1420.[44] Lydgate's perspective on the Trojan material is fundamentally shaped

---

43. For an excellent overview of how the *House of Fame* informs the *Troy Book*, see Bernadette C. Vankeerbergen, "Rhetoric, Truth, and Lydgate's *Troy Book*" (Ph.D. diss., The Ohio State University, 2009), esp. 123–43. Lydgate's creativity and poetics have often been regarded as inferior to Chaucer's; see, e.g., David C. Benson, "Critic and Poet: What Lydgate and Henryson Did to Chaucer's *Troilus and Criseyde*," *Modern Language Quarterly* 53 (1992): 23–40; Derek Pearsall, "Chaucer and Lydgate," in *Chaucer Traditions: Studies in Honour of Derek Brewer*, ed. Ruth Morse and Barry Windeatt (Cambridge: Cambridge University Press, 1990), 39–53.

44. For the historical context in more detail, see Alan S. Ambrisco and Paul Strohm, "Succession and Sovereignty in Lydgate's Prologue to *The Troy Book*," *The Chaucer Review* 30, no. 1 (1995): 40–57, with special emphasis on the Prologue; Colin Fewer, "John Lydgate's *Troy Book* and the Ideology of Prudence," *The Chaucer Review* 38, no. 3 (2004): 229–45; Lee Patterson, "Making Identities in Fifteenth-Century England: Henry V and John Lydgate," in *New Historical Literary Study: Essays on Reproducing Texts, Representing History*, ed. Jeffrey N. Cox and Larry J. Reynolds (Princeton: Princeton University Press, 1993), 69–107, with reference to

by Chaucer, and perhaps via Chaucer, or via additional sources, by Ovidian and Virgilian influences. Lydgate's indebtedness to Chaucer comes to the fore in the engagement with a line of tradition Chaucer does *not* use: the Latin tradition since Dares and Dictys. Christopher Baswell has demonstrated, correctly I believe, that Lydgate pays homage to Chaucer by 'translating' him into "Latin," that is, by inserting Chaucerian material into the translation of Guido's Latin account.[45] In doing so, Lydgate attempts to change the register of Chaucer's *Troilus and Criseyde*—which, after all, recounts only one episode of the Trojan War, and the war itself is but a general frame for the tragic love story. While Chaucer tells a romance, Lydgate reintroduces the 'epic' dimension of the larger context, which in Lydgate materializes as a historical, often moralizing perspective.[46] Lydgate's reinvention of Chaucer's Trojan story also extends to the formal dimension of the narrative: Lydgate exploits the tendency of epic to contain long descriptions and catalogues, thus emulating Chaucerian list-making propensity by elevating it to the form of the epic catalogue. Lydgate's approach to epic narrative and self-understanding as a poet come to the fore in his translation—and expansion—of the catalogues and enumerations. Behind Lydgate's copiousness, as we shall see, there is a deep-rooted suspicion towards his sources.

Lydgate's technique of amplification can be observed in the first major catalogue of the work in Book 2, the Catalogue of the Greek allies and their descriptions (2.4509–5066). In the verbose introduction to the purpose of the catalogue's content and its source (ll. 4509–21), Lydgate shows full awareness of the catalogue form offering a site for poetological statements and self-reflection. He uses the catalogue form to create an interlaced web of

---

the *Siege of Thebes*; Larry Scanlon and James Simpson, eds., *John Lydgate: Poetry, Culture, and Lancastrian England* (South Bend, IN: University of Notre Dame Press, 2006); Paul Strohm, "Hoccleve, Lydgate, and the Lancastrian Court," in *The Cambridge History of Medieval English Literature*, ed. David Wallace (Cambridge: Cambridge University Press, 1999), 640–61.

45. Christopher Baswell, "*Troy Book*: How Lydgate Translates Chaucer into Latin," in *Translation Theory and Practice in the Middle Ages*, ed. Jeanette Beer (Kalamazoo, MI: Medieval Institute Publications, 1997), 215–37.

46. Lydgate's clear preference for verbosity and amplification can at times lead to a certain "dullness," the term David Lawton famously used to describe Lydgate's (and other fifteenth-century writers') learned but overly moralistic, serious engagement with their sources ("Dullness and the Fifteenth Century," *ELH* 54, no. 4 [1987]: 761–99). For Lydgate and his treatment of the classical material, see, e.g., Benson, *The History of Troy*, 106–13, and John Studer, "History as Moral Instruction: John Lydgate's Record of *Troie Toun*," *Emporia State Research Studies* 19, no. 1 (1970): 5–13. On Lydgate's techniques of amplification, see Derek Pearsall, *John Lydgate: Medieval Authors: Poets of the Later Middle Ages* (London: Routledge and Kegan Paul, 1970), 129–32; on his aureate style, Robert J. Meyer-Lee, "Lydgate's Laureate Pose," in *John Lydgate: Poetry, Culture, and Lancastrian England*, ed. Larry Scanlon and James Simpson (South Bend, IN: University of Notre Dame Press, 2006), 36–60.

translation and reference from Dares through Guido to Chaucer and finally to himself. Dares's eyewitness account is acknowledged as the ultimate source of the catalogue, which begins with Helen. Once he reaches Cressid (Briseida in Dares), the catalogue, which in itself has already ground the narrative to a halt, is further digressed upon by a long reflection on Chaucer and his ingenuity in describing Criseyde (2.4677-90). This is a decisive point in the *Troy Book* because Lydgate is confronted with two conflicting authorities: his (Latin) source's, Guido's, and ultimately Dares's, description, and Chaucer's English one.[47] The solution lies in Lydgate's own linguistic and poetic abilities, which he hides behind the humility topos: he announces that he is unable to hold a candle to Chaucer's style, yet after a long praise of Chaucer paired with an apology for his own mediocre writing, Lydgate nevertheless provides his own description (2.4691-735). The catalogue closes, several hundred lines later, with another reference to Dares:

> In special he [*Dares*] putte no mo in mynde
> Þan ȝe haue herde, saue, as ȝe schal fynde
> In þis story, whan it cometh þer-to,
> Of hir knyȝthod & who þat best hath do,
> Lastyng þe sege, þe maner euerydel.
>   (2.5059-63)

The catalogue ends because Dares does not provide any more information. This is an odd way of closing a catalogue, which shows a distrust of Dares and his textual reliability: Lydgate seems to imply that there must have been additional information, yet he could not find it in his source. Lydgate's verbose and amplificatory style may be indicative almost of an angst with regard to both textual incompletion and the unreliability of poetic truth. At the same time, the catalogue makes obvious Lydgate's struggle to claim a place for himself in the literary tradition.

In Book 2, Lydgate presents his audience with the Catalogue of Ships (2.5105-98). Here, too, he stresses that he relies on his source, Dares: "myn auctor telleth" (2.5106). The source is followed closely, yet the presentation of the leaders' names and their homes is subtly changed. Lydgate does not *narrate* the Catalogue of Ships but present it with a markedly *explanatory* attitude. Since demonstratives are used throughout, the names and places become items of reference quite distant from the speaker and by extension also distant

---

[47]. See Baswell, "*Troy Book*," 232-4, for a detailed analysis of the imagery used in the passage.

from the audience. Menelaus, for instance, is said to come "out of his londe þat callid is Sparten" (2.5111), and, some lines later, we learn: "from þe lond, called Sycomenye, . . . / Of þe duke þat hiȝte Achalapus" (2.5115; 5117). Salamis, from where Ajax is coming, is described as "his royal chef cyte" (2.5126), and "þe duke namyd Prothisalus" also makes his way "to þe hauene þat callid was Athene" (2.5154–5). This distance between the poet and his material provides evidence for what Derek Pearsall has described as Lydgate's interest in Guido not as a story but as a text: "It may be history, but it has no historical reality."[48] This qualification, however, should not be seen as a sign of Lydgate's inferior style or lack of creativity. Rather, in that historical reality becomes subsumed under the controlling hands of the poet, Lydgate highlights the constructedness of narrative and its unstable, uncertain truth claims. Lydgate's technique here points to the scepticism which with he views the contradictory accounts of the Trojan tradition.

The fifth and final book mentions the statistics we have encountered already, that is, the overall number of deaths on both sides and the duration of the war (5.3341–59). However, while Lydgate mentions Dares's numbers, we are not given any names. Whether Lydgate's source did not include the list of names here, or whether he chose not to translate it (rather untypically), cannot be said with certainty. Lydgate closes by implicitly inscribing himself into two lists:

> I haue no more [of] latyn to translate
> After Dites, Dares, nor Guydo,
> And me to adden any more þer-to
> Þan myn auctours specefie & seyn,
> Þe occupacioun, sothly, wer but veyn,
> Lik a maner of presumpcioun.
>   (5.3360–5)

The first list is that of literary history: upon Dictys, Dares, and Guido (and Chaucer, we may add) now follows Lydgate, too. The second list is history and historical time, as suggested by the statistics. Lydgate adds the year AD 1420, when he completed the work (5.3366–8), and praises Henry V, whose reign he hopes will be a restoration of the golden age in England (5.3999–401). Even though it is a topos to end on a devotional note—Lydgate first apologizes, once more, to his readers, just in case, and then prays to God—the ending of the *Troy Book* is a battle ground of authorities in conflict. Lydgate wrestles

---

48. Pearsall, *John Lydgate*, 127.

with his material, his predecessors, his position towards his patron, who happens to be king, politics, and ultimately even God. This is quite a list, too, which demonstrates the extent to which Lydgate was caught between different poles and expectations, and, as a result, deeply suspicious of fixed truths and stable authorities.

CONCLUSION

Having taken Chaucer's list of epic poets in the *House of Fame* as our vantage point, we have moved backwards and forwards in the Middle English tradition of the matter of Troy. While Chaucer is an extreme example of exploiting the list form in order to destabilize truth claims and the reliability of sources, references, and discourses, there is evidence of a more general trend discernible in Middle English accounts of the Trojan War to assume a sceptical perspective on the war and on narrating the Trojan story in the handling of the epic catalogue. As we have seen, epic catalogues become means to communicate criticism. As they do not narrate but enumerate, they stand out from the rest of the narrative material and also invite a different approach to how they are received. The poets' skepticism towards authority, authorial truth, and fame is directed at three issues: the Trojan War and its necessity, the genre of epic, and the form of the catalogue itself. The first is content-related, the second and third are instances of form, on a macro and micro level respectively. What is more, the degree of scepticism certainly increases over time. In the *Seege*, the scepticism targets the level of content primarily in critiquing the war and its necessity, albeit in an indirect way. In the *Laud Troy Book*, the poet is sceptical of the catalogue form and its close ties with epic traditions, which he actively suppresses in favor of a romance retelling of the story. In the *Gest*, by contrast, which dates to the second half of the fourteenth century, the poet uses the catalogue form to openly criticize the necessity of the Trojan War and its claims to fame through fatalities. Lydgate's *Troy Book*, finally, is written in full awareness of Chaucer's playful negotiation and negation of poetic fame and authorial control. The *Troy Book* is a decidedly epic poem that through its catalogues lays claim to the epic tradition while at the same time exhibiting a strong sense of scepticism towards the authority and truth claims of its predecessors. All poets and their works under scrutiny here are actively engaged in making literary history—by adding themselves, ultimately, to the list of poets who have written on the Trojan War in Middle English literature.

CHAPTER 7

Performing Generic Exhaustion
Implosive Households in Gavin Douglas's Palice of Honour

WOLFRAM R. KELLER

The "basic structural device ... is the list," Denton Fox observes with a view to Gavin Douglas's *Palice of Honour*.[1] To a certain extent, the omnipresence of lists in Douglas's dream poem is motivated generically, since lists are a recurring feature in dream poetry in general and in poems taking their cue from Geoffrey Chaucer's *House of Fame* in particular. What interests me about the lists in *Fame* and *Palice* is how they are related to the poems' epistemological underpinnings, to the representation of the three ventricles of the brain—imagination, logic, and memory—and the metapoetic relevance thereof. In Chaucer's *Fame*, lists are a prominent feature in the description of architectural spaces, including the temple of Venus, the palace of Fama, and the wicker house of Rumor. These spaces can be read as representations of the three cells of the brain—a brain busy penning poetry. The individual ventricles are thereby represented as households that should be ideally governed by the precepts of traditional household management, by *oikonomia*. In the case of Chaucer's *Fame*, however, the lists come with a dis-

---

I would like to thank Eva von Contzen, Andrew James Johnston, James Simpson, and the anonymous reviewers for their generous and helpful feedback on my thoughts concerning (post-)Chaucerian imaginational chrematistics.

1. Denton Fox, "The Scottish Chaucerians," in *Chaucer and Chaucerians: Critical Studies in Middle English Literature*, ed. D. S. Brewer (London: Thomas Nelson and Sons, 1996), 198.

order and excessiveness that are characteristic of a different mode of economic activity, namely, commerce or, in Aristotle's term, *chrematistike*. What ensues in Chaucer's dream poem could thus be described as a commercial transformation of the poet's brain. And this commercial transformation results in a poetry, first and foremost the *House of Fame* itself, driven by an uncurbed imagination, by an excess that comes into view primarily (albeit not exclusively) through lists.

Post-Chaucerian dream poetry seems to be intent on imposing order upon the metapoetic chaos and disharmony besetting Chaucer's dream poetry. Douglas's *Palice* (c. 1501) is no exception. The poem seems to celebrate harmonic relationships everywhere—the harmony of body and soul, and celestial harmony—in terms of instrumental music. Moreover, the dreamer's journey through different spaces in the *Palice*'s three parts appears to be leading toward spiritual enlightenment. At a first glance, the rather long, often unwieldly lists singled out by Fox as a defining feature of the *Palice* reinforce this sense of harmony—at least initially. This is supposed to be true even of the poem's longest list, listing what the dreamer beholds in Venus's mirror. By virtue of its placement and, literally, by its framing (by way of three posts), this mirror-list yields insights into the epistemological and metapoetic status of lists and listing within the poem as a whole. Venus's mirror not only relocates the excess generally associated with the faculty of imagination within the realm of memory; furthermore, the proliferation of images in the mirror is reflected in the poem's proliferation of mirrorings, including the repeated representations of the ventricles. That is, the tripartite frame of Venus's excessive mirror-list spotlights a different form of listing within the poem: the replication of the three ventricles within the three parts of the poem includes *en miniature* a second-order representation of the three ventricles. An imaginational excess familiar from Chaucer's *Fame*, then, threatens to dissolve from within what seemed to be a harmonious mental *oikonomia*. The metapoetic correlative of this is the *Palice*'s performance of its own representational exhaustion, the wholesale destabilization of the genre of faculty allegory itself.

MENTAL HOUSEHOLD MANAGEMENT IN LATE-MEDIEVAL DREAM POEMS

Douglas's *Palice* belongs to the genre of allegorical dream poetry, in which a protagonist journeys through an imaginary landscape. As such, Douglas's poem frequently references earlier (Chaucerian) dream poems. Scholars usually see *Fame* as the most important intertext for the Middle Scots poem,[2] not least because the *Palice*, like *Fame*, renders the protagonist's dream journey *explicitly* as a means to educate the poet, poetry being the pathway toward (poetic) honor.[3] Like *Fame*, the *Palice* is littered with lists, which have generally begun to attract scholarly attention again.[4] In Stephen Barney's view, "medieval poets generally, and Chaucer especially, were list-makers."[5] Chaucer's *Fame* is one of the dream poems brimming with lists: the list of what the dreamer sees in the temple of Venus, including a list of abandoned women that interrupts the narrator's summary of the *Aeneid* (388–426);[6] the lists in the course of the Eagle's lecture; the more excessive lists in the description of the palace of Fama; the lists of innumerable personified narratives—that is, *tidings*—that keep whirring around in the wicker house of Rumor. All of these lists effect chaos and disharmony, as, for instance, in the case of the list of hundreds of musicians simultaneously and cacophonously using their instruments or in a list of Trojan authorities. Thus, these (and other) lists in *Fame* are more often than not associated both with disharmony and excess. Moreover, the proliferation and excessiveness of the images flooding Geffrey's senses is intrinsically related to the poem's representation of cognitive processes, which are mapped within the poem by means of representing the ventricles of the brain as households that are ultimately dissolved by forms of excess they prove unable to contain.

Allegorical dream visions like Chaucer's *Fame* usually feature the journey of a protagonist through an unfamiliar landscape, through architectural

---

2. See, e.g., Chelsea Honeyman, "*The Palice of Honour*: Gavin Douglas' Renovation of Chaucer's *House of Fame*," in *Standing in the Shadow of the Master? Chaucerian Influences and Interpretations*, ed. Kathleen A. Bishop (Newcastle upon Tyne: Cambridge Scholars Press, 2010), 65–81, here 68; 71; Gregory Kratzmann, *Anglo-Scottish Literary Relations, 1430–1550* (Cambridge: Cambridge University Press, 1980), 104–28; but cf. also David J. Parkinson, introduction to *Gavin Douglas: The Palyce of Honour*, ed. David J. Parkinson, 2nd ed. (Kalamazoo, MI: Medieval Institute Publications, 2018), 48–52.

3. Priscilla Bawcutt, *Gavin Douglas: A Critical Study* (Edinburgh: Edinburgh University Press, 1976), 52; Mark E. Amsler, "The Quest for the Present Tense: The Poet and the Dreamer in Douglas' *The Palice of Honour*," *Studies in Scottish Literature* 17, no. 1 (1982): 186–208, here 186–7.

4. See esp. Robert Belknap, "The Literary List: A Survey of Its Uses and Deployments," *Literary Imagination* 2, no. 1 (2000): 35–54; Eva von Contzen, "The Limits of Narration: Lists and Literary History," *Style* 50, no. 3 (2016): 241–60.

5. Stephen A. Barney, "Chaucer's Lists," in *The Wisdom of Poetry: Essays in Early English Literature in Honour of Morton W. Bloomfield*, ed. Larry D. Benson and Siegfried Wenzel (Kalamazoo: Western Michigan University Press, 1982), 189–223, here 194.

6. Chaucer's works are cited from *The Riverside Chaucer*, 3rd ed., gen. ed. Larry D. Benson (Boston: Houghton Mifflin, 1987).

spaces, through houses, temples, and gardens, for example. The latter are frequently representations of the protagonist's (and the poet's) mind. More specifically, as Kathryn Lynch notes, these spaces stand in for the cells of imagination, logic, and memory.[7] The theory of the three ventricles was the most widely accepted and disseminated model of cognition in the Middle Ages. According to this model, the brain was subdivided into three discrete ventricles, associated with different cognitive abilities.[8] In his popular encyclopedia *De proprietatibus rerum*, Bartholomaeus Anglicus (here in John Trevisa's fourteenth-century translation) writes that the inner wit is divided into three "regiouns of þe brayn" in which one finds three cells. First, the ventricle of imagination, which receives, in an unordered manner, sense impressions from the "vttir witte." The second "chambre" is called "*logica*," in which "þe vertu estimatiue is maister." Third, there is the cell of memory, "þe vertu of mynde. Þat vertu holdiþ and kepiþ in þe tresour of mynde þingis þat beþ apprehendid and iknowe bi þe ymaginatif and *racio*."[9] Medieval dream poems stage journeys through these ventricles. At the outset of their journeys, dreamers tend to be confused or to suffer mental imbalances that are eventually resolved, as the charted journey culminates in the reestablishment of order, in spiritual enlightenment, in a reharmonized household of the soul.[10] That Chaucer's dream poetry depicts journeys through the three ventricles and is heavily invested in epistemological questions has been repeatedly observed.[11] Notably, Chaucer's (and subsequent Middle English) dream poems depict the ventricles in terms of the management of (courtly) households. That is, foregrounded in the representation of the ventricles are the processes by means of which these mental households are managed.

Lists in Chaucer's poetry are frequently means to organize, to order knowledge, and thus gesture towards processes of *oikonomia*. The lists in Chaucer's

---

7. For high medieval dream visions and faculty psychology, see esp. Kathryn L. Lynch, *The High Medieval Dream Vision: Poetry, Philosophy, and Literary Form* (Stanford: Stanford University Press, 1988), esp. 21–45.

8. See, e.g., Murray W. Bundy, *The Theory of Imagination in Classical and Medieval Thought* (Urbana: University of Illinois Press, 1927); E. Ruth Harvey, *The Inward Wits: Psychological Theory in the Middle Ages and the Renaissance* (London: Warburg Institute, 1975).

9. John Trevisa, trans., *On the Properties of Things: John Trevisa's Translation of Bartholomaeus Anglicus "De proprietatibus rerum,"* ed. M. C. Seymour, 2 vols. (Oxford: Clarendon Press, 1975), 2:98.

10. Lynch, *Dream*, esp. 42–5. See further Aristotle, *Politics* 1254b.

11. Kathryn L. Lynch, *Chaucer's Philosophical Visions* (Cambridge: Brewer, 2000), 61–82; Robert R. Edwards, *The Dream of Chaucer: Representation and Reflection in the Early Narratives* (Durham: Duke University Press, 1989); Frank G. Hoffman, "The Dream and the Book: Chaucer's Dream-Poetry, Faculty Psychology, and the Poetics of Recombination" (Ph.D. diss., University of Pennsylvania, 2004).

Fame (and in other dream poems) are especially relevant epistemologically, insofar as they ideally order and organize the disparate images received by the senses, provided that the ventricles of logic and memory are managed by the precepts of traditional household management, by *oikonomia*: the appropriate allocation of value (proper placement); proportional modes of exchange (reciprocity); and moderate gain. All of these processes of allocation are also characteristic of allegory, the chosen representational mode for most medieval dream poetry.[12] Moreover, the many lists in (Chaucerian) dream poetry become metapoetically relevant insofar as they list materials available for poetic composition. In Chaucer's *Fame*, however, nothing ever appears to be in the right place in the dreamer's mental household. In fact, the main modes of economic operation rather appear to be misevaluation and excess, operations well familiar to a late fourteenth-century audience from the world of commerce.

In the Middle Ages, the household was the central economic category. The management of a household, especially a courtly household, entailed appropriate allocation, proportional reciprocity, and moderate gain, that is, *oikonomia*. This form of household management, though, increasingly came under pressure in the later Middle Ages on account of increasing commercialization and monetization.[13] Trade was expanding and monetary values and evaluations penetrated all areas of life, leading to an increasing awareness of the arbitrariness of monetary valuations, not least the fluctuating value of money itself. Money became the (problematic) measure of all things.[14] On the one hand, money was seen as a practical instrument that facilitated economic transactions; on the other hand, money was considered to generate chaos and pervert order. Increasingly, it became more difficult for royal households to put a price on money, to regulate commerce, to keep gain to what appeared as acceptable in terms of a 'natural' amount. Continued revaluations of the value of money were one of the results across Europe, making everyone aware of the lack of stable allocations of value.[15] Nothing was wrong with the accumulation of things necessary for maintaining the household, which was seen as natural. The surplus generated by a commercial world, artificial wealth gener-

---

12. For faculty households, see further Verena O. Lobsien, *Shakespeares Exzess: Sympathie und Ökonomie* (Berlin: Berlin University Press, 2015), 149–56.

13. See Richard H. Britnell, *The Commercialisation of English Society, 1000–1500*, 2nd ed. (Cambridge: Cambridge University Press, 1996); Diana Wood, *Medieval Economic Thought* (Cambridge: Cambridge University Press, 2002).

14. Joel Kaye, *Economy and Nature in the Fourteenth Century: Money, Market Exchange, and the Emergence of Scientific Thought* (Cambridge: Cambridge University Press, 1998), 17; 47–50; Wood, *Medieval Economic Thought*, 69.

15. Kaye, *Economy*, 18; 23–35.

ated by greed was, however, seen as inherently problematic. These different forms of economic experience were conceptualized by way of the Aristotelian distinction between *oikonomia* and *chrematistike* (chrematistics).[16] In Thomas Aquinas's words, "The appetite for natural wealth is not unlimited, for a fixed measure is enough for nature. The appetite for artificial wealth, however, may know no bounds, but panders to an unregulated concupiscence which, as Aristotle brings out, is without measure."[17] The latter corresponds with medieval theories of usury, money that unnaturally generates more money out of itself.[18] Despite an actual economic condition in which chrematistic practices abounded, *oikonomia* was still cherished, specifically in courtly contexts. Especially problematic in Chaucer's London, but also in Douglas's Edinburgh, was the imbalance between the household of the Crown and the lifestyles of the rich merchants. Chaucer would have been keenly aware thereof, given his job at the Customs House (1374–86), which marked an important intersection between the worlds of the court and the merchants:[19] as controller of the wool tax, Chaucer would have been familiar with the differences between *oikonomia* and *chrematistike*, and with many merchants' amassing of material wealth that articulated itself, among other things, in account books, in lists.[20] Chaucer, moreover, would have known that the Crown increasingly borrowed money from the merchants, while trying to limit their political influence.[21] These lending practices notwithstanding, the aristocracy clung to the ideals of *oikonomia*, (the illusion of) natural gain and proportional reciprocity.[22] The tensions between *oikonomia* and *chrematistike* persisted well into the early modern period, and were thrown sharply into relief on account of the scar-

---

16. Aristotle, *Politics* 1256b; 1257–8a.

17. Thomas Aquinas, *Summa Theologiæ*, vol. 16, ed. and trans. Thomas Gilby (London: Eyre and Spottiswoode, 1969), Ia2æ, 2.1.3. See further João César Das Neves, "Aquinas and Aristotle's Distinction on Wealth," *History of Political Economy* 32 (2000): 649–57; S. Todd Lowry, *The Archaeology of Economic Ideas: The Classical Greek Tradition* (Durham: Duke University Press, 1987), 230–2.

18. See, e.g., Jacques Le Goff, *Your Money or Your Life: Economy and Religion in the Middle Ages*, trans. Patricia Ranum (New York: Zone Books, 1998).

19. David R. Carlson, *Chaucer's Jobs* (New York: Palgrave Macmillan, 2004), 1–31.

20. David Matthews, "Enlisting the Poet: The List and the Late Medieval Dream Vision," *Style* 50, no. 3 (2016): 280–95, here 284–5; Anke Bernau, "Enlisting Truth," *Style* 50, no. 3 (2016): 261–79, here 261–2.

21. David Wallace, *Chaucerian Polity: Absolutist Lineages and Associational Forms in England and Italy* (Stanford: Stanford University Press, 1997), 188–99.

22. See Felicity Heal, "Reciprocity and Exchange in the Late Medieval Household," in *Bodies and Disciplines: Intersections of History and Literature in Fifteenth-Century England*, ed. Barbara A. Hanawalt and David Wallace (Minneapolis: University of Minnesota Press, 1996), 179–98; Elliot Kendall, *Lordship and Literature: John Gower and the Politics of the Great Household* (Oxford: Oxford University Press, 2008), 1–27.

city of silver and the rampant conspicuous consumption of the wealthy. While Douglas's world was naturally different from Chaucer's, economic conditions in late medieval Scotland were dramatically affected by the shortage of silver as well as by several (unsuccessful) attempts of the court to impose order on commercial chaos. The increasing loss of the value of money, for instance, led to the traumatic introduction of the "black penny" in 1480.[23] Scottish writers of the day, moreover, frequently touched upon the tensions between *oikonomia* and *chrematistike*.[24] It is a tension that is palpably present in the representation of mental households, both in Chaucer's *Fame* and in Douglas's *Palice*.

CHAOTIC HOUSEHOLD MANAGEMENT IN CHAUCER'S *HOUSE OF FAME*

The excessive lists in Chaucer's *Fame* are part and parcel of a poetic program driven by the commercialization of (mental) households, that is, the poet's brain at work.[25] The problem which Chaucer's dreamer Geffrey has to grapple with at the outset of *Fame* consists of contradictory images impressing on his faculty of imagination.[26] It is the inability of higher-order cognitive processes to regulate and order the proliferation of contradictory images—by means of moderation, appropriate evaluation, and proper allocation—that ultimately generates the poem itself. The mental inability to order things is anticipated at the outset, first, when the dreamer muses on the uncertain epistemological status of dreams and, second, when Geffrey finds himself in a temple of Venus where brass tablets seem to represent Virgil's *Aeneid*; the dreamer here articulates, in a humble authorial gesture, his inability to verbalize what he sees: "I wol now synge, yif I kan, / The armes and also the man" (142–3). Verbs relating to sense perception, especially visual perception, are used almost excessively at this point; the dreamer has entered his/the ventricle of imagination, Venus being traditionally associated with the world of the senses. Sud-

---

23. Jenny Wormald, *Court, Kirk, and Community: Scotland 1470–1625* (Edinburgh: Edinburgh University Press, 1981, repr. 2005), 41–55.

24. See esp. Louise Olga Fradenburg, *City, Marriage, Tournament: Arts of Rule in Late Medieval Scotland* (Madison: University of Wisconsin Press, 1991), 19.

25. For a more comprehensive account of Chaucer's commercialized poetics, see Wolfram R. Keller, "Re-Novating Troy: Chrematistics, Imagination, and Hybrid Temporalities in Chaucer's Troy Stories," *Working Papers der FOR 2305 "Diskursivierungen von Neuem"* 7 (2018), DOI:10.17169/ FUDOCS_document_000000028572.

26. For an instructive account of the different ways in which imagination was conceptualized in medieval culture, see Michelle Karnes, *Imagination, Meditation, and Cognition in the Middle Ages* (Chicago: University of Chicago Press, 2011), esp. 1–110.

denly, the summary of what Geffrey sees (the *Aeneid*) is interrupted by what he hears, namely, Dido's different, negative assessment of Aeneas, recalling Ovid's *Heroides*.[27] While Geffrey is eventually able to complete the summary of the *Aeneid*—with the appropriate inclusion of Aeneas's loss of his helmsman—the strange new hybrid Virgilian-Ovidian narrative ("Non other auctour alegge I" [314]) confuses him; he, too, is without a "stiryng man" (478). In the remainder of the poem, this confusion is not resolved but compounded, as Geffrey moves to the ventricles of logic and memory, a movement indicated by the proem to Book Two, when Geffrey asks for the assistance of the muses to properly retrieve the dream from memory: "O Thought, that wrote al that I mette, / And in the tresory hyt shette / Of my brayn" (523–5).[28] Now, it is time to see if his dream can be retrieved correctly: "Now kythe thyn engyn and myght!" (528).

As Geffrey is picked up and transported in the claws of an Eagle to visit the realm of Fama, where he is supposed to witness the processing of tidings, spiritual enlightenment seems close at hand, which is underlined by frequent allusions to Boethian philosophy (762; 765–8, etc.). First, though, the Eagle literally evaluates Geffrey's poetry, criticizing the latter for lacking lived experience. With a nod to Chaucer's job at the Customs House, the Eagle complains that Geffrey, when he returns home from his "rekenynges" (653), immediately buries his head in another book. Nonetheless, the journey to Fama is meant as a reward for Geffrey's continued, albeit flawed service. It is a reward that is ambiguously contextualized concerning different modes of household management: the journey is meant for Geffrey's "lore and for thy prow" (579), *prow* meaning both "reward" (reciprocity) and "monetary gain."[29] And while the reward is later couched more explicitly in terms of proportional reciprocity—"In som recompensacion / Of labour and devocion / That thou hast had, loo causeles, / To Cupido the rechcheles" (665–67)—Geffrey appears to be overly compensated. For instead of spiritual enlightenment and harmony, Geffrey's senses are drowned in the cacophonous symphony of incongruous tidings. Fama's realm is characterized mainly by the incessant increase of tidings—"multiplicacioun," "multiplying," "multiplicacioun" (784; 801; 820)—and the problematic commingling of "fals and soth" (1029). Approaching Fama's palace, Geffrey notices in the pinnacles "sondry habitacles, / In which stonden, al without / . . . / Of alle maner of mynstralles" (1194–7), all longing for fame. A list of no fewer than eighty lines follows, beginning

---

27. John Fyler, *Chaucer and Ovid* (New Haven: Yale University Press, 1979), 37–9.

28. See further Barney, "Chaucer's Lists," 200; Rebecca Davis, "Fugitive Poetics in Chaucer's *House of Fame*," *Studies in the Age of Chaucer* 37 (2015): 101–32, here 120–1.

29. *MED*, entry "prōu n. 1 and 2."

with Orpheus and other musicians whom the dreamer can identify followed by groups of unnamed musicians (1201–81). Their plenitude manifests in a cacophonous soundscape, since all of them use their instruments at the same time: "Many thousand tymes twelve, / That maden lowde mynstralcies / In cornemuse and al shalemyes / And many other maner pipe" (1216–19). Chaos and dissonance continue as Geffrey steps into the palace of Fama and, later, the wicker house of Rumor, the former representing the process of memorial allocation, the latter the retrieval of tidings for the purposes of poetic composition. Clearly, neither household is governed by the precepts of *oikonomia*, even though the palace of Fama has the appearance of a traditional treasury of memory.

In classical antiquity and the Middle Ages, architectural spaces are frequently used as grids to systematically memorize things, to organize knowledge. Underlining the (ethical) importance of memory, such mnemonic spaces were frequently conceptualized as treasuries or purses with subdivisions to group things according to their value.[30] Fama's palace, however, is a disordered treasury at best. For all its seemingly traditional conceptualization of memory as a treasury, commerce and chrematistics are tangible everywhere. Every wall, roof, and floor of the edifice "Was plated half a foote thikke / Of gold, and that nas nothyng wikke," with gold "As fyn as ducat in Venyse, / Of which to lite al in my pouche is" (1345–9). The comparison of the gold to Venetian ducats clearly alludes to the world of commerce: ducats were a much-coveted commercial currency, too little of which can be found in Chaucer's *pouche,* a subdivided bag or purse for carrying money. A further indication of the instability of values in the palace is the goddess herself: her size keeps fluctuating (3.1368–76; see *Aen.* 4.249–52). For the time being, though, illusions of "memorial *oikonomia*" are maintained when Geffrey sees and lists several pillared authorities of biblical, Jewish, and Trojan history, the latter including Homer, Dares, Dictys, Lollius, Guido delle Colonne, and an "Englyssh Gaufride" (1466–70).[31] While the chronology is somewhat shaky, Geffrey also notices that there is disagreement among the authorities: "Betwex hem was a litil envye. / Oon seyde that Omer made lyes, / Feynynge in his poetries, / And was to Grekes favorable" (1476–9). What at first seems to be a well-ordered list emerges to be the articulation of an historiographical relativism clearing space for authors to create new poetry, notably along the lines of

---

30. See Edwards, *Dream,* 114; Mary Carruthers, *The Book of Memory: A Study of Memory in Medieval Culture,* 2nd ed. (Cambridge: Cambridge University Press, 2008), 45–6; 89–98; Frances A. Yates, *The Art of Memory* (London: Routledge and Kegan Paul, 1966), 63–113.

31. For Chaucer's list of the authorities of Trojan historiography as an epic catalogue, see also Eva von Contzen's contribution to this volume.

the excess tangible everywhere in the poem. The list of the Trojan authorities culminates with Virgil and Ovid, the former on a pillar of "tynned yren cler" and bearing the fame of "Pius Eneas" (1481–5), the latter, as "Venus's clerk" (1487), on a pillar of copper, representing changeability, thereby replicating in the realm of memory the antagonism between Virgil and Ovid in the Temple of Venus, the cell of imagination. Thus, imaginational dissonance is not resolved, but rather amplified.

Excess and arbitrary evaluations also affect the collaboration of logic and memory, that is, of Fama's allocation of reputation. Flocking to Fama from all corners of the earth ("Auffrike, Europe, and Asye," 1339), the assembled tidings render Fama's court an international marketplace. The tidings request proportional reciprocity, as is to be expected in courtly worlds: "In ful recompensacioun / Of good werkes, yive us good renoun" (1557–8). (In)famously, though, Fama is unperturbed by the actual worth of the petitioners, dealing out reputations on the basis of arbitrary principles (1532–867) in what amounts to a noisy parody of cosmic harmony.[32] The result of the excessive multiplication and increase of tidings as well as their arbitrary evaluations and spatial misallocations in the realm of memory is a poetry that is best represented by *Fame* itself; the poem is the product of the chrematistic epistemological and metapoetic processes it describes.

The poem's chrematistic poetics is represented in abstracted form in the wicker house of Rumor, which depicts tidings as they try to force their way back into the world. Given the wicker dwelling's source—Orosius's labyrinth of historiography[33]—the processes described delineate the poem's poetics in a nutshell. The wicker dwelling is overcrowded with tidings; it is a repository of all known narratives, listed in fifteen anaphoric lines all beginning with "Of" (1961–76).[34] The tidings multiply incessantly: "more encres," "enresing ever moo" (2074; 2077). As two tidings that are structurally opposed to each other—recalling the opposition between Ovid and Virgil, that is, one is true, one is false—simultaneously reach an opening through which they want to escape into the world, they combine themselves into one tiding, since they would not fit through the opening side-by-side: "We wil medle us ech with other / That no man, be they never so wrothe, / Shal han on [of us] two, but

---

32. For Chaucer's parody of *musica mundana*, see Wolfram Keller, "'Therout com so gret a noyse': The Harmony of the Spheres and Chaucerian Poetics," in *Sing Aloud Harmonious Spheres: Renaissance Conceptions of the Pythagorean Doctrine of Cosmic Harmony*, ed. Jacomien Prins and Maude Vanhaelen (London: Routledge, 2018), 80–98, here 89–91.

33. Lee Patterson, *Chaucer and the Subject of History* (Madison: University of Wisconsin Press, 1991), 99–104.

34. For the lists in the wicker house of Rumor, see James Simpson's contribution to this volume.

bothe / At ones" (2102–5). Welded into one, as if they were different metals or coins, "fals and soth compouned / Togeder fle for oo tydynge" (2108). At the end of *Fame*, then, the poem represents its own poetics, which is driven by excess and arbitrariness, processes that become tangible in the poem's many lists. It is a poetics driven by the processes it describes, processes familiar from the world of commerce. And it is a poetics advanced in an allegorical dream poem that literally recalibrates the poet's brain, insofar as the orderly world of *oikonomia* reveals itself to be infiltrated by chrematistics. And lastly, it is a poetics that apparently attracted many post-Chaucerian poets, all of whom at least *seem* to have been troubled by its excessiveness.

EXCESSIVE MIRRORING IN DOUGLAS'S *PALICE OF HONOUR*

Douglas's *Palice*, too, stages a poet's journey through the ventricles of his brain. In contrast to Chaucer's *Fame*, however, the prevailing attitude in the Middle Scots poem—a disorienting look in Venus's mirror notwithstanding—is harmony, which is *inter alia* tangible in the poem's frequent allusions to musical harmony.[35] Most importantly, perhaps, and also unlike *Fame*, the *Palice* is a dream journey at the end of which the poet's confusion seems to be remedied: "The poem defines the development of the narrator as a man and poet from a state of conflict, despair, and poetic dryness to inner harmony, a devotion to honor, and restored poetic power."[36] Following the Prologue, the focus of the dreamer's journey in Part One is on what he observes, beginning with an invocation of the cognitive apparatus: "Thow barrant wyt ouerset with fantasyis, / Schaw now the craft that in thy memor lyis" (127–8).[37] As he tries to find his bearings, the dreamer hears something, alerting him to an approaching company. He hides in a tree stump, from which he watches the peripatetic court of the Queen of Sapience, of Minerva, the nature and members of which are explained to him by the traitors Ahithophel and Sinon (who

---

35. For the *Palice*'s emphasis on harmony generally, see Kratzmann, *Anglo-Scottish*, 128; for musical harmony, see esp. Alice Miskimin, "The Design of Douglas's *Palice of Honour*," in *Actes du 2e Colloque de Langue et de Littérature Écossaises (Moyen Age et Renaissance)*, ed. Claude Graf and Jean Jacques Blanchot (Strasbourg: Université de Strasbourg, 1978), 396–421.

36. Lois Ebin, *Illuminator, Makar, Vates: Visions of Poetry in the Fifteenth Century* (Lincoln: University of Nebraska Press, 1988), 92. See further Amsler, "Quest," 187; Honeyman, "*Palice*," 72.

37. This and all following quotations from and references to Douglas's *Palice* are to the London edition in Priscilla Bawcutt, ed. and introd., *The Shorter Poems of Gavin Douglas*, 2nd ed. (Edinburgh: Scottish Text Society, 2003).

obviously do not belong in this ordered court): everyone rides "In stedfast ordour" (209); members are grouped by rank (221). Next, Actaeon passes by as a transformed hart, indicating the arrival of the court of Diana, the latter identified as rendering women's hearts "stabil and na way inconstant" (333). Lastly, his "fantasy" (358) perceives a bright light and a wonderful sound, prompting a short lecture on musical harmony (360–81) and a description of the angelic music he experiences: "of angellys," "armony fordynnand all the skyis," "So dulce, so swete, and so melodious," et cetera (389; 390; 391, etc.). These sense impressions dull the higher-order faculties: "The heuinly soundis of their armony / Has dymmyt so my drery fantasy / Baith wit and reason, half is lost of all" (412–14). Further descriptions of harmony follow: as bells remind him of the hierarchies of the nine orders of the angels (444); as the numerical proportions of music are explicated; as the lack of dissonance is emphasized (490–534). And while the court includes all manner of folk, it is unanimous in the judgment of the dreamer for his performance of a blasphemous song (646–53). Part One closes with the dreamer's worries about Venus's potential punishments floating in his imagination: "And rolland thus in diuers fantasyis, / Terribil thochtis oft my hert did gryis / For all remeid was alterit in dispare" (763–5). Appropriate to the cell of imagination (and for this stage of the dream journey), the predicament to be resolved by the higher-order faculties is also articulated as follows: "My febyll mynd seand this gret suppris / Wes than of wit and euery blys full bare" (770–1).

At the outset of Part Two, the dreamer recognizes that God has provided for him, so that now he "foryet[s] all Imagination" (780). The dreamer progresses from the realm of imagination to the cell of evaluation and logic, literally in terms of Venus's judgment (she wants the dreamer to die), metaphorically by way of the poetic assignment the latter entails. While in Part One, the dreamer mainly perceives harmony, he is now included in the well-ordered court of Rhetoric—"Of a fassoun and all of stedfast hew, / Arrayit weil" (791–2)—which is immediately also described in terms of (musical) harmony (795–807). Members of Venus's court are reported to emphasize Rhetoric's orderly household: the Nine Muses (and their association with celestial harmony) are observed (835–85);[38] a list of the preeminence of the poet-members is furnished (895–924). Seemingly along the lines of proportional reciprocity, Venus is willing to let the dreamer live, provided he compose a ballad in her praise and fulfill her "nixt resonabil command" (997). After performing two (rather clumsy) songs in gratitude, the dreamer joins the Muses on their aerial journey: knowledge of the world is retrieved by means of logic.

---

38. See also Ebin, *Illuminator,* 93.

Toward the end of Part Two, while the court rests at Hippocrene's fountain, (musical) harmony is stressed yet again (1153–66; 1234–6; 1251–69).

Part Three opens with an invocation of the Nine Muses, who help him refresh his memory, the latter epitomized by Honor's highly organized household: "Len me a recent scharp fresch memory / And caus me dewly til indyt þis story" (1291–2). While the ascent to the palace of Honor includes some terrifying images, those are now allegorically explained by the dreamer's guide, the Nymph. That is, the images are correctly allocated and consequently less alarming (1380–404; 1760–4). Correct allocation is also characteristic of the palace of Honor, where everything finds its right place, including the traitors Ahithophel and Sinon, whom the dreamer sees again as they fail to access Honor's realm. The Nymph's explanation of how Honor's household works— Loyalty as the Keeper, Patience as Doorkeeper, Liberality as the Treasurer, Discretion as Comptroller, et cetera (1789–827)—further generates an atmosphere of harmony. It is a "short allegorical passage based on the hierarchies of a royal household,"[39] describing a strictly managed court: "And schortly euery vertew and plesance / Is subiect to 3one kyngis obbeysance" (1826–7). By means of the Nymph's allegorical explications, the conceptual overlap between *oikonomia* and allegory comes into view: both are self-sustaining systems of reciprocal exchange and the clear allocation and valuation of meaning. Through a peephole the dreamer then marvels at the lavishly decorated hall of Honor, but is unable to look at the householder himself, the "god armypotent" (1921). Lastly, the dreamer witnesses the household of the Muses, the garden of Rhetoric: "My lydyis court in thair gudly array. / For till behald thair myrth cum on thy way" (1957–8). The "ladies" are busy gathering "The swete florist colouris of rethoreis" (2066) in a garden that renders bland and uninspiring the luxurious garden which the dreamer fell asleep in at the beginning of the poem.

Sitting somewhat oddly with the poem's frequent protestations of harmony and its (re)constitution of what seems to be a harmonious ventricular household are some of the poem's (longer) lists and catalogues, including lists of philosophers (250–62), instruments (501–5), clothing (537–43), lovers (562–89), places (1086–133), poets (896–924), and heroes (1194–215). The overabundance of lists has been frequently seen as an aesthetic blemish.[40] Recently, David Parkinson has emphasized the lists' coordination of classical and Chris-

---

39. Joanna Martin, *Kingship and Love in Scottish Poetry, 1424–1540* (Aldershot: Ashgate, 2008), 132. See further Honeyman, "Palice," 77; Kratzmann, *Anglo-Scottish*, 117.

40. For the lists in general, see Fox, "Scottish Chaucerians." For the (lack of) aesthetic quality, see J. Norton-Smith, "Ekphrasis as a Stylistic Element in Douglas's *Palis of Honoure*," *Medium Ævum* 48 (1979): 240–53, here 240–1; Kratzmann, *Anglo-Scottish*, 114; Anthony J.

tian figures as well as the inclusion of problematic individuals, arguing that "the way inconsistency acts throughout the poem as a stimulus to the reader to seek additional levels of signification" makes "such moments of dissonance seem entirely fitting."[41] The most striking list within the poem is undoubtedly the list of what the dreamer beholds in Venus's mirror. Totaling 236 lines, it is the longest, the most excessive list in the *Palice*. A "dementedly compendious account of all styles, genres and 'materes' known to medieval literary production, secular and sacred," the list can be quickly summarized as "a compilation that catches up an entire medieval library within the loose and permeable bounds of universal history,... which is then named, retroactively, as the face of the beloved" by the Nymph.[42] With a view to the latter, Priscilla Bawcutt opines that "the Nymph's explanation of the Mirror's significance ... is lame and unconvincing. It seems to serve chiefly as a decorative digression."[43] In my opinion, the mirror episode actually contains Douglas's poetic program *in nuce*: Douglas employs the form of the list in order to strategically recuperate Chaucerian imaginational chrematistics, thereby destabilizing from within the genre of faculty allegory itself.

The dreamer encounters Venus's mirror in Part Three, as he is traveling with the Nymph toward the palace of Honor.[44] As the dreamer admires the palace from afar, the Nymph pushes him onward, reminding him that there is much more to see, to which he should pay close attention. Moreover, she commands, "Quhat thow seyst, luke eftirwartis thow write" (1464), which highlights the metapoetic relevance of the subsequent mirror scene. The mirror is set before Venus on a slightly raised area, "Quhare on thare grew, thre curius goldyn treis. / Sustenttand weil the goddis face aforne. / A fair myrrour be thaym quently vpborn" (1474–6). After describing the material appearance of this "riall rillik," the dreamer begins to list at length what he sees reflected within the mirror. As he turns away from the mirror, Venus asks him how he liked his journey and its entertainments, before reminding him of her second task for him. She hands him a book that he has to "put in ryme" (1752). Whether, as Johnston and Rouse surmise, the book in question is the *Palice* itself,[45] the reference to writing tasks again spotlights the metapoetic relevance

---

Hasler, *Court Poetry in Late Medieval England and Scotland: Allegories of Authority* (Cambridge: Cambridge University Press, 2011), 100.

41. Parkinson, introduction, 46.

42. Hasler, *Court Poetry*, 105.

43. Priscilla Bawcutt, introduction to *Shorter Poems of Gavin Douglas*, 2nd ed. (Edinburgh: Scottish Text Society, 2003), xlv.

44. For the centrality of Venus in all three parts of the *Palice*, see Miskimin, "Design," 400.

45. Andrew James Johnston and Margitta Rouse, "Facing the Mirror: Ekphrasis, Vision, and Knowledge in Gavin Douglas's *Palice of Honour*," in *The Art of Vision: Ekphrasis in Medi-*

of the mirror scene. Eventually, the Nymph offers the mentioned "allegorical" interpretation of the mirror:

> ȝone myrrour clere,
> The quhilk thow saw afore dame Venus stand
> Signifyes nothyng ellis till vnderstand
> Bot the gret bewty of thir ladyis facis
> Quhairin louers thinkis thay behald all gracis.
> (1760–4)

Compared to her other allegorizations, this one is curiously brief and remarkably unhelpful. At the very moment when the poem reaches the climax of its poetic self-reflexivity, hermeneutic certainties are withheld.

The mirror's metapoetic relevance has already been stressed by Johnston and Rouse. With a view to the poem's conceptualization of ekphrasis, they discuss the interplay between the mirror and its frame as "one costly mirror [being] reflected within another in the style of... Chinese boxes." Moreover, the three trees holding the mirror, they argue, "mirror... the three-part structure of the narrative."[46] What precisely, though, is the relationship between mirror and poem? The fact that it is the metapoetic mirror episode that fails to elicit a clear-cut interpretation locates the list outside of the realm of the secure allegorical explanations otherwise offered by the Nymph. This finds an analogue on the plot level, given that the poet is and *is not* part of the household of Rhetoric. He travels with the Muses, but he does not drink from their fountain, he cannot experience fully Honor's household, and he cannot cross the bridge into the garden of Rhetoric.[47] The dreamer's relationship with Venus comes closest to patronage. However, the dreamer does not enter Venus's court through service. Furthermore, a comparison with the judgment scene in Chaucer's Prologue to the *Legend of Good Women* (henceforth *LGW*), on which the scene in the *Palice* is modeled, quickly shows Venus to be much more "exacting," requesting two writing tasks instead of merely one.[48] More importantly, in the *Palice* no future relationship of reciprocity is envisaged; unlike Alcestis and the God of Love in Chaucer's poem, Venus does

---

eval *Literature and Culture,* ed. Andrew James Johnston, Ethan Knapp, and Margitta Rouse (Columbus: The Ohio State University Press, 2015), 166–83, here 180–1.

46. Johnston and Rouse, "Ekphrasis," 169.

47. For the dreamer's exclusion, see David Parkinson, "The Farce of Modesty in Gavin Douglas's *The Palis of Honoure,*" *Philological Quarterly* 70, no. 1 (1991): 13–25, here 22; but cf. Amsler, "Quest," 196.

48. For *LGW* as source, see esp. Bawcutt, *Douglas,* 55; for the more exacting Venus in the *Palice,* see Kratzmann, *Anglo-Scottish,* 115.

not promise to further the poet's reputation as compensation for his (future) labor (*LGW,* G 491–3). The poetry that is the *Palice* is thus different from the allegorical poetry that enables access to courts and to courtly patronage. The underlying poetic program of the *Palice* comes into view more clearly when one follows up on the mirror scene's intratextual referencing, which brings into play two related aspects: increase and the replication of tripartite structures.

Apart from Venus's mirror, the *Palice* includes only one other reference to a mirror. In the Prologue, the dreamer admires a wondrous garden when he suddenly hears a hymn to May praised as the "myrrour of soles" (64), at once drawing attention to the soul and to matters of "encres" (68) with which May is associated. Such increase can be seen in the (in all senses) increasingly harmonious journey of the dreamer toward the perfection of Honor's household, but also in the plethora of lists. One of the many lists recalled especially by Venus's mirror is the list of places traveled at the end of Part Two, the second longest list in the poem. In both cases, the dreamer beholds everything at once, in an instantaneousness that dissolves geographical and temporal boundaries. In the mirror, the dreamer sees everything—past, present, and future[49]—"at a sycht" (1495); the journey with the court of Rhetoric ensues "Als swyft as thocht" and "in twynkling of ane E" (1077; 1084), taking the dreamer "out of linear time."[50] Moreover, the journey's itinerary in no way corresponds to any real-world geography.[51] The sudden, excessive increase of images in the form of lists is indeed a characteristic of *Palice,* which is underlined by the three trees framing the mirror, which bring into focus the poem's excessive replication of threes. Given the mapping of the respective ventricular processes within the three parts of the poem, in turn, the poem's genre is spotlighted: faculty allegory. While the three-part frame of Venus's mirror may seem to contain the excessiveness therein, a closer look at the three parts of the poem and their representation of the ventricles challenges from within what initially seems like an orderly ventricular *oikonomia*.

What comes into view by way of the tripartite structure of Venus's excessive mirror and its relation to the tripartite structure of the poem is a different kind of listing, insofar as the ventricular structure actually is mirrored *en min-*

---

49. See Parkinson, *Palyce,* 149–50n.

50. Amsler, "Quest," 197. For the capacity of lists to open up atemporal, spatial dimensions, see Eva von Contzen, "Theorising Lists in Literature: Towards a Listology," in *Lists and Catalogues in Ancient Literature and Beyond: Towards a Poetics of Enumeration,* ed. Rebecca Lämmle, Cédric Scheidegger Lämmle, and Katharina Wesselmann (Berlin: de Gruyter, 2021), 35–54.

51. Hasler, *Court Poetry,* 104.

iature in each part of the poem, like the Chinese boxes mentioned by Johnston and Rouse. Space limitations prohibit a full account of the intricacies of this second-order ventricular representation, which can only be indicated here by way of a few examples.

In Part One, which is characterized by a focus on imagination, the dreamer witnesses three courts, each of which alludes to different cognitive processes.[52] Minerva is traditionally associated with Reason and represents processes of evaluation insofar as this passage is dominated by the (exclusion of) the traitors. The arrival of the court of Diana is announced by the transformed Actaeon, by means of which the dreamer recollects his Ovid; the hart is a memory *topos*. In passing, it should be mentioned that this scene is one of many other mirrorings within the *Palice,* since the dreamer's spying on Diana replicates Actaeon's spying on Diana (319–27; *Met.* 3.131–257). Finally, and appropriately, the extensive description of the court of Venus spotlights the faculty of imagination, and it does so also on account of Venus's connection with uncurbed and infinite increase, of images, of desire.[53]

Part Two opens with various kinds of abstractions, allocations, and evaluations, befitting the ventricle of logic, including Venus's and Calliope's evaluations of the dreamer and the way in which members of Venus's court identify individuals within the court of Rhetoric. Thus framed, Part Two continues with the dreamer's already discussed journey in the company of the court of Rhetoric, which has been suitably described as a journey of the imagination.[54] The journey ends with a pastoral scene with all manner of plants and humming bees—that is, typical memory *topoi* (1135–52)[55]—as well as with the assembled court wondering which individuals were the greatest in their respective times. This question prompts the interplay of memory and logic in the evaluation of several individuals' deeds.

Part Three then opens with the appeal to the dreamer's memory. Before the dreamer beholds the mental *oikonomia* of the palace of Honor, however, the focus first falls on sense perception with a Scipionian view of a little earth (1344; 1348–50) and on Venus's mirror. Interspersed with references to the palace's preservation of the past, the dreamer also focuses on Honor's mechanisms of exclusion (logic), not only in terms of the negative assessment of oth-

---

52. For ventricular courts, see esp. Elizabeth Elliott, "'This is myn awin ymaginacioun': The Judgment of Paris and the Influence of Medieval Faculty Psychology on *The Kingis Quair*," in *Fresche Fontanis: Studies in the Culture of Medieval and Early Modern Scotland,* ed. Janet Hadley Williams and J. Derrick McClure (Newcastle upon Tyne: Cambridge Scholars Press, 2013), 3–15.

53. For the Scottish context, see esp. Elliott, "'This is myna win ymaginacioun," 11–12.

54. See A. C. Spearing, *Medieval Dream-Poetry* (Cambridge: Cambridge University Press, 1976), 223.

55. Carruthers, *Memory,* 41–5.

ers, but also of his own inability to enter Honor's hall. The dreamer voices his regret at this point, because he would have loved to see the torment of those impairing Honor (2058–9; 2109–10). The *Palice* ends with the Nymph's list of those who have been received in the hall of Honor and the description of the garden of Rhetoric. Again, one encounters the memory *topoi* already familiar not only from the pastoral scene at the end of Part Two, but also from the Prologue's garden scene. In fact, the opening garden scene with its reference to the "mirror of souls" constitutes the first in the poem's long sequence of various representations of increase.

The self-replication of the three ventricles is, in a way, anticipated in the Prologue, which is also divided into three distinct parts, each alluding to a different faculty. The dreamer first recollects his Ovid (*Met.* 13.621–2) and "roams" among the bejeweled plants of the garden, bees collecting material (memory). He then becomes fearful on account of his lack of devotion and poetic activity (logic). And lastly, he focuses on a sound he hears, which he is unable to bear and which is followed by his perception of a blinding light ("impressioun") that strikes him down into his swoon (102; 105–6). The Prologue thus moves the dreamer from the cell of memory toward imagination, with(in) which the dream proper begins. Furthermore, multiplications of three are characteristic of the dreamer's poetic output within the *Palice*: three stanzas on the inconstancy of Venus in Part One (607–36) lead to three hastily composed ("als swyth") stanzas "thanking" Venus (conceptualized as his "Vnwemmyt wit, deliuerit of dangear") in Part Two (1014–44), which then lead to "versis thre" on Honor at the end of Part Three (2115–42), to which one could add the Epilogue's three stanzas in praise of James IV (2143–69). "Schaw now thy beggit termis, mare than thryis," the dreamer suitably requests of his "wyt" at the beginning of Part One (131; 127).

As Alice Miskimin has argued, numerologically, the proliferation of threes could be seen as reinforcing Pythagorean harmony,[56] the "speres thryes thre" of Chaucer's *Parliament of Fowls* (61). The mirroring and multiplication of the ventricular underpinning of Douglas's poem, however, challenge the depicted harmony and orderliness of households, as imaginational excess erupts forcefully into the realms of logic and, by way of Venus's mirror, memory. Since Venus's mirror becomes the poet's mirror, it brings into purview a poetics that is self-consciously located outside of the courtly system of *oikonomia*, a poetics that is ultimately just as driven by imaginational chrematistics as Chaucer's *Fame*. But in the *Palice*, this poetics of excess goes beyond that of Chaucer's *Fame* by destabilizing the genre of faculty allegory as such. The pro-

---

56. Miskimin, "Design."

liferation of images in the mirror finds a correlative in the poem's proliferation of mirrorings, including the repeated representations of the ventricles. The excess results in a *mise-en-abyme*-like structure threatening infinite regress. The mirrorings of the poem's ventricular architecture thus question the capacity of faculty allegory to generate and sustain harmony, to deliver any meanings beyond self-replication. Finally, then, Venus's mirror brings into view the *Palice*'s performance of its own representational exhaustion, an exhaustion perfectly encapsulated in the poem's proliferation of lists.

CHAPTER 8

The Epic Tree Catalogue from Chaucer to Spenser

INGO BERENSMEYER

This essay has its origin in a moment of surprise; or, to be precise, two moments: the first one was seeing so many similarities between the catalogues of trees in Spenser's *Faerie Queene* and Sidney's *Arcadia*, and the second one was finding how little attention these similarities and their potential reasons had received. Literary critics should perhaps not be so surprised that a wider public has little time for even their favorite objects of study. But, given the vast amount of scholarship devoted to Sidney and Spenser, this did come as a surprise. My initial question was purely textual: who copied from whom? Which of these two major Elizabethan poets had priority? Little enough is known about their relationship as men and as writers, so my hope was that their tree catalogues might reveal something about this relationship. I have to admit, from the start, that my research did not lead to such a revelation, devoutly to be wished for though it may be. But, as my enquiry expanded, I was able to provide not only a more systematic overview of the parallels between their respective lists and their use of common sources (particularly in the work of Chaucer), but also a better sense of the historical origins of the tree catalogue as a generic element in epic poetry, and of its changing functions in the early modern period. Thus, though this essay may not be particularly revealing about Sidney and Spenser as biographical subjects, I do hope that it can shed some light on a literary form—the tree catalogue—that can tell us more about early modern English culture and some of its key assumptions.

The epic catalogue has been a hallmark of narrative poetry since antiquity: a rhetorical device of amplification that extends the scope of the poem towards the encyclopedic. As Gordon Campbell explains, it is a "division of material into lists, and the parallel expression of that material."[1] Perhaps its most famous instance is the catalogue of Greek ships in the second book of the *Iliad*. The tree catalogue in particular has its roots in Virgil's *Aeneid* and Ovid's *Metamorphoses*. In the Middle Ages and the Renaissance, this tradition is continued in, among others, the *Roman de la rose*, Boccaccio's *Teseida*, and the twelfth-century English cleric Joseph of Exeter's (Iosephus Iscanus) *De bello Troiano*. It enters the English vernacular tradition with Chaucer, who includes tree catalogues in *The Knight's Tale* and the *Parliament of Fowls*. Chaucer's lists of trees are strongly influenced by Boccaccio.[2] In the early modern period, both Sidney and Spenser include lists of trees in their work. Both Chaucer's and Spenser's tree catalogues will continue to influence later poets and translators. As is the case with many features of poetic tradition, and literary tradition more widely, such elements, beyond their more concrete functions in a particular text, also serve as beacons by which one poet sends signals to both past and present, participating in a community of poets and developing a tradition. Once their serial recurrence has established them as generic features of a particular text type, they become entrenched, indispensable: every poem should have one.[3] The list, in the form of the epic catalogue, itself becomes an item in a longer list or series of epic catalogues. Among the "affordances" of such catalogues, then, is a metareferential and metapoetic act of insertion into the tradition of (narrative or epic) poetry.[4]

If texts are conversations—with readers, but also among themselves and with their predecessors—the catalogues of early modern epic romance are conversation pieces of a particular kind, holding converse with an extensive tradition of verse and, in doing so, marking their own place within it. As a subtype of the epic catalogue, the list of trees in a narrative poem marks that

---

1. Gordon Campbell, "Catalogues," in *The Spenser Encyclopedia*, ed. A. C. Hamilton (Toronto: University of Toronto Press, 1990), 137; see also Eva von Contzen, "The Limits of Narration: Lists and Literary History," *Style* 50, no. 3 (2016): 241–60, and, by the same author, "Die Affordanzen der Liste," *Zeitschrift für Literaturwissenschaft und Linguistik* 47, no. 3 (2017): 317–26.

2. Piero Boitani, "Chaucer and Lists of Trees," *Reading Medieval Studies* 2 (1976): 28–44; for an account of Old English catalogue poems, see Nicholas Howe, *The Old English Catalogue Poem* (Copenhagen: Rosenkilde and Bagger, 1985).

3. See Jonathan Culler's classic essay on "Apostrophe," *diacritics* 7, no. 4 (1977): 59–69.

4. von Contzen, "Affordanzen."

poem as belonging to a tradition, an extended series of similar, earlier as well as contemporary and, possibly, future textual performances. The list, or *articulus*, not only has a referential function in associating different tree types with certain qualities or cultural meanings; it also has a metareferential function of articulating the text in relation to its predecessors, contemporaries, and successors as belonging to a common genre. It is at least as much about *recognition* as it is about cognition; its goal may be the didactic transmission of knowledge about different trees and their uses, or their symbolic meanings, but it also serves to identify the poem and the poet as participants in a literary transaction or a cultural performance.

The tree catalogue not only causes textual expansion and descriptive expansiveness within the poem; in its shade, there thrives a dense and lively undergrowth of annotation: marginal notes in manuscripts and explanatory notes in later editions. These add further annotations to what is often not only a form of rhetorical amplification but already a form of annotation within the poetic text.[5] In their retardation of the action and their enumeration of detail, epic tree catalogues invite readers to lose sight of the larger whole, the purpose or *telos* of the narrative. But readers who follow them into the wandering wood of a literary arboretum can perhaps learn something important about reading narrative poetry and the function or functions of lists in premodern literary texts.

In this essay, I am more concerned with the literary, semiotic, and textual specifics of tree catalogues than the actual and ecological significance of trees. Nevertheless, a few remarks on the latter may be useful by way of contextualization. In early modern Europe, trees were an important natural resource for construction work, particularly house- and shipbuilding, and highly relevant for colonial forays into the New World. Thomas Harriot's *Briefe and True Report of the New Found Land of Virginia* famously includes a list of tree species native to the future colony and commercially useful for the colonists: walnut, fir, cedar, maple, holly, willow, beech, and ash, and the more exotic-sounding "Rakiock," from which the indigenous population is said to build their canoes.[6] Faustus in Marlowe's *Doctor Faustus* asks Mephistopheles for

---

5. On annotation as a public rather than a private practice in the early modern period, see Jason Scott-Warren, "Unannotating Spenser," in *Renaissance Paratexts*, ed. Helen Smith and Louise Wilson (Cambridge: Cambridge University Press, 2011), 153–64.

6. Thomas Harriot, *A Briefe and True Report of the New Found Land of Virginia* (London, 1590), 22–3. "This was almost certainly the tulip tree (*Liliodendron tulipifera*), unknown in Europe," according to David Quinn, *Set Fair for Roanoake: Voyages and Colonies, 1584–1606* (Chapel Hill: University of North Carolina Press, 1985), 179.

a complete list of "all the plants, herbs, and trees that grow upon the world,"⁷ probably for similarly utilitarian, medicinal, or commercial purposes.

But there is a highly valued symbolic dimension to the early modern arboretum that is at least as, if not more, significant than the economic and material. When Charles II hides in an oak tree in Boscobel Wood to escape Parliamentarian forces after the Battle of Worcester in 1651, the fact that the oak is, traditionally, the most 'royal' of trees and, for Spenser, associated with epic battle scenes,⁸ is of no small importance. Trees in Renaissance literature can be carriers of allegorical meaning and heraldic emblems. Emblem books contain numerous trees of symbolic significance, from the biblical Tree of Life to a tree shaken by the winds as a symbol of fortitude,⁹ the palm tree—which is difficult to climb—as a symbol of the reward of hardship, or an almond tree as a symbol of precocity,¹⁰ among many others. Such emblems are frequently employed also by poets and dramatists, as by Marlowe in *Edward II*, where Mortimer junior describes his device as "A lofty cedar tree, fair flourishing, / On whose top branches kingly eagles perch."¹¹ This literary usage of trees forms a sharp contrast to the reality of merciless deforestation and exploitation of natural resources that begins in the early modern period and that is lamented already in Drayton's *Poly-Olbion* of 1612.¹²

Furthermore, since antiquity, different species of trees could be used to designate different literary styles: pastoral poetry is set among beeches, poplars, and willows, "middle poetry" in orchards, and epic in forests of more 'heroic' trees like ash, oak, or pine.¹³ Trees can also serve as material carriers of written texts. It was a common practice to carve verses or names into trees, as Spenser's Colin promises to do for Queen Elizabeth: "Her name in euery tree I will endosse / That as the trees do grow, her name may grow."¹⁴ In *As You Like It*, trees are the recipients and media of love poetry, used by

---

7. Christopher Marlowe, *The Complete Plays*, ed. Mark Thornton Burnett (London: Dent; Vermont: Tuttle, 1999), A.2.1.170.

8. Marillene Allen, "Trees," in *The Spenser Encyclopedia*, ed. A. C. Hamilton (Toronto: University of Toronto Press, 1990), 698.

9. Mario Praz, *Studies in Seventeenth-Century Imagery*, 2nd ed. (Rome: Edizioni di Storia e Letteratura, 1975), 114; 124.

10. Andrea Alciato, *Emblems*, Alciato at Glasgow, Glasgow University, https://www.emblems.arts.gla.ac.uk/alciato/iconclass-browse.php?id=25G3(PALM-TREE).

11. Marlowe, *The Complete Plays*, 2.2.16–17; cf. Praz, *Studies in Seventh-Century Imagery*, 215.

12. Andrew McRae, "Tree-Felling in Early Modern England: Michael Drayton's Environmentalism," *The Review of English Studies* 63, no. 260 (2012), 410–30.

13. Allen, "Trees," 698.

14. Edmund Spenser, "Colin Clouts Come Home Againe," in *The Shorter Poems*, ed. Richard A. McCabe (Harmondsworth: Penguin, 1999), 362, lines 632–3.

Orlando to distribute his poems throughout the Forest of Arden. Trees are also regularly kissed, by human lips or by the wind (as in *The Merchant of Venice*, 5.1.2). Moreover, the tree is a symbol of the Cross, and also of the Tree of Life and the Tree of Knowledge in Paradise, and thus an important object of Christian reflection and meditation, with different kinds of trees carrying different possible meanings and typological layers of significance. In Aemilia Lanyer's country-house poem "The Description of Cooke-ham" (1611), the central oak tree on the grounds of Margaret Clifford's estate is likened to the biblical cedar and palm tree (ll. 55–62), with the cedar representing "the building material for the temple of God, and the palm . . . the symbol of spiritual victory"[15] and also "an emblem of female chastity."[16] Various trees and other flora imbued with symbolic or allegorical significance are planted throughout Shakespeare's plays, from Ophelia's rosemary for remembrance and pansies for thoughts to Desdemona's willow song. How clear and present these meanings were to early modern (urban) audiences and readers is a fairly open question; certainly, knowledge of plant lore was widely disseminated in herbals and husbandry manuals, which formed a strong presence on the early modern English book market, beginning with William Turner's *Libellus de re herbaria* (1538) and his *A New Herball* of 1551. Thomas Tusser's *A Hundred Good Pointes of Husbandrie*, first printed in 1557, was "one of the fifteen top-selling books in Elizabethan England."[17]

It is part of the generic makeup of a tree catalogue that it glosses the meanings of trees. Lists and catalogues are descriptive, but they are also forms of annotation, marking what is notable about each item. Frequently, these meanings are conventional, stock associations. In *The Knight's Tale*, Chaucer includes this *articulus* of twenty-one tree names: "As ook, firre, birch, aspe, alder, holm, popler, / Wylugh, elm, plane, assh, box, chasteyn, lynde, laurer, / Mapul, thorn, bech, hasel, ew, whippeltree."[18] In the *Parliament of Fowls*, he

---

15. Elaine Beilin, *Redeeming Eve: Women Writers of the English Renaissance* (Princeton: Princeton University Press, 1987), 204.

16. Patrick Cook, "Aemilia Lanyer's 'Description of Cooke-Ham' as Devotional Lyric," in *Discovering and (Re)Covering the Seventeenth Century Religious Lyric*, ed. Eugene R. Cunnar and Jeffrey Johnson (Pittsburgh, PA: Duquesne University Press, 2001), 104–18, here 111; see Angelika Zirker, "Aemilia Lanyer, 'The Description of Cooke-ham' (1611)," in *Handbook of English Renaissance Literature*, ed. Ingo Berensmeyer (Berlin / Boston: De Gruyter, 2019), 478–95.

17. Todd Andrew Borlik, "Mute Timber? Fiscal Forestry and Environmental Stichomythia in the Old Arcadia," in *Early Modern Ecostudies: From the Florentine Codex to Shakespeare*, ed. Thomas Hallock, Ivo Kamps, and Karen L. Raber (New York: Palgrave Macmillan, 2008), 31–53, here 38.

18. Geoffrey Chaucer, *The Riverside Chaucer*, 3rd ed., ed. Larry D. Benson (Oxford: Oxford University Press, 1988), 64, ll. 2921–3; see Boitani, "Chaucer and Lists of Trees." On the metrical challenges of Chaucer's catalogues, see Ad Putter, "In Appreciation of Metrical Abnormality:

gives us fourteen species, among which the cypress is associated with death, the yew with archery, and the olive with peace:

> The byldere ok, and ek the hardy asshe;
> The piler elm, the cofre unto carayne;
> The boxtre pipere; holm to whippes lashe;
> The saylynge fyr; the cipresse, deth to playne;
> The shetere ew; the asp for shaftes pleyne;
> The olyve of pes, and eke the dronke vyne;
> The victor palm, the laurer to devyne.[19]

This list of trees clearly left its mark on the Elizabethan poets, who were avid readers and admirers of Chaucer. In the first eclogue in the *Old Arcadia*, Sidney skillfully inserts a tree catalogue that taps into the symbolic resources of arboreal lore when Musidorus, disguised as the shepherd Dorus, recognizes "part of [his] estate represented" in trees. There follows a list of trees and their symbolic significance for Musidorus:

> Laurel shows what I seek, by the myrrh is showed how I seek it,
> Olive paints me the peace that I must aspire to by conquest;
> Myrtle makes my request, my request is crowned with a willow,
> Cypress promiseth help, but a help where comes no recomfort.
> Sweet juniper saith this, though I burn, yet I burn in a sweet fire.
> Yew doth make me bethink what kind of bow the boy holdeth
> Which shoots strongly without any noise and deadly without smart.
> Fir trees great and green, fixed on a high hill but a barren,
> Like to my noble thoughts, still new, well placed, to me fruitless.
> Fig that yields most pleasant fruit, his shadow is hurtful,
> Thus be her gifts most sweet, thus more danger to be near her,
> But in a palm when I mark how he doth rise under a burden,
> And may I not (say I then) get up though griefs be so weighty?
> Pine is a mast to a ship, to my ship shall hope for a mast serve?
> Pine is high, hope is as high; sharp-leaved, sharp yet be my hope's buds.
> Elm embraced by a vine, embracing fancy reviveth.
> Poplar changeth his hue from a rising sun to a setting:

Headless Lines and Initial Inversion in Chaucer," in *Engaging with Chaucer: Practice, Authority, Reading*, ed. C. W. R. D. Moseley (New York / Oxford: Berghahn, 2021), 65–85, here 66–8, who argues that the intellectual work of sorting items into a list is mirrored by the metrical problems of Chaucer's catalogues. Thanks to James Simpson for pointing this reference out to me.

19. Chaucer, *The Riverside Chaucer*, 387, ll. 176–82.

Thus to my sun do I yield, such looks her beams do afford me.
Old aged oak cut down, of new work serves to the building:
So my desires, by my fear cut down, be the frames of her honour.
Ash makes spears which shields do resist, her force no repulse takes:
Palms do rejoice to be joined by the match of a male to a female,
And shall sensitive things be so senseless as to resist sense?[20]

Potentially limitless, this list is motivated by the enamored Musidorus as an illustration of how his thoughts are "dispersed" rather than straightforward: "thus thinking nurseth a thinking, / Thus both trees and each thing else be the books of a fancy." The passage culminates in his praise of the cedar, the anthropomorphized "queen of woods" and the worthiest recipient of Dorus's "plaints," whose response is imagined as a gentle nod. Seventeen types of trees, among which the palm is mentioned twice, make up this nursery of bittersweet human desire and passion, a "dense semantic thicket" and "a place of pure poetry."[21]

This tree catalogue was cut in the 1590 quarto but restored, by Mary Sidney, in the folio of 1593.[22] What is striking is that four of the extant manuscripts of the *Old Arcadia*[23] contain marginal glosses that explain the allegorical meanings of seven species: laurel = victory, myrrh = lamentation, olive = quietness, myrtle = love, willow = refusal, cypress = death, palms = happy marriage. These interpretative glosses are not necessarily authorial. With the—curious—exception of the palms, they are reproduced in Katherine Duncan-Jones's Oxford Classics edition[24] and have now entered the modern textual history of the *Arcadia*. But even if one disregards these marginal annotations, the catalogue itself contains numerous glosses that explain the individual tree species' mythological, psychological, or allegorical significance, for example, comparing the yew to the wood of Cupid's bow, or the height of the pine to the speaker's high hopes, or the cutting of "old, aged oak" to the speaker's "desires, by [his] fear cut down," and so on. There might even be a bawdy joke in the palm's 'rising' "under a burden." As they are in Chaucer, the cypress is here associated with death, the yew with archery, and the olive with peace.

---

20. Sir Philip Sidney, *The Countess of Pembroke's Arcadia (The Old Arcadia)*, ed. Katherine Duncan-Jones (Oxford: Oxford University Press, 1999), 77.
21. Borlik, "Mute Timber?," 34.
22. Borlik, "Mute Timber?," 47–8 n. 5.
23. St John's College, Cambridge, MS I.7; Jesus College MS 150; Helmingham Hall MS; Bodleian Rawlinson Poetical MS 85; see Borlik, "Mute Timber?," 47 n. 5.
24. Sidney, *Arcadia*, 77.

We find another Chaucerian tree catalogue in Spenser's *Faerie Queene*. In the first canto, Redcrosse and Una (and the dwarf, lagging behind) enter a "shadie grove,"[25] the first of the poem's many enclosed natural spaces. As the travelers traverse this forest, time in the epic narrative slows down, and readers are invited to wander through a textual grove of thirteen lines, in which they find the following:

> The sayling Pine, the Cedar proud and tall,
> The vine-propp Elme, the Poplar neuer dry,
> The builder Oake, sole king of forrests all,
> The Aspine good for staues, the Cypresse funerall.
>
> The Laurell, meed of mightie Conquerours
> And Poets sage, the Firre that weepeth still,
> The Willow worne of forlorne Paramours,
> The Eugh obedient to the benders will,
> The Birch for shaftes, the Sallow for the mill,
> The Mirrhe sweete bleeding in the bitter wound,
> The warlike Beech, the Ash for nothing ill,
> The fruitfull Oliue, and the Platane round,
> The caruer Holme, the Maple seeldom inward sound.[26]

Critics have noted the ways in which Spenser uses trees in his work, "in epic catalogues, for their emblematic meanings, for their heraldic significance, as devices to identify poetic landscapes, and for the conventions associated with them";[27] while indebted to a tradition of tree catalogues from Virgil, Ovid, Statius, Claudian, Boccaccio, and Chaucer, only Chaucer's catalogue in the *Parliament of Fowls* has been identified as "a direct source."[28]

I began this essay by stating that the tree catalogue functions as a metareferential, metapoetic act of self-insertion into the poetic tradition. Here, it also arguably serves a narrative function. Spenser's trees might be read in connection with Dante's *selva oscura*, the dark forest in which the speaker finds himself at the beginning of the *Divine Comedy*, as a symbolic location. Thus they have been read as "symbols of our passage through life, being emblems

---

25. Edmund Spenser, *The Faerie Queene*, rev. 2nd ed., ed. A. C. Hamilton, text ed. Hiroshi Yamashita and Toshiyuki Suzuki (London / New York: Routledge, 2013), 1.1.7.

26. Spenser, *Faerie Queene*, 1.1.8–9.

27. Allen, "Trees," 697.

28. Allen, "Trees," 697; cf. Anthony M. Esolen, "The Disingenuous Poet Laureate: Spenser's Adoption of Chaucer," *Studies in Philology* 87, no. 3 (Summer 1990): 285–311.

of secular activities—shipbuilding, agriculture, love, and warfare—set against reminders of human mortality and weaknesses," and also as a foreshadowing of Redcrosse's fight against Error after finding his way out of the Wandering Wood.[29] It might be argued that, as Redcrosse and Una lose their path in the forest, wandering "too and fro in waies vnknowne,"[30] the reader is given a similar experience of no longer seeing the wood for the catalogue of trees: twenty different species, in this case, from ash to yew. Spenser could have picked this up from Dante, or from Ariosto's *Orlando furioso,* or from Horace's *Satire* 2.3: "velut silvis, ubi passim / palantis error certo de tramite pellit, / ille sinistrorsum, hic dextrorsum abit, unus utrique / error, sed variis illudit partibus" ("just as in a forest, where some error drives men to wander to and fro from the proper path, and this one goes off to the left and that one to the right: both are under the same error, but are led astray in different ways").[31]

The overlap between Sidney's and Spenser's tree catalogues is intriguing. Both writers had at least begun to compose their respective *magnum opus* in 1579, and Spenser was moving in circles close to Sidney and probably knew him in person, although their social distance in rank was considerable, and they may not have been all that close.[32] However, the connections between them extend beyond the personal; the pastoral mode of the *Shepheardes Calender,* printed in 1579 and dedicated to Sidney, offers a poetic analogue to the latter's *Arcadia,* and its woodcuts are modeled on the 1571 edition of Sannazaro's *Arcadia,* itself an obvious influence on Sidney's book.[33] In his *Defence*

---

29. Allen, "Trees," 697.

30. Spenser, *Faerie Queene,* 1.1.10.

31. Horace, *Satires,* in *Satires; Epistles; The Art of Poetry,* trans. H. Rushton Fairclough (Cambridge, MA: Harvard University Press, 1926), 156–7. Cf. John Upton, ed., *Spenser's Faerie Queene: A New Edition with a Glossary, and Notes Explanatory and Critical,* 2 vols. (London, 1758), 2:338–9.

32. Andrew Hadfield puts it thus: "It was assumed for a long time that Spenser must have been an intimate associate of Sir Philip Sidney because they were both poets who had Irish connections, and that Sidney must have eased his entry into court society, but many have questioned how well they could have known each other, given their obvious difference in class and status." See Hadfield, *Edmund Spenser: A Life* (Oxford: Oxford University Press, 2012), 1. The first biographical source that reports on the first encounter between Spenser and Sidney dates from 1679; for details, see Hadfield, *Edmund Spenser,* 419–20.

33. Ruth Samson Luborsky, "The Illustrations to *The Shepheardes Calender,*" *Spenser Studies* 2 (1981): 3–53; Ruth Samson Luborsky, "The Illustrations to *The Shepheardes Calender* II," *Spenser Studies* 9 (1988): 249–53; S. K. Heninger Jr., "The Typographical Layout of Spenser's *Shepheardes Calender,*" in *Word and Visual Imagination: Studies of the Interaction of English Literature and the Visual Arts,* ed. Karl Josef Höltgen et al. (Erlangen: Universitätsbund Erlangen-Nürnberg, 1988), 33–71.

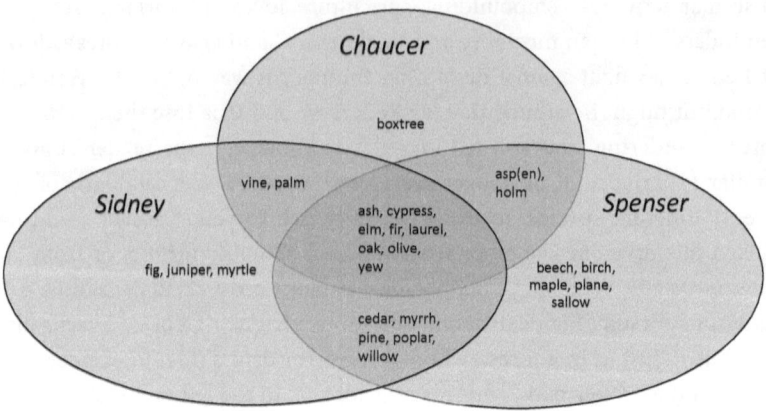

FIGURE 8.1. Tree species featured in Sidney's, Spenser's, and Chaucer's tree catalogues.

of Poesy, Sidney compares Spenser to Sannazaro, recognizing the parallel.[34] Moreover, Spenser and Sidney shared the same publisher, William Ponsonby, whose editions of Sidney's *Arcadia* and the *Faerie Queene* appeared in the same year (1590) and were printed in the same format (quartos in eights) and the same roman typeface, unusual at the time for works in the vernacular, for which black-letter would have been the norm.[35] In his dedicatory sonnet to the Countess of Pembroke, Spenser invokes Sidney's memory as the one "Who first my Muse did lift out of the flore."[36] Thus, it is intriguing to speculate about intertextual connections between Spenser's and Sidney's arboreal lists. In their respective tree catalogues, five species are exclusive to Sidney, seven to Spenser, and thirteen occur in both texts. As the Venn diagram shows, eight of the thirteen tree species that Spenser and Sidney have in common are also shared by Chaucer (in the *Parliament of Fowls*). Five other trees are shared by Spenser and Sidney that are not in Chaucer, but Sidney also shares two others with Chaucer (the vine and the palm), as does Spenser (the aspen and the

---

34. Sir Philip Sidney, "A Defence of Poetry," in *Miscellaneous Prose of Sir Philip Sidney*, ed. Katherine Duncan-Jones and Jan van Dorsten (Oxford: Clarendon Press, 1973), 73–121, here 112.

35. Mark Bland, "The Appearance of the Text in Early Modern England," *Text* 11 (1998): 91–154, here 107–13. Sidney's *Arcadia* was printed for Ponsonby by John Windet, *The Faerie Queene* by John Wolfe. While work on the *Faerie Queene* must have started earlier, both were finished at roughly the same time, with *The Faerie Queene* appearing "immediately after the publication of the *Arcadia*" (Bland, "Appearance," 111). It has been argued that "a deliberate decision was taken to associate Spenser with Sidney through typography and format" (Bland, "Appearance," 110). By publishing both, Ponsonby secured "a monopoly on the work of the two most celebrated poets of the 1590s" (Hadfield, *Edmund Spenser*, 237).

36. Spenser, *Faerie Queene*, 734, 1.6.

holm, or holly). A comparison of the meanings associated with these trees in the three texts shows even more parallels:

Meanings associated with trees in Sidney (Si),[37] Spenser (Sp), and Chaucer

Ash: spears (Si),[38] 'for nothing ill' (Sp), hardy (C),
Cedar: queen of woods (Si), proud and tall (Sp)
Cypress: 'promiseth help' / death (Si), 'funerall' (Sp),[39] death to plain (C)
Elm: 'embraced by a vine' (Si),[40] 'vine-propp' (Sp), pillar (C)
Fir: 'great and green . . . to me fruitless' (Si), 'weepeth still' (Sp), sailing (C)
Laurel: 'shows what I seek' / victory (Si), 'meed of mightie Conquerours
     and Poets' (Sp),[41] divine (C)
Myrrh: shows 'how I seek it' / lamentation (Si), 'sweete bleeding in the bitter wound' (Sp)
Oak: building (Si), builder (Sp), builder (C)
Olive: peace / quietness (Si), fruitful (Sp), peace (C)
Pine: 'a mast to a ship' (Si), 'sayling' (Sp)[42]

---

37. Where two meanings are given for Sidney, the second one refers to the marginal notes in the manuscripts, as printed in Duncan-Jones's edition.

38. Cf. Ovid, *Metamorphoses*, 2 vols., trans. Frank Justus Miller, rev. G. P. Goold (Cambridge, MA: Harvard University Press, 1916), 2:10.93: "fraxinus utilis hastis" ("the ash, suitable for spear-shafts").

39. Claudian, *Rape of Proserpine*, in *On Stilicho's Consulship 2–3; Panegyric on the Sixth Consulship of Honorius; The Gothic War; Shorter Poems; Rape of Proserpina*, trans. M. Platnauer (Cambridge, MA: Harvard University Press, 1922), 2.108: "tumulos tectura cupressus" ("the cypress, sentinel of graves"); Silius Italicus, *Punica*, 2 vols., trans. J. D. Duff (Cambridge, MA: Harvard University Press, 1934), 2:10.534: "ferale decus, maestas ad busta cupressos" ("cypresses that deck the funeral train and mourn beside the pyre"). In Spenser's version of *Virgil's Gnat*, the cypress is a "signe of deadly bale" (l. 216), translating from pseudo-Virgil's *Culex*, in *Aeneid: Books 7–12; Appendix Vergiliana*, trans. H. Rushton Fairclough, rev. G. P. Goold (Cambridge, MA: Harvard University Press, 1918), 140: "nec laeta cupressus" ("the cypress of grief").

40. The most persistent association throughout this tradition: Ovid, *Metamorphoses*, 2:10.100, "amictae vitibus ulmi" ("the elm-trees, draped with vines"); Statius, *Thebaid*, in *Thebaid, Volume I: Thebaid: Books 1–7*, ed. and trans. D. R. Shackleton Bailey (Cambridge, MA: Harvard University Press, 2004), 6.106, "nec inhospita vitibus ulmus" ("the vine-welcoming elm"); Claudian, *Rape of Proserpine*, 2.111, "hic pampinus induit ulmos" ("here the vine clothes the elm"); Boccaccio, *Teseida*, 11.24.8, "l' olmo che di viti s'innamora."

41. A possible source for this, noted by Upton, is Statius, *Achilleid*, in *Thebaid, Volume II: Thebaid: Books 8–12; Achilleid*, ed. and trans. D. R. Shackleton Bailey (Cambridge, MA: Harvard University Press, 2004), 1.15–16: "cui geminae florent vatumque ducumque / certatim laurus" ("for whom the twin laurels of bards and captains flourish in rivalry").

42. Possible sources for this are Claudian, *Rape of Proserpine*, 2.107: "apta fretis abies" ("the pine, useful for seafaring") or Silius Italicus, *Punica*, 2:10.522: "amantem litora pinum" ("pine-trees that love the shore"). The botanical distinction between *abies* and *pinus* leads to Chaucer attributing "sayling" to the fir-tree rather than the pine.

Poplar: 'changeth his hue' (Si), never dry (Sp)

Willow: 'my request is crowned with' / refusal (Si), 'worne of forlorne Paramours' (Sp)

Yew: bow [of Cupid] (Si), 'obedient to the benders will' (Sp), shooter (C)

Table 8.1 shows this overlap more clearly; an 'x' in each row marks verbal or conceptual identity (with 'y' and 'z' as alternatives in each case), a '0' indicates a tree not included in Chaucer. An 'x' in parentheses marks a case where the identity is not immediately evident, as it is in the case of the cypress (death/funeral), but still likely, as in the cases of myrrh and willow.

TABLE 8.1. Semantic agreement among shared tree species epithets in Sidney, Spenser, and Chaucer

TREE	SIDNEY	SPENSER	CHAUCER
Ash	x	y	z
Cedar	x	y	0
Cypress	x	x	x
Elm	x	x	(x)
Fir	x	y	z
Laurel	x	x	z
Myrrh	x	(x)	0
Oak	x	x	x
Olive	x	y	x
Pine	x	x	0
Poplar	x	y	0
Willow	x	(x)	0
Yew	x	x	x

Complete verbal and conceptual overlap between all three texts occurs three times (cypress, oak, and yew), four if the elm is included on the basis of understanding Chaucer's "piler" (pillar) to mean "support (for vines)"; between Chaucer and Sidney, five times (with the olive added); between Chaucer and Spenser, four times; and between Sidney and Spenser, six times (or eight if the less certain cases of myrrh and willow are included). In the case of the yew, the association with archery, taken from Chaucer, is both Virgilian[43] and

---

43. Virgil, *Georgics*, in *Eclogues; Georgics; Aeneid: Books 1–6*, trans. H. Rushton Fairclough, rev. G. P. Goold (Cambridge, MA: Harvard University Press, 1916), 2.448: "Ituraeos taxi torquentur in arcus" ("yews are bent into Ituraean bows"); also noted in Upton, *Spenser's Faerie Queene*, 2:340.

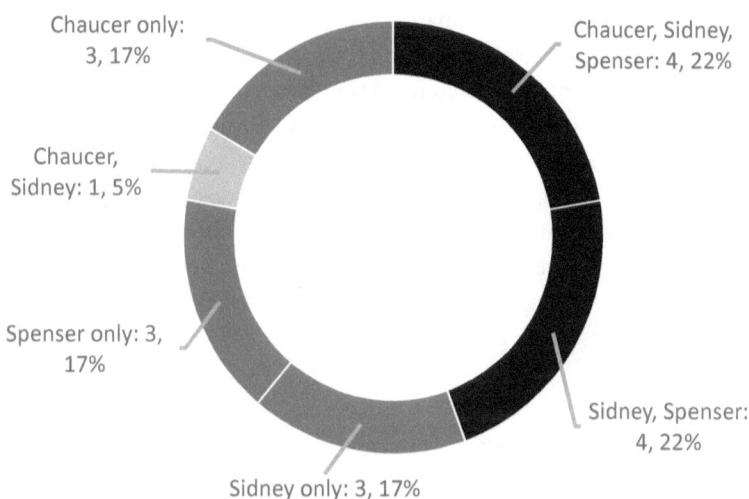

FIGURE 8.2. Distribution of shared tree epithets.

thoroughly English, as Upton explains: "Our forefathers, so famous for their skill in the bow, used the yew-tree; and that yew-trees might never be wanting, they ordered one at least to be planted in every church-yard in England."[44] All in all, at least 44%—according to the narrow approach—of the meanings of trees shared by Spenser and Sidney are in agreement (see Figure 8.2). However, the question remains what, if anything, this agreement signifies: did Sidney's tree catalogue influence Spenser's or vice versa (either case is possible, assuming early manuscript circulation), or were both independently inspired by the shared repertoire of poetic epithets and figurative meanings of trees from classical, biblical, and modern sources, with some—in Spenser's case, less considerable—input from Chaucer? In any case, they have more in common with each other than either of them has with Chaucer's model. There is no epithet that Spenser shares with Chaucer that he does not also share with Sidney. This might support his statement in the sonnet to the Countess of Pembroke that Sidney not only acted as his patron but also "raised" him through poetic inspiration. Although unsurpassed in their scope and detail, A. C. Hamilton's annotations disappoint in this regard. While he traces Spenser's arboreal epithets to Chaucer, Virgil, Ovid, the Old and New Testament, the *Iliad*, Plato's *Phaedrus*, Pliny's *Natural History*, and the sixteenth-century treatise *Batman vppon Bartholome*, he fails to mention Sidney's *Arcadia* at this

---

44. Upton, *Spenser's Faerie Queene*, 2:340.

point.[45] Readers convinced of the existence of a fairly coherent late medieval or early modern world picture may find it easier to believe that all these references came naturally to a Sidney or a Spenser; others may find some form of intertextual transmission or conversation between the two to be the more likely scenario. As it happens, post-Spenserian translations of classical or modern verse narratives often continue this intertextual conflation by projecting Spenser's descriptions back onto the source texts, as Edward Fairfax does, for example, in his translation of Tasso's *Gerusalemme liberata* of 1600, which includes both the "funeral cypress" and "sailing pine."[46] Similarly, John Dryden, in his reworking of *The Knight's Tale*, cuts Chaucer's list of trees by half and adds Spenserian epithets:

> the trees were unctuous fir,
> And mountain ash, the mother of the spear;
> The mourner yew, and builder oak were there;
> The beech, the swimming alder, and the plane,
> Hard box, and linden of a softer grain,
> And laurels, which the gods for conquering chiefs ordain.[47]

Even the eighteenth-century prose version of the *Faerie Queene* by Alexander Bicknell, intended to present Spenser's story without his "antique Language," cannot dispense with the tree catalogue,[48] which is taken almost verbatim from the original:

> Pleased with the beauty of the place, and charmed with the music of the birds, of which an infinite number filled every spray, the Knight and damsel forgot, for a moment, their more important concerns, and roved, enraptured, through many different avenues, admiring the beauties of the various trees which composed their assylum [*sic*]. The sailing pine, the cedar proud and tall, the vine-propped elm, the knotted oak king of the forest, the mournful cypress, the laurel meed of conquerors and poets, the weeping fir, the willow worn by love-lorn paramours, the yew obedient to the bender's will, the myrrh sweet bleeding at each bitter wound, the fruitful olive, and the warlike beech, by turns attract their notice, and engage their admiration.[49]

---

45. Spenser, *Faerie Queene*, 33–4.
46. Torquato Tasso, *Jerusalem Delivered: A Poem: Translated by Edward Fairfax*, ed. Henry Morley (London: Routledge, 1890), 3.75.
47. John Dryden, *Selected Poems*, ed. Paul Hammond and David Hopkins (Harlow: Pearson, 2007), 680, ll. 959–64.
48. Alexander Bicknell, "To the Honourable Lady Howe," in *Prince Arthur: An Allegorical Romance, The Story from Spenser*, 2 vols. (London, 1779), 1:n.p.
49. Bicknell, *Prince Arthur*, 1:7–8.

Bicknell's prose version reminds us in passing that the catalogue allows the poet, the characters, and the reader "a moment" in which to "forg[e]t . . . their more important concerns" and enjoy the richness of description or what Bicknell also calls "a Kind of Poetical Magic."[50] The epic catalogue in Spenser is more than a source of mere historical information; beyond its semantic content and verbal display, it often has a structural function for the narrative, giving it an expansive scope and providing an intense sense of world-production or of what Eric Hayot has termed "worldedness."[51]

There are, despite all they have in common, differences between Sidney's and Spenser's catalogues beyond the purely lexical dimension. Whereas, in Sidney, the catalogue is connected to the speaker's psychological and emotional state in an elaborate back and forth between the human and the natural world, there is no such pathetic fallacy in Spenser; and yet the trees in the Wandering Wood are more than merely ornamental. They are not linked to Redcrosse's subjectivity; in their sheer diversity, they exceed any particular allegorical significance that they might otherwise have for understanding his quest or the poem as a whole. They may, as Peter Remien argues, present an economic, instrumental view of the material world that is about to be contrasted with the "grotesque ecology of Error," and what Spenser may be doing here is to stage a self-aware literary confrontation between the danger of sterile imitation on the one hand and "chaotic formlessness" on the other.[52] Spenser's trees, then, are less an emblem of human life than they are, perhaps, emblematic of the act of poetic creation as such, and of inserting the *Faerie Queene* firmly into the epic tradition; they "make claims of literary tradition and poetic succession."[53] As some scholars believe, the catalogue may even represent the oldest surviving layer of the ancient epics,[54] thus touching the deepest level of poetry as the incantatory magic of naming. Be that as it may; what is certain is that, like the epic simile—another hallmark of Spenser's art—the catalogue halts the narrative progression and introduces a moment of reflection in which the net of allusion can be cast wide and the horizon of reference expanded, in this case making the wood invisible because the focus

---

50. Bicknell, *Prince Arthur*, 1:vii.

51. Eric Hayot, *On Literary Worlds* (Oxford: Oxford University Press, 2012); scholarship on the epic catalogues in Spenser has focused on the historical catalogue, e.g., in the marriage of the Thames and the Medway in *FQ* 4.11: see Michael O'Connell, "History and the Poet's Golden World: The Epic Catalogues in *The Faerie Queene*," *English Literary Renaissance* 4, no. 2 (1974): 241–67; Gordon Braden, "Riverrun: An Epic Catalogue in *The Faerie Queene*," *English Literary Renaissance* 5 (1975): 25–48.

52. Peter Remien, "Silvan Matters: Error and Instrumentality in Book I of *The Faerie Queene*," *Spenser Studies* 28 (2013): 119–43, here 119.

53. von Contzen, "Limits of Narration," 250.

54. Campbell, "Catalogues," 137.

is on each and every individual tree. Beyond this certainty of being able to name tree species and assign them their correct attributes, Error awaits.

And yet, as we learn from Upton, the connection between woods and error has a long (Horatian) tradition:

> Methinks in this poetical description of various trees, Spenser is superior to all the poets who have indulged their luxuriant fancy in such descriptions, because his allegory so naturally led him to the subject: for what are these trees and labyrinths, but the various amusements and errors of human life? So Horace and Dante apply the similitude. But what fury possesses other poets to suffer their Muse to run riot, and to expatiate, upon the very mentioning of trees? Let me except Virgil, G. ii. 440. Æn. vi. 180. xi. 135. and Homer, Il. xxiii. 118. where Mr. Pope's notes are well worth consulting. How chaste and short is Milton; Par. Lost, iv. 137. And likewise Tasso, Gierus. Liberat. Canto iii. St. 75, 76. Let me do justice to Lucan likewise, who is very short, where he mentions the trees which Cæsar ordered to be cut down in the grove of Marseilles, L. iii. 440. As to Statius, in Theb. vi. 98, he seems plainly to have Ovid in his eye, who describes the various trees which assembled on the mountain of Thrace to hear the musick of Orpheus. The passage is too long to transcribe; the reader may consult it at his leisure, Ov. Met. Lib. x. Fab. 2. The reader too if he chooses it may consult Claud. de Rapt. Proserp. iii. 107, and the moral Seneca, who introduces Creon running out into a florid description of trees at the mentioning of a grove, at a time when Oedipus is in the utmost expectation of what Tiresias had been transacting in the grove.... Is not my reader already tired with these trees? I think we are got into a WOOD as well as our knight; it will be well for us if we get out of it again: for THIS WOOD *is human life with its various bewildering amusements, and full of* ERROUR.[55]

Arboreal annotation is here understood to deal with nothing else other than human life itself, its "various amusements and errors,"[56] and the eighteenth-century annotator toys with the difficulty of extricating himself from this textual "labyrinth," which ensnares readers as well as Spenser's unlikely heroes.

In its amusing form, the tree catalogue survives even into the twentieth century, at least with parodic intent, when James Joyce includes a tree catalogue of sorts in *Ulysses,* listing the guests at the wedding between the "grand high chief ranger of the Irish National Foresters" and "Miss Fir Conifer of Pine

---

55. Upton, *Spenser's Faerie Queene,* 2:339–40.
56. Upton, *Spenser's Faerie Queene,* 2:339.

Valley," who all have tree-related names such as "Lady Sylvester Elmshade, Mrs Barbara Lovebirch, Mrs Poll Ash," etc.[57]

With the catalogue, the ancient poets may have found a perfect generic design feature, a form and a format to allow "their Muse to run riot" in endless "labyrinths,"[58] transcending any expectations of narrative realism and inviting readers intent on narrative progression—just get on with the plot, bard!—to stop and enjoy the view from here, or, perhaps, merely to focus on the mellifluous sound of tree names and their attributes, and notice how skillfully they are integrated into the poem's meter and rhythm. Beyond the verbal feats of imitation and emulation, in the age of the codex—a word derived from the Latin for "tree trunk"[59]—the epic tree catalogue also points to the material and metaphorical connections between literary texts and the books in which they are carried.

Ranging from texts and books to relationships between individual poets, readers, and annotators, and their roles in the making of poetic conventions and traditions, this essay has explored sources and functions of the tree catalogue in early modern England. Unless more conclusive evidence turns up, we may never be able to establish whether Sidney copied from Spenser (as seems rather more likely to me) or vice versa. But, in the end, what matters more is that we learn to pay attention to minor forms like the tree catalogue and their small but not entirely insignificant role in shaping poetic traditions.

---

57. James Joyce, *Ulysses, the Corrected Text*, ed. Hans Walter Gabler with Wolfhard Steppe and Claus Melchior (Harmondsworth: Penguin, 1986), 268 (I would like to thank Hans Walter Gabler for reminding me of this passage); cf. Brigitte L. Sandquist, "The Tree Wedding in 'Cyclops' and the Ramifications of Cata-logic," special issue of *James Joyce Quarterly* 33, no. 2 (Winter 1996): 195–209, as well as James Fairhall, "Ecocriticism, Joyce, and the Politics of Trees in the 'Cyclops' Episode of *Ulysses*," *Irish Studies Review* 20, no. 4 (November 2012): 367–87.

58. Upton, *Spenser's Faerie Queene*, 2:339.

59. Amaranth Borsuk, *The Book* (Cambridge, MA / London: MIT Press, 2018), x. On meter, see Putter, "In Appreciation of Metrical Abnormality."

CHAPTER 9

What's in a List?
Erasmus, Cromwell, Bale

ALEX DAVIS

"What's in a list?" asks Jack Goody.[1] That is: what might a list contain, and what is the significance of listing? Goody's discussion of the list in *The Domestication of the Savage Mind* is part of an argument about the ways in which graphic formats such as lists and tables acted as agents of social transformation during the advent of literacy in the ancient world. The written list opens up possibilities for the manipulation of information that oral discourse lacks, and Goody observes that administrative lists are one of the earliest extant uses of writing, dominating the bureaucracies of ancient Mesopotamia. His principal interest is in the list as an instrument for sorting and storage. For Goody, the list collects. It sorts and ranks. It is defined by its boundaries. But, as Eva von Contzen and James Simpson observe in their introduction to this volume, the list exists poised between two formal possibilities: "satisfying completeness" on the one hand, and "dispersal and entropy" on the other. What of the latter? Following hints laid down in Goody's discussion, I want to move beyond the stocktaking activities that are his primary concern to explore questions of potentiality, unpredictability, and imagination. Goody's key perception concerns the way in which forms such as the list might interact with wider processes of histori-

---

1. Jack Goody, *The Domestication of the Savage Mind* (Cambridge: Cambridge University Press, 1977), 74.

cal change. This is fundamentally a creative function. This essay argues that both properties of the list—the regularizing and the anarchic—had a role to play within a much later moment of intensive state centralization and reform.

My scene is the England of Henry VIII, in particular the crucial decade of the 1530s; my interest is in projects of religious reconstruction and pedagogic reform. The 1530s saw the declaration of the monarchy's supremacy over the English church and the beginnings of the dissolution of English religious houses; in tandem with this, there was also an extension of humanist education through a program of grammar school reform, undertaken with royal approval. Humanism and the Reformation were in principle distinct projects of cultural and spiritual transformation. In the 1530s, however, they both became the objects of the exertion of state power. In what follows, I survey three moments of list-making within this field of Henrician governmentality. The first concerns the rhetorical lists in Desiderius Erasmus's pedagogic classic *De copia*, produced for St Paul's School in London; the second looks at the lists produced in the office of Thomas Cromwell, Henry VIII's chief minister during these crucial years; and the third deals with the lists in John Bale's allegorical history play, *King Johan*. These moments form a loosely connected group. T. W. Baldwin identifies the period 1530–45 as that in which the Erasmian educational program began to be regularized and institutionalized in England.[2] Meanwhile, Cromwell sponsored a series of Erasmian publications throughout the 1530s, and arranged an Erasmian education for his son Gregory.[3] Bale was in effect hired by Cromwell to write and perform plays that propagandized for evangelical reforms.[4] Finally, although Bale was too old to have benefitted from a humanistic education in letters himself, he was certainly aware of Erasmus as a biblical scholar and a critic of the church.[5] The claim is not that Erasmus, Bale, and Cromwell were participating in a shared project. Their affiliations are looser and more contingent than that. Rather, they offer three different views on the functions of the list in a shared moment of historical

---

2. T. W. Baldwin, *William Shakspere's Small Latine & Lesse Greeke*, 2 vols. (Urbana: Illinois University Press, 1944), 1:164.

3. On Erasmus and Cromwell in general, see James Kelsey McConica, *English Humanists and Reformation Politics Under Henry VIII and Edward VI* (Oxford: Clarendon Press, 1965), 150–99.

4. On Cromwell and Bale, see Paul Whitfield White, *Theatre and Reformation: Protestantism, Patronage, and Playing in Tudor England* (Cambridge: Cambridge University Press, 1993), 13–27.

5. Stylistically, Bale tends to be classed as prehumanist. John N. King argues that "sixteenth-century Ciceronianism made Bale's Latin prose style, which descended from the learned tradition of medieval universities and monasteries, seem old-fashioned" (*English Reformation Literature: The Tudor Origins of the Protestant Tradition* [Princeton: Princeton University Press, 1982], 60–6).

crisis and transformation. In the 1530s, I argue, there was a moment when it seemed like lists might help to change the face of a nation entirely.

THE PEDAGOGIC LIST: ERASMUS'S *DE COPIA*

> Your letter mightily pleased me; to a wonderful degree did you letter please me; me exceedingly did your letter please . . . By your letter was I mightily pleased; I was exceedingly pleased by your letter . . . Your epistle exhilarated me intensely; I was intensely exhilarated by your epistle; your brief note refreshed by spirits in no small measure; I was in no small measure refreshed in spirit by your grace's hand; from your affectionate letter I received unbelievable pleasure; your affectionate letter brought me unbelievable pleasure . . . Your pages engendered in me an unbelievable delight; I conceived a wonderful delight from your pages; your lines conveyed to me the greatest joy.[6]

Desiderius Erasmus's demonstration of how to amplify the simple phrase "your letters have pleased me mightily" (*tuae litterae me magnopere delectarunt*)—some 150 alternatives, beginning with simple variations such as those quoted above and culminating in the deeply obscure "your letter was to me a positive Διὸς ἐγκέφαλος [choice morsel] for a Persian, as the Greeks say"[7]— has a good claim to be *the* quintessential Renaissance list. Here, in the *De copia,* Erasmus's treatise on abundant style, we find a point of origin for the lists of Rabelais and of Shakespeare. Here we find a culprit in relation to Francis Bacon's accusation that the sixteenth century was a moment of "affectionate study of eloquence and copie of speech," when "men began to hunt more after words than matter."[8] Erasmus's list is open-ended and endlessly generative, confounding expectations about the list as an instrument for ordering a preexisting body of content. In it, we encounter a sequence in which fractional technical modifications of grammar and vocabulary (such as the swapping of subject and object, or a shift from active to passive voice) produce a chain of variations marked by a flowing, organic character. Words are shuffled; epithets change; tenses and moods realign . . . and so phrase blooms into phrase, but

---

6. Desiderius Erasmus, *De copia,* in *The Collected Works of Erasmus,* various eds., 72 vols. to date (Toronto: Toronto University Press, 1974–), 24:349.

7. Erasmus, *De copia,* 24:354. Betty I. Knott's parenthetical gloss in the quotation minimizes the oddity of the phrase in order to explain it. More literally, the letter is compared to "the brain of Zeus." The saying is discussed in Erasmus's *Adage* I.vi.60, *Jovis et regis cerebrum* (Erasmus, *Adages,* 32:43).

8. Francis Bacon, *The Major Works,* ed. Brian Vickers (Oxford / New York: Oxford University Press, 2002), 139.

never in an absolutely predictable way. It would be wrong to suggest that there is no overall trajectory to these variations. Erasmus's list presents a staged run-through of sixteenth-century grammar school teaching, beginning with basic experiments with vocabulary, tense, and mood; then adding in figures of speech; and eventually abstruse mythological allusions, with a little bit of Greek. But there is no rule governing the production of this list, nor any obvious halting point for its iterations. It could, in principle, carry on reinventing itself forever.

In his discussion of listing Jack Goody identifies three types of list: the inventory; the shopping list (which includes to-do lists, agendas, and itineraries); and the lexical list. The first two are structured in relation to the categories of temporality and possession. They itemize what one currently has (the inventory) and what one will acquire (the shopping list). They also have obvious practical uses. The lexical list seems the odd man out in this scheme, not least because it really looks like a kind of inventory. Nonetheless, it is important in opening up Goody's discussion towards kinds of functionality not otherwise central to it. The lexical list is where we enter a space of play and exploration, such as a list of words beginning with y-.[9] It foregrounds considerations of conceptual pleasure rather than immediate utility. Erasmus's list belongs here. It is not, quite, a list of things that one has, although it certainly offers a prodigious demonstration of the author's verbal resources. Instead, "your letters have pleased me mightily" is a list of things that one might say or write. It is a catalogue of possible utterances, generated by unlocking the verbal potential latent within a simple Latin sentence. From this swarming multiplicity of phrases the orator selects, and then realizes his choice in eloquent speech.

The *De copia* was a staple of the sixteenth-century grammar school classroom. However, as Terence Cave has shown, it is as much a work of poetics as it is a schoolboy's textbook. It mythologizes verbal creativity through a series of symbolic oppositions. For Cave, copious language has two negative counterparts: "*inopia*, poverty of diction, is its antithesis; empty prolixity (*loquacitas*), *copia* without *varietas*, or Asiatic over-elaboration are its inversions."[10] Another significant Other for *copia* is the heap or pile—or, to put it another way, the list in its most open and unarticulated form. In his dedication of the *De copia* to John Colet, Erasmus disclaims any absolute novelty for his material. Other writers have offered sound advice on achieving the abundant style.

---

9. Goody, *Domestication*, 89.

10. Terence Cave, *The Cornucopian Text: Problems of Writing in the French Renaissance* (Oxford: Clarendon Press, 1979), 5.

What I can really claim is that I have been the first to envisage the subject and give an account of it. For anyone may see how different from my purpose was that of the ancient Greek writer, Julius Pollux, when he classified under topics the names of different things and made up neat piles, so to speak, of a number of synonyms and related terms.[11]

The boast here is that the *De copia* offers the first truly methodical treatment of its subject matter, and if a reader should find this portrait of Erasmus's organizational genius slightly implausible it would be with good reason, since Pollux's "neat piles" actually look like a rather good description of much of the *De copia*'s content, which frequently comprises page after page of lists of metaphors, adjectives, similes, or phrases. Erasmus's text is troubled throughout by the thought of a merely additive structure. As the letter to Colet goes on to admit: "I confess with regret that the present work has not received the careful revision it should have had. It is some time since I unsystematically amassed the raw material for my future work, seeing that I should require a great deal of time to polish it and must read through a great many authors."[12] This is not just a question of presentation. Simple accumulation is a persistent object of anxiety in the *De copia* because it signifies rhetorically. Erasmus goes on to note that those who try but fail to achieve the abundant style "pile up a meaningless heap of words and expressions without any discrimination."[13] Ungoverned profusion indicates a failure of expression, clearly enough. The problem is that it can't be completely disentangled from the conditions of successful eloquence. Erasmus must know that a fully rationalized treatment of his subject matter is beyond his reach: an exhaustive account of the variations on *tuae litterae me magnopere delectarunt* is an impossibility; so too is a systematic analysis of the forms of variation that could be deployed throughout such a sequence. *Copia* cannot be fully rule-governed, and the heap or pile therefore remains an indelible possibility in the *De copia*'s poetics of productivity, which are shadowed throughout by the threat of descent into a mere, sprawling listiness.

Questions of what can be reduced to order and what might resist regimentation thus play a key role in Erasmus's literary theory. They also signify in terms of the sociology of the humanist project more generally, as Erasmian curricula began to be rolled out into schools across Europe throughout the first half of the sixteenth century. In their groundbreaking study *From Humanism to the Humanities*, Lisa Jardine and Anthony Grafton argued that

---

11. Erasmus, *De copia*, 24:285.
12. Erasmus, *De copia*, 24:285–8.
13. Erasmus, *De copia*, 24:295.

the spread of humanist pedagogy ultimately served the needs of early modern governing elites:

> It stamped the more prominent members of the new élite with an indelible cultural seal of superiority, it equipped lesser members with fluency and the learned habit of attention to textual detail and it offered everyone a model of true culture as something given, absolute, to be mastered, not questioned—and thus fostered in all its initiates a properly docile attitude towards authority. The education of the humanists was made to order for the Europe of the Counter-Reformation and of late Protestant orthodoxy. And this consonance between the practical activities of the humanists and the practical needs of their patrons, we argue, was the decisive reason for the victory of humanism. Scholasticism bred too independent an attitude to survive.[14]

Under the influence of Rudolph Agricola and his successors, it is argued, Northern European humanism became distinctively preoccupied with themes of method and pedagogical organization. It became a thing of curricula, drills, epitomes, handbooks. The *De copia* itself was one of the most successful textbooks of all time: it was printed and revised and reprinted and translated and digested and adapted over and over again throughout the sixteenth century. In Jardine and Grafton's reading, the ends of humanism and a centralizing bureaucracy are aligned; so too are the forms of writing that they propagate, via a shared interest in system and method.

The humanist pedagogy of the early sixteenth century thus occupies a landscape shaped by the opposing qualities of creativity and control. On the one hand, Erasmus's demonstration of the powers of rhetoric is marked by something unquantifiable that can never quite be reduced to order; Erasmus speaks of a phrase taking on "a Protean variety of shapes."[15] On the other hand, the humanist program is driven by the promise of systematic instruction, aiming to provide a reliable education for the administrative classes of early modern Europe. It is this ambition that, in England, gives rise to a Tudor pedagogic literature seemingly convinced of the intimate connection between linguistic fluency and sound government. In the 1530s, there was a conscious effort to reorganize and standardize grammar school teaching along Eras-

---

14. Anthony Grafton and Lisa Jardine, *From Humanism to the Humanities: Education and the Liberal Arts in Fifteenth- and Sixteenth-Century Europe* (Cambridge, MA: Harvard University Press, 1986), xiv.

15. Erasmus, *De copia*, 24:348.

mian lines.[16] In 1540, Henry VIII mandated a standard textbook for grammar schools; this textbook opens with a preface celebrating Henry's imposition of "one bryef, plaine, & vniforme grammer" across the nation.[17] Once the linguistic basics were acquired, instruction was devoted to developing pupils' eloquence. Thomas Elyot's *Boke named the gouernour*, dedicated to Henry VIII and directed towards the education of the Tudor elites, recommends that after learning the basic rules of grammar, young gentlemen should aim to acquire "plentie of the tongues called Copie" by reading Aesop; having passed into the study of rhetoric, they are directed to "the litle boke made by the famous Erasmus . . . whiche he calleth *Copium verborum et Reurm* / that is to say / plenty of words and maters."[18]

The form of the list helps identify a paradoxical quality lying at the heart of this movement towards uniformity and regulation. A list might, as in Jack Goody's account, operate as a device for sorting and storing information; yet it can never eradicate the possibility of a mere, unorganized accumulation of material. In Erasmus, as we have seen, this formal option is in many ways the point. If *copia* is constantly under threat from a descent into heaping and mindless aggregation, that is because it contains within itself something— some generative principle—that is fundamentally unpredictable. Although it is a negative quality in itself, the presence of mere listiness within the *De copia* thus points towards the existence of a creative force that operates beyond the bounds of the classificatory impulse. The Tudor educationalists' conviction was that these playful energies could be harnessed and directed towards the ends of sound government. We might wonder about the plausibility of this move. Even the Tudor pedagogues don't always sound fully convinced. Thomas Elyot claims that because the orator must praise and dispraise, exhort and dissuade, accuse and defend, he "is required to be a heape of all maner of lernyng."[19] The comment is intended as praise; it also echoes some of the worries about unstructured knowledge that inflect Erasmus's *De copia*. Nonetheless, the association is foundational for early modern education. It also exemplifies a dialectic of creation and control that plays itself out in a number of other scenes of early Tudor list-making, to which I now turn.

---

16. See Baldwin, *Small Latine & Lesse Greeke*, 1:79–80 (on grammar school Erasmianism), and 1:164–84 (on moves towards standardization under Henry VIII).

17. William Lily et al., *An introduction of the eyght partes of speche, and the construction of the same* (London: Thomas Berthelet, 1542), A2v.

18. Sir Thomas Elyot, *The boke named the gouernour* (London: Thomas Berthelet, 1531), D4r; E4r.

19. Elyot, *The boke*, F8v.

THE ADMINISTRATIVE LIST: THOMAS CROMWELL AND TUDOR GOVERNMENT

We move into the heart of Henry VIII's government. Here is a rather different list, much closer to the kind of document that interested Jack Goody:

> ffirst that I haue depeched the money into Ireland.
> Item that I haue delyuered to Will' Gonson CCCli.
> Item that I am redy to send on M'li for the buyldinges at Calais.
> Item that I haue also made redy M'li to be imployed vppon the making of the haven at Dover.
> Item that will Gonson hath couented wth Cavendish for the provision of Ros Ropes and Cables to be provyded in Esteland, wherein will' Gonson sayeth wilbe saved the costes of the rigging of the Mynyon now into those partes, the which charges for one Moneth will amount to xxxv^{li} xi^s viij^d / and it requireth at the lest provision of the same charges for iij Monethes, which amountith to Cvj^l xv$^{s\,20}$

Drawn up in April 1535, this is one of several lists of "remembrances" preserved in the papers of Henry VIII's chief minister, Thomas Cromwell. In this case, what we have is a note of actions taken, used as an agenda to structure Cromwell's meetings with Henry VIII. Once discussed, such a list might be signed by the king and filed in Cromwell's "book of remembrance" for later reference; other documents in this category comprised lists of things to be done.[21] The remembrance was thus a form that encompassed the first and second of Jack Goody's principal types of list, the inventory and the shopping list; and that indeed might transition from one form to the other, as a to-do list was repurposed as a memorandum of tasks accomplished.

Ireland, Calais, and Dover; this messenger and that building; ropes, cables, and rigging; pounds, shillings, and pence: the sheer range of subject matter

---

20. Cromwell, "Remembrances," BM Cotton MS Titus B. I. 433r. This note also appears in G. R. Elton, *The Tudor Revolution in Government: Administrative Changes in the Reign of Henry VIII* (Cambridge: Cambridge University Press, 1953), 153, and I have relied heavily on Elton's transcription. When referring to documents viewed in the *State Papers Online 1509–1714* database, as here, I use the folio numbers stamped in print by archivists at the Public Record Office in preference to other numbering systems if available. I also give the title, volume, and entry numbers from Brewer et al., abbreviated as *LP* (J. S. Brewer et al., eds., *Letters and Papers, Foreign and Domestic, of the Reign of Henry VIII, 1509–47,* 1862–1932, 21 vols. and 2 vols. of addenda [Vaduz: Kraus Reprint Ltd, 1965]).

21. On Cromwell's "book of remembrances" and its place in Cromwell's papers, see Diarmaid MacCulloch, *Thomas Cromwell: A Life* (London: Penguin Books, 2018), 2.

and intricate detailing preserved in these documents is all the more impressive when one considers the duties that Thomas Cromwell was performing in Henry VIII's government by 1535, when he was serving both as the king's principal secretary and as Vicegerent and Vicar-General, with authority over the ecclesiastical institutions of the realm. As Geoffrey Elton noted in his classic 1953 account of *The Tudor Revolution in Government,* "Cromwell ... attended personally to the routine of a subordinate office even after he had achieved pre-eminence amongst the king's ministers."[22] Elton's famous thesis was that Cromwell's time as Henry VIII's chief minister saw the beginnings of a distinctively modern form of rationalized state administration, used to put into effect the king's will. The key to this argument was not just Cromwell's mastery of detail or his tireless diligence in office. Elton's conception of Cromwell's transformative role in English history was at its core technical and procedural. For Elton, what underpinned Cromwell's reforms, his restructuring of the king's finances, and ultimately the dissolution of the monasteries and the first phase of the English Reformation in general, was his ability first to intuit the potential for innovation latent in old court offices and then to realize it through an array of bureaucratic innovations. The Tudor revolution in government was, Elton argued, as much as anything a paper revolution. Throughout the 1530s documentary instruments such as the list of remembrances permitted Henry VIII and his chief minister to reshape the nation.

In this section, I want to use *The Tudor Revolution in Government* as a key, hugely influential historical reading that can be used to think through the significance of list-making at a moment of historical transformation. We will be moving, therefore, from pedagogy to politics, with all the realignments in the function of a list that entails. The entries in Cromwell's remembrances are entirely distinct from Erasmus's unpredictable, self-proliferating sequence of copious variations. On one hand, we have something functional, bureaucratic, closely anchored to the administration of the things of this world; on the other, a list endowed with the power to create its own world of significance. At the same time, though, as we track Elton's discussion, I want to show that the themes we identified in our discussion of Erasmus are not left behind. On the contrary: questions of individual creativity, predictability, and control are central to the historiography of the 1530s.

Geoffrey Elton's argument in *The Tudor Revolution in Government* offers a sixteenth-century analogue for what Jack Goody identified in ancient Assyria or Sumer: the affinity between a graphic format and the demands of developing state organization. His discussion proceeds via a series of bureaucratic

---

22. Elton, *Tudor Revolution,* 154.

vignettes. Very often these involve different forms of listwork: Sir Brian Tuke's book of "receipts and paymentes dailly entred and made" as Treasurer of the Chamber;[23] a procedural list, setting down the method for making acquittances in the newly established Court of Augmentations;[24] Thomas Cromwell's careful shaping through multiple drafts of the agenda for a meeting of the privy council in 1533.[25] The 1535 list of "remembrances" quoted above is another of these. In Elton's framing, it speaks to Cromwell's almost superhuman meticulousness and attention to detail. It also helps to advance a larger argument about the shifting nature of state finance and the discrediting of the idea that national expenditure could be identified with the king's personal outlay. It functions as part of a narrative about the role of bureaucratic activity within the emergence of modernity.

That might sound incongruous. Elton's scholarly reputation is that of a master of the archive; his own account of the historian's work, entitled *The Practice of History*, gives primacy to engagement with documentary sources, with large-scale abstractions very much relegated to the back seat.[26] Nonetheless, we can identify some of the key conceptual architecture that organized Elton's work with the English State Papers. For Elton, the transition to a modern form of state administration involved government's decoupling from the sphere of the household. "Where we find administration in and through the household," Elton writes, "there we have medieval government; where there are plentiful signs of emancipation from the household, however mingled they may be with survivals from the past, we may justly suspect the beginnings of a new attitude to government which for want of a better word we call modern."[27] There is nothing new about bureaucracy. But in Elton's historiography, medieval listwork serves a conception of government in which the king's revenues and those of his kingdom are coextensive; in which the king's household is the king's government; and in which any idea of the state is subsumed under the person of the monarch. The modern bureaucratic list, by contrast, operates within an environment where these functions have been distinguished.

That political maturity should involve the discrimination of political life from the life of the household is one of the oldest motifs in Western political theory; it may even be foundational of it, as with the Greek idea that the bar-

---

23. Elton, *Tudor Revolution*, 178.
24. Elton, *Tudor Revolution*, 208.
25. Elton, *Tudor Revolution*, 361–4.
26. G. R. Elton, *The Practice of History* (Oxford: Blackwell, 2002).
27. Elton, *Tudor Revolution*, 19–20.

barian ruler treats the state as his personal possession, as the *polis* does not.[28] It also has its more recent exemplars. Geoffrey Elton was on the whole disparaging about the thought of Max Weber, but as a scholar born in 1921 and educated in Germany until the age of eighteen, it is not implausible that Elton should have encountered at least some of Weber's ideas about the modern administrative state. They certainly offer an analogue for his thinking about the historical effects of bureaucracy.[29] Bureaucracy has a bad name nowadays, and a well-earned one. It is a byword for obfuscation, petty humiliation, and Kafkaesque futility.[30] It is therefore both bracing and a little disorienting to pass from this popular reputation to the judgements of Max Weber in his essay on 'Bureaucracy' concerning the technical superiority of a bureaucratic organization over competing administrative formats. "A strictly bureaucratic administration," Weber writes, "produces an optimal efficiency for precision, speed, clarity, command of case knowledge, continuity, confidentiality, uniformity, and tight subordination. This is in addition to minimization of friction and the costs associated with materials and personnel."[31] What bureaucracy promises is the maximized and regularized realization of the potential latent in the resources (natural, human, or institutional) that it administers. That is not how Thomas Cromwell could ever have put it, of course; but it is very much what Elton's Cromwell understands to be the case. Furthermore, in Weber's thinking early modernity is understood precisely as the period that initiates the turn away from household government towards government that is not dependent upon individual personalities. As administrative business increases and expert knowledge becomes essential to the task of government,

---

28. See, e.g., Brendan Nagle: "It was a commonplace among Greeks that the members of these types of households [non-*polis* households] were slaves because everyone in the state, except the ruler himself, was a slave: 'Among the barbarians all are slaves save one,' said Helen in the play of that name by Euripides, lamenting her fate as a subject of the king of Egypt. The state itself was in the nature of a giant household, a family writ large" (*The Household as the Foundation for Aristotle's Polis* [Cambridge: Cambridge University Press, 2006], 135–6).

29. See Patrick Collinson, "Geoffrey Rudolph Elton (1921–1994)," *Proceedings of the British Academy* 94 (1997): 429–55, here 433, for the claim that Elton "despised and radically misrepresented" Weber. Arthur J. Slavin, "G. R. Elton and His Era: Thirty Years On," *Albion* 15, no. 3 (1983): 207–29, here 222, argues that "the pattern of Professor Elton's reading of the 1530s might easily be expressed in Weberian terms." By contrast, Ian Harris, "Some Origins of a Tudor Revolution," *The English Historical Review* 126, no. 523 (2011): 1355–85, emphasizes William Stubbs's *Constitutional History* and T. F. Tout's *Chapters in the Administrative History of Medieval England* as the key precursors for Elton's thinking on modernity and the household.

30. For a penetrating account see David Graeber, *The Utopia of Rules: On Technology, Stupidity, and the Secret Joys of Bureaucracy* (Brooklyn / London: Melville House, 2015).

31. Max Weber, "Bureaucracy," in *Weber's Rationalism and Modern Society: New Translations on Politics, Bureaucracy, and Social Stratification*, ed. and trans. Tony Waters and Dagmar Waters (Basingstoke: Palgrave Macmillan, 2015), 73–128, here 96.

the monarch can no longer rely on traditional confidantes. He therefore establishes permanent advisory bodies. Weber writes: "'Privy Councils' [*Räte von Haus*] are examples of characteristic transitional phenomena."[32] That is, institutions such as the English Privy Council—the body whose Cromwellian reconstruction is the subject of the fifth chapter of *The Tudor Revolution in Government*—are identified as key staging posts on the way to a fully rational bureaucratic structure.

Like Max Weber, then, and like Ernst Kantorowicz, whose classic study of *The King's Two Bodies* was first published in 1957, four years after *The Tudor Revolution in Government*, Geoffrey Elton is interested in the emergence of the state as a political entity conceivably distinct from the persons who man it. His thesis of governmental revolution is over half a century old now, and has not worn well in every respect. Attacks on his argument since the 1980s and 90s have succeeded in putting questions of household politics—of affect and intimacy—back onto the historical map.[33] Meanwhile, although Diarmaid MacCulloch's recent biography of Thomas Cromwell is presented as a "conscious tribute" to Elton,[34] it nonetheless concludes by arguing that the thesis of administrative revolution has been "dispersed"[35]—although the central importance of Cromwell himself is retained. And yet the argument of *The Tudor Revolution in Government* is more nuanced than Elton's opponents sometimes concede. Let us consider one final list, the "Accompt of Thomas Cromwell," in which Cromwell recorded expenditures and outlays made in the king's service, and from which Elton excerpted as an appendix in the *Tudor Revolution*.[36] These include: £24,606 of "sondry payments . . . for the Affaires of oure saide soueraigne lord the king"; £2,253 "remayning in the Custody and charge of William Body"; £593 lent by Cromwell himself "of his owne moneye"; £2,180 of "*ffynes* for knyghtes Sessid . . . to the kings vse and nat paid."[37] The "Accompt" offers a "view" or abstract drawn from more detailed accounts dealing with payments made in late 1532. Elton uses it and Cromwell's other account books to map the increasing sums of money that he, Cromwell, ended up administering for the purposes of the state. It is a moment that should suggest just how far Elton's account is from a narrative of smoothly advancing

---

32. Weber, "Bureaucracy," 119. "Privy Council" is Tony and Dagmar Waters's translation of "*Räte von Haus*," literally a "house council"; they offer the original in parenthesis.

33. See, e.g., Christopher Coleman and David Starkey, eds., *Revolution Reassessed: Revisions in the History of Tudor Government and Administration* (Oxford: Clarendon Press, 1986).

34. MacCulloch, *Cromwell*, 3.

35. MacCulloch, *Cromwell*, 543.

36. See Appendix II A in Elton, *Tudor Revolution*. For Elton's discussion, see 140–50.

37. Cromwell, "Accounts," SP 1/72, f. 136r–v.

bureaucratic depersonalization. Cromwell's activity in relation to the king's finances derived from his position as master of the king's jewels, acquired on April 12, 1532. This was a minor household office, dating back to the reign of Richard II, which he exploited in unorthodox directions. "In Cromwell's hands," Elton writes, "the mastership of the jewels became one of the leading financial ministries of state through which Cromwell rivalled, and in a measure superseded, the treasurer of the chamber as the head of a standing department which financed wars and garrisons and paid the better part of day-to-day expenditure on embassies, reward, buildings, naval affairs, and a dozen other purposes."[38] It developed into an office in which Cromwell could act "in personal charge of money for the king."[39] That is, Cromwell's list of accounts is part of a story about an improvisatory genius capable of grasping the unexploited potential latent in a traditional office. Geoffrey Elton's account of the Tudor revolution in government may involve a movement away from the personal towards the administrative state, but, in a counterintuitive twist, the mechanisms that drive this process of historical transformation are themselves highly individualistic and contingent. As Elton says at the start of his book: "It is one of the paradoxes of sixteenth-century history that a dynasty, which saw the personal power of the monarchy at its height and the importance of court life greater than ever, could also transcend the purely personal view of the royal duty and treat England and the nation as the true basis of the state."[40] Cromwell's lists are bureaucratic, individualistic, monarchical, impersonal—all at once.

If *The Tudor Revolution in Government* remains compelling history, it is in part because of this paradoxical knot, which allows Geoffrey Elton to give an account of the relationship between the historical actor and wider historical processes that doesn't simply absorb the former into the latter or vice versa. It allows the minutiae of administration—such as Cromwell's lists—to play a key role in Elton's historiography, as he moves between the realm of the particular and general historical claims. We can note, too, that if Elton's vision is paradoxical, it is also tacitly ironic. One thing that Cromwell's work at the heart of Tudor government suggests is that "bureaucratic creativity" is anything but an oxymoron; yet to chart the emergence of the modern state as a structure of depersonalized paperwork is also to gesture towards a comprehensively administered society in which the genius of a Thomas Cromwell might be radically constrained, or indeed never find any expression at all. In

---

38. Elton, *Tudor Revolution*, 111.
39. Elton, *Tudor Revolution*, 140.
40. Elton, *Tudor Revolution*, 4.

the historical long term, just as in his service to Henry VIII, we might judge that Thomas Cromwell worked to his own destruction.

We are maybe now in a position to see that the questions that lie at the heart of Geoffrey Elton's portrait of Tudor government are not entirely dissimilar from those that structure Lisa Jardine and Antony Grafton's contribution to the historiography of Tudor humanism; and to map the terms on which the Cromwellian list might resemble its Erasmian counterpart. In each case, we are being asked to consider to what extent processes of regimentation and reorganization might either be bound up with, or exist in antithesis to, a creativity that is fundamentally unpredictable. Can this generative principle be harnessed, or is it something that the desire for ever-more-meticulous close supervision of human action must ultimately begin to snuff out? The final panel in our triptych of sixteenth-century list-makers offers a different view of these questions, exploring the imaginative dimensions of listing as the state's energies are directed to the task of reconstructing a competing system of institutionalized control.

THE REFORMER'S LISTS: JOHN BALE'S *KING JOHAN*

What might a literature of administrative reformation look like? Some time around 1536, the scholar John Bale renounced his vows as a Carmelite friar, married, and embarked on a new career producing Protestant drama. By 1537, he was clearly operating within the sphere of Thomas Cromwell's patronage and in the interests of evangelical factions within the Henrician government. *King Johan,* the history play that is my primary focus in this section, was almost certainly performed in Thomas Cranmer's household on Christmas 1538. Bale offers an opportunity to examine the literary and imaginative aspects of Cromwell's project for reform. His interest, furthermore, is not just ideological but also formal, because Bale's Protestantism exists intertwined with an obsessive impulse towards list-making. "There is no doubt," writes Honor McCusker, "that Bale was a collector all his life; few men have suffered more acutely from the disease."[41] John Bale might, in fact, be the most committed maker of lists in all of early Tudor literature. His early historical research involved a survey of Carmelite authors. His records of British writers, such as the *Scriptorum illustrium maioris Britannie catalogus,* are essentially annotated lists. We know of many of Bale's own works only from the four sep-

---

41. Honor McCusker, *John Bale: Dramatist and Antiquary* (Baltimore: J. H. Furst, 1942), 29.

arate lists of his plays that he compiled during his lifetime.[42] And his plays are full of lists—none more so than *King Johan*, which offers an allegorical representation of the conflicts between crown and papacy in thirteenth-century England. *King Johan* propagandizes for Cromwell's reforms. It also offers a surprisingly rich account of the affects elicited by this attempt to overthrow the past, and the play's lists are central to its combination of polemical intent and emotional complexity.

Early in *King Johan,* Clergy lists the different religious orders that flourish under the Pope's authority:

> Munkes, chanons and fryeres, most excellent dyvynis,
> As Grandy Montensers and other Benedictyns,
> Premonstratensers, Bernardes and Gylbertynys,
> Jacobytes, Mynors, Whyght Carmes and Augustynis,
> Sanbonites, Cluniackes, with holy Carthusyans,
> Heremytes and Auncors, with most myghty Rodyans,
> Crucifers, Lucifers, Brigettes, Ambrosyanes,
> Stellifers, Ensifers, with Purgatoryanes,
> Sophyanes, Indianes and Camaldulensers,
> Jesuytes, Joannytes, with Clarimontensers,
> Clarynes and Columbynes, Templers, Newe Ninivytes,
> Rufyanes, Tercyanes, Lorytes and Lazarytes,
> Hungaryes, Teutonyckes, Hospitelers, Honofrynes,
> Basyles and Bonhams, Sclavons and Celestynes,
> Paulynes, Hieronymytes, and Monkes of Josaphathes Valleye,
> Fulygynes, Flamynes, with Bretherne of the Black Alleye,
> Donates and Dimysynes, with Canons of S. Marke,
> Vestals and Monyals, a worlde to heare them barke,
> Abbottes and doctors, with bysshoppes and cardynales,
> Arche decons and pristes, as to ther fortune falls.[43]

In his essay in this volume, James Simpson will consider Bale's lists as instruments of iconoclastic polemic. How does this function relate to bureaucratic listing of the kind that interested Geoffrey Elton? We might think of Clergy's list in terms of the paperwork generated by Thomas Cromwell's office as Vice-

---

42. See John Bale, *The Complete Plays of John Bale*, ed. Peter Happé (Cambridge: D. S. Brewer, 1985–6), 1; 8–9.

43. Bale, *Plays*, ll. 441–60. Quotations from *King Johan* are taken from volume 1 of this edition, and refer to line numbers when quoting the text, page when referencing Happé's editorial matter.

Gerent in Spirituals, held from 1535. Bale came into possession of some of the lists generated at this time; in his autobiographical text *The vocacyon of Johan Bale*, he states that "I haue the registre of ye visitacions of ye cloysters of Englande."[44] It is not implausible that Cromwell's office might have held, somewhere, a complete list of all the religious orders operating in England and Wales. But Clergy's list is not really an inventory of this sort. It is not exhaustive. It is not organized. It could contain three items fewer, or six more, and have roughly the same effect. Most importantly, several of its items may be fictitious. The Benedictines and Gilbertines and the Carthusians are straightforward enough. The Lucifers sound intriguing, but the play's editor Peter Happé suggests they were a real monastic order founded by Lucifer, Bishop of Cagliari in the fifth century. Nonetheless, as the list progresses, it is increasingly pocketed with what Happé judges to be obscure or fantastical entries. The Flamynes "are perhaps included to suggest pagan origin for monks"; the Donates were an "ancient sect"; while the Clarimontensers, the Lorytes, the Dimysynes, and the Canons of Saint Mark remain unidentified.[45]

In short, this is not an administrative list, and the point is not to be able to place every reference within it. Instead, it achieves its effect by setting the bureaucratic function of the list in opposition to its disintegrative, chaotic properties. Seemingly aiming at the form of the exhaustive catalogue, in reality it proceeds under its own steam, laced together not by any administrative or classificatory logic but by patterns of rhyme, alliteration, and assonance. Consider the frequency with which the first two items in a line in particular form a sonic pair, as with the Stellifers and the Ensifers, or the Jesuits and the Johannites. Crucifers, Lucifers, Brigettes, and Ambrosians: as Clergy proceeds through his speech, the monastic orders are reduced to sound effects, like items in a nursery-rhyme. Bale was too old to have benefitted directly from an Erasmian education, but he understood perfectly well how a list might be possessed of a ludic, self-generating character. In *King Johan*, this playfulness is harnessed to bitter satirical intent. Proliferating via a logic of aural pleasure and association, the religious orders are voided of meaning; repackaged as nonsense verse, they are presented to Bale's audience as all and equally pointless. So many orders, and to so little good effect. Away with them!

Bale's intent is clear. Yet behind the scenes, Bale's catalogue of monastic orders is charged with complex affects, although in ways that may be ultimately indecipherable. As Thora Balslev Blatt has shown, Clergy's list derives from the historical studies of monasticism that Bale had begun to produce

---

44. John Bale, *The vocacyon of Johan Bale* ([Wesel?: J. Lambrecht for Hugh Singleton?], 1553), B6v.

45. Bale, *Plays*, 1:10–11.

before his conversion. A manuscript of notes on the Carmelite order, drawn up in Bale's hand and held in the Bodleian Library, contains a catalogue of religious orders that feeds into the list in *King Johan*: "Ordo hospitaliorum sancti Antonij sub regula sancti Augustini / Ordo sancti Lazari sub regula Sancti Augustini."[46] Clergy's list originates in the scholarly activities of a shameful, unregenerate past. It was also a speech that kept growing beyond its point of first composition. *King Johan* exists in a single manuscript, held in the Huntington Library, the history of which is not entirely clear. It was first copied by a scribe around 1538, and subsequently revised by Bale himself, who inserted lines and added new sheets, ultimately canceling the ending of the play in favor of an extended plotline and new denouement. This was a process of revision extending over two decades (the final version of the play culminates with references to Elizabeth I). In its initial phases, however, it seems to date from the period following Thomas Cromwell's fall from power and execution in 1540, when Bale fled to the continent in order to avoid a resurgent theological conservatism under Henry VIII. It was in this period, Peter Happé conjectures, that Clergy's original list was expanded to more than twice its original length, with lines 447–58, comprising forty extra monastic orders, added in the margin.

Clergy's list is thus the product of a deep psychic knot, one that draws together Bale's first historical researches, their reconfiguration at the point of Bale's conversion and the disavowal of his identity as a Carmelite friar (the "Whyght Carmes," name checked at line 444), and then extends into the period of religious reaction that followed Cromwell's fall from power—a period, now, of ungodly Protestantism, in which it became clear just how resistant to change some of the practices and institutions targeted by reformers might be. There are layers upon layers of revisions of attitude sedimented in this speech. What effect *does* adding to Clergy's list have? It is not that any single element is essential to the meaning of the speech. On the contrary, they could be swapped in or out, almost at will. But for the list to more than double in size must make it feel somehow weightier, more intransigent, more monolithic: more like the administrative inventory of actually existing institutions that it in some sense parodies. Viewed from the anxious perspective of the 1540s, this is a list of institutions and offices that offsets a gleeful collapse into absurdity against intimations of the persistence of a past that was proving less repudiable than Bale and others like him had hoped it might be during

---

46. See Thora Balslev Blatt, *The Plays of John Bale: A Study of Ideas, Technique and Style* (Copenhagen: G. E. C. Gad Publishers, 1968), Appendix I, 235–38. The plate facing p. 8 offers a reproduction of a folio from this manuscript.

the years of Thomas Cromwell's ascendancy. King John, we remember, dies a failure in Bale's play.

Clergy's speech sets the tone for the other lists in *King Johan*, the effects of which are often just a little bit more complex than they need to be. They also often constitute additions: Bale's play gets more list-ridden as he revises it. Here, for instance, is Sedition's list of relics, the final fifteen lines of which constitute an expansion of the original play-text:

> Here ys fyrst a bone of the blyssyd Trynyte,
> A dram of the tord of swete Seynt Barnabe;
> Here ys a feddere of good Seynt Myhelles wyng,
> A toth of Seynt Twyde, a pece of Davyds harpe stryng,
> The good blood of Haylys, and owre blyssyd ladys mylke,
> A lowse of Seynt Fraunces in this same crymsen sylke,
> A scabbe of Saynt Job, a nayle of Adams too,
> A maggott of Moyses, with a fart of Saynt Fandigo;
> Here is a fygge leafe, and a grape of Noes vyneyearde,
> A bede of Saynt Blythe with the bracelet of a berewarde,
> The Devyll that was hatcht in maistre Iohan Shornes bote,
> That the tree of Jesse ded plucke up by the roote;
> Here ys the lachett of swett Seynt Thomas shewe,
> A rybbe of Seynt Rabart with the huckyll bone of a Jewe;
> Here ys a joynt, of Darvell Gathyron
> Be sydes other bonys and relyckes many one.
> (1215–30)

Adam's nail, Moses's maggot, Saint Fandango's farts: this time the list is fantastical and obscene. Its scurrilities aim to skewer the materialism and implausibility of late medieval relic culture. Developing a tendency in Clergy's speech, its entries are dominated by imaginary items. Significantly, though, it comes to a head with a real-life object of veneration, the wooden statue of the sixth-century monk Derfel Gardarn, which was publicly burned on Cromwell's orders in 1538 alongside the friar John Forest.[47] Sedition's list thus moves from the fictional to the literal, in order to argue for their equivalence. A devil hatched in a boot, or the image of a Welsh saint: what's the difference? Brutal judicial remedies for this plague of fantasies hover at the edges of awareness.

Primed to collapse into one another, the fantastical and the everyday constitute important conceptual poles in Bale's writing, and it is notable that

---

47. See MacCulloch, *Cromwell*, 459–60.

elsewhere in *King Johan* the play's lists take on a much more mundane and documentary character. Dissymulacyon lists all the offices instituted by Usurpid Powre (991–1010) in another insertion comprising three rhyme royal stanzas, and although the intent driving the speech is again satirical—Dissymulacyon openly admits that monastic orders were instituted "to corrupt cyties and townes" (995)—much of its detail is simply a realistic accounting of offices and practices within the Catholic Church: doctors, monks, and canons; friars, matins, and Mass; rosaries and pardons and Latin and fasting and blessings. Meanwhile, Treason offers a parallel account of the "ceremonies" of the church (1828–38: another insertion). Here we read of "crowchynges, with kyssynges, and settynge up of lyghtes, / Bearynge them in processyon, and fastynges upon their nyghtes" (1835–36), and also of "Your fyers, your waters, your oyles, your aulters, your ashes, / Your candlestyckes, your cruettes, your salte" (1829–30). The list is densely material, aggressively desublimatory. This is all there is to it, Bale implies: crouching and carrying, candles and salt. Household stuff, nothing more.

It is surely no coincidence that one of the key early pieces of criticism on Bale's play, "The Roman Rite in Bale's *King John*" by Edwin Shepard Miller, should be dominated by a list of Roman Catholic practices and rituals— around 107 items in all, ranging from Mass and matins, lauds, prime, and vespers to shrines, tonsure, torches, the triple crown, vestments, and wax: a great, wall-like block of text that dominates the second page of Miller's article. These are all, Miller comments, the means by which "the Church prostitutes its rites to dominion over the state."[48] They function through their infiltration of the everyday lives of Catholic believers: an intricately detailed, utterly absorbing universe of practice and meaning within which divinely sanctioned royal authority can be usurped by its demonic Roman Other. "Latin epistles, Latin gospels, Latin sermons, lections, offertories, the paternoster, psalms, sequences, the *Te Deum,* and tracts. The litany of the saints. Rites for the dead: vespers, matins, Mass, and burial. Prayers for the dead and devices to promote them: bequests, legacies, mortuaries, the Mass of Scala Caelo, perpetuities, and trentals": Miller's list can, and does, go on.

What effect is produced by this great heaping up of listed items? In a famous essay, Roland Barthes once identified the insertion of superfluous detail into a fictional narrative as productive of a "reality effect." "Insignificant gestures, transitory attitudes, insignificant objects, redundant words . . . The pure and simple 'representation' of the 'real,' the naked relation of 'what is' (or

---

48. Edwin Shepard Miller, "The Roman Rite in Bale's *King John*," *PMLA* 64, no. 4 (1949): 802–22, here 803.

has been) thus appears as a resistance to meaning," he writes.[49] The lists that dominate Bale's play, and Miller's article on it, don't assemble purely contingent details in quite the way Barthes describes—on the contrary, their entries tend to be invested with ritualistic and symbolic significance, which Bale hopes to dispel—but their overall effect is perhaps not dissimilar. Bale's lists evoke a world. In a bizarre way, with its emphasis upon the complete institutional saturation by the Roman Church of the everyday life of its victims and the all-encompassing character of the universe it offers them, *King Johan* reads like a Protestant version of Eamon Duffy's classic of revisionist Tudor history, *The Stripping of the Altars*. Duffy's argument is animated by a kind of pragmatism. The worldview of late medieval Catholicism was, it is argued against its critics, fit for purpose. "Vigorous, adaptable,"[50] it offered a coherent and anthropologically satisfactory account of the universe for its believers, extending from birth to marriage and death and beyond. So too in *King Johan*. The ideological system of Roman Catholicism structures believers' experience of time. It resides in the material reality of objects. It is written into the fabric of day-to-day life. The "real-life" entries in Bale's lists catalogue the properties of this virtual reality; their imaginary items and absurdities aim to disrupt and defamiliarize it. Flamens, vestals, Saint Francis's louse, and Moses's maggot—these are like glitches in the matrix, flickers of surreal incongruity and scabrous humour that query the verisimilitude of the illusion. Bale's contempt is palpable. But one cannot but sense, too, the insidiousness, the sheer ubiquity, and the institutional weight of what he is fighting against. There is nothing opposed to his literary project here, but once again the list reveals unexpected dimensions within the desire to administer and reconstruct. John Bale is the great bureaucrat of a world he aims to sweep aside.

CONCLUSION

"To reformers of the sixteenth century it was a truism that in order to build it was necessary to destroy." Thus Margaret Aston in her great, posthumous survey of English iconoclasm, *Broken Idols of the English Reformation*.[51] John Bale wouldn't disagree. Indeed all the lists surveyed in this essay occupy the

---

49. Roland Barthes, "The Reality Effect," in *The Rustle of Language*, trans. Richard Howard (Oxford: Basil Blackwell, 1986), 141–8, here 146.

50. Eamon Duffy, *The Stripping of the Altars: Traditional Religion in England c. 1400–c.1500*, 2nd ed. (New Haven / London: Yale University Press, 2005), 5.

51. Margaret Aston, *Broken Idols of the English Reformation* (Cambridge: Cambridge University Press, 2016), 17.

territory Aston's comment identifies, marked by a dialectic of creation and destruction. Lists that inventory the old prior to its demolition; lists that direct resources towards the construction of something new: these are very much the administrative operations of the list as explored by Jack Goody. What I have tried to add to his account is a suggestion that the functionality that connects the list to wider historical movements need not be purely a question of gathering, sorting, and organization. It can also be a matter of play and paradox, of an imaginative dimension whose presence can be identified even in Thomas Cromwell's most brutally instrumental documentation. This too, I argue, is a key characteristic of listing. The list is a form that ties together the impulse towards methodical organization with the potential for moments that cannot be predicted within any system of protocols for inclusion and exclusion. As such it opens out to view the complex operations of the gratuitous and the unpredictable within even the most brutally disciplinary—the most coercively enlisting—of historical processes.

CHAPTER 10

Reformation Lists

Syntax, the Sacred, and the Production of Junk

JAMES SIMPSON

How much deceleration can a single sentence bear before it stops being a sentence? The multi-action force of syntax normally does at least two things: it takes us along a narrative road, *and* it proactively plugs syntactic holes in that road even as we travel along it. Syntax, that is, keeps us moving steadily forward along the road of a sentence by filling potential holes in the road. Need an adjective for the noun "tree" coming up, for rhythmic and/or conceptual reasons? Here! quickly throw "green" into that potential hole, and just keep this sentence going! Or, a good deal more urgently, need a main verb? Here it is! With the syntactic hole-filler working at full tilt, we avoid the retardation of our conceptual voyage through every sentence.

Every now and again, however, the efficient, propulsive force of syntax is stymied. Every now and again, that is, the syntax machine suffers a breakdown of sorts. Perhaps it fails to supply the necessary main verb, in which case it breaks down altogether. Alternatively, it fills the pothole, to be sure, but goes into overdrive as it does so; it fills the hole so energetically as to produce an obstructive mound of surplus syntactic junk on the road. We do not end up with a smooth road surface that permits fluid, forward syntactic drive; on the contrary, we end up with an obstructive list plumb in the middle of our way. We end up slowly having to negotiate piles of syntactic refuse. Our voyage is slowed down as the sentence must, unavoidably, change down syntactic gears in order to deal with much less tractable road conditions of suddenly obstructive, appositively posed information (i.e., lists). At worst, we move into neutral and are unable to move forward at all, stuck by the obstructive junk piles.

The classic form of syntactic junk is the list. Many lists are purposive, such as the much-maligned laundry or shopping list. Those lists are useful; they do not slow sentences down, since they were never part of sentences in the first place. They are also useful because they are examples of the complete list. The complete and independent list offers comfort—everything is, or soon will be, under control; the mess of the world will be set to rights. With the help of the shopping list, the gaps in the kitchen will be filled.

Lists within sentences are, by contrast, threatening. Those lists are the potential enemy to fluid, forward moving syntax. They pose an obstruction that has us moving into neutral, with something that makes us very uneasy—a potentially unfinishable sentence. To be sure, in the legal prose of a contract or statute, the laborious intra-sentence list might offer comfort, as it covers every eventuality. Or the complete catalogue of tree species in a garden, such as we find in Chaucer's *Parlement of Foules*, for example, offers ecological reassurance.[1] Complete lists that form a contained part of narrative, such as the muster of navies in Homer's *Iliad*, imply unified purpose from multiple sources.[2] There is no comfort to be derived, however, from the potentially unfinishable intra-sentence list, the list that could, in principle, carry on *ad infinitum*. Such lists often lurk on the edges of narratives that do make it home, but only by managing to get past the potholes of gaping lists.[3] In this essay I look, then, to

---

1.
The bilder ook, and eek the hardy asshe;	*serviceable for building*
The piler elm, the cofre unto careine;	*serviceable for supports; coffin*
The boxtree piper; holm to whippes lasshe;	*boxtree for pipe making; holly bush*
The sailing fir; the cipres, deth to pleine;	*fir tree good for making boats; lament*
The sheter ew, the asp for shaftes pleine;	*yew tree good for archery equipment*
The olyve of pees, and eek the drunken vine,	
The victor palm, the laurer to devine.	*prophesy*

Geoffrey Chaucer, *The Parlement of Foules*, in *Geoffrey Chaucer, The Oxford Chaucer*, ed. Christopher Cannon and James Simpson (Oxford: Oxford University Press, forthcoming), ll. 176–82. All citations from the works of Chaucer in this essay are drawn from this edition. For tree catalogues, see the essay by Ingo Berensmeyer in this volume. For anxieties about the open-ended list in early modern writing, see the essay by Alex Davis in this volume.

2. Homer, *Iliad*, ed. William F. Wyatt, rev. ed., 2 vols. (Cambridge, MA: Harvard University Press, 2014), 1:2.494–75.

3. Three of many possible examples: (1) Bunyan's description of the list of things on sale in Vanity Fair in *Pilgrim's Progress* (John Bunyan, *The Pilgrim's Progress*, ed. David Hawkes [New York: Barnes and Noble, 2005], 102)—for discussion of this list, see James Simpson, *Permanent Revolution: The Reformation and the Illiberal Roots of Liberalism* (Cambridge, MA: Belknap Press of Harvard University Press, 2019), 195–96; (2) Swift's list of the elements of war, and of

the list, but not just any list: I look to the open-ended list that forms part of a sentence, and I calibrate the effect of deceleration that a potentially unfinishable list imposes on sentences.

The topic of lists is huge. By looking only to potentially unfinishable lists within sentences, we delimit the huge topic of the list. Even with that delimitation, however, the topic remains too big for one essay. I therefore narrow it in a further way. I will look to intra-sentence lists in revolutionary periods. Such periods are especially revealing for the obstructive list mound, or what I have been calling the retarding, syntactic junk of the list. Why? Because revolutionary moments always face a challenge of cultural road cleaning. The syntactic road of the revolutionary regime will inevitably be obstructed, that is, by piles of junk. The revolution must redescribe the entire material and institutional apparatus of the *ancien régime* as bric-à-brac. What was numinous and what upheld the symbolic order of the old dispensation must be visibly taken apart. One way of managing that undoing is precisely to undo the syntax, both the literal and the metaphorical syntax, of that discarded dispensation, so as to undo its structure of meaning. One does that in various ways, most obviously by the material dismantling of the old order through iconoclasm.

There is also literal syntactic work to be done. One does that work principally by apposition: all items of the repudiated order are set in syntactic apposition, so rendering them each equal with each other. And as they are made equal, so too are they made meaningless. Perhaps syntactic equality, indeed, is part of the very definition of junk—endless piles of stuff, each item of which is equally meaningless and equally useless. Sentence-threatening lists that itemize new-made detritus of this kind are, needless to say, potentially infinite. And such lists are, as we shall see, especially frequent in moments of sudden cultural upheaval.

The cultural revolution I have in mind is the beginning of the sixteenth-century Reformation in England, across the 1530s and 40s. Negotiating the new-made detritus was not easy work. The syntactic machines of cultural hygiene and road cleaning went into overdrive as they suddenly produced so much cultural rubbish on the sixteenth-century syntactic roads. Objects that had been considered sacred suddenly needed to be recycled or disposed of. The objects designated for recycling needed to be literally listed lest they be swept forever into oblivion, such as the book lists of English authors com-

---

the potential assailants of European existence, in *Gulliver's Travels* (Jonathan Swift, *Gulliver's Travels*, ed. Albert J. Rivero [New York: Norton, 2002], 209; 233); and (3) Joyce's plethora of lists in *Ulysses*, especially in Episode 17 (James Joyce, *Ulysses: A Critical and Synoptic Edition*, ed. Hans Walter Gabler, 3 vols. [New York: Garland, 1984], 3:1455–633).

piled by John Bale and John Leland from the books dispersed from monastic libraries.[4]

Other objects were not regarded as in any way precious, and needed to be transformed into detritus. The list of such objects was potentially infinite, and the destructive act of transforming the objects into detritus was in part syntactic. By setting the list of such objects *within* sentences, the work of devaluation was effected. Polemicists piled up the syntactic junk deliberately, so as to destroy the meaning—the "sentence" if you will, of the old order. Especially brilliant literary artists could make art of waste within the sentence.

MESS AND MANAGEMENT: SYNTAX AND HISTORY

I begin with two passages on either side of our chosen period by way of getting the formal properties of our subject into sharp focus. The first, from Chaucer's *House of Fame*, illustrates the challenges of the intra-sentence list. The second, from Milton's *Paradise Lost*, models syntax in its maximally efficient operation, utterly determined to avoid the obstructive list.

Chaucer's narrator in the *House of Fame* (early 1370s) describes the House of Rumor as a porous construction into which crowds news of infinitely various kinds. He attempts to enumerate the different kinds of news that ends up there thus:

And by day, in every tyde,	*at all times*
Ben al the dores opened wide,	
And by night, echoon unshet;	*each one left open*
Ne porter ther is non to let	*nor is there any porter to hinder*
No maner tidings in to pace;	*to come in*
Ne never reste is in that place,	
That hit nis fild ful of tidinges,	*it is not filled*
Other loude, or of whispringes;	*cries*
And, over alle the houses angles,	*nooks and corners*
Is ful of rouninges and of jangles	*whisperings . . . chatterings*
Of werres, of pees, of mariages,	*wars*
Of reste, of labour, of viages,	*voyages*
Of abood, of deeth, of life,	*waiting*

---

4. For which see James Simpson, "Ageism: Leland, Bale and the Laborious Start of English Literary History, 1350–1550," *New Medieval Literatures* 1 (1997): 213–35, and further references. See also Jennifer Summit, *Memory's Library: Medieval Books in Early Modern England* (Chicago: University of Chicago Press, 2008).

Of love, of hate, acorde, of strife,	*harmony . . . conflict*
Of loos, of lore, and of winninges,	*fame . . . loss*
Of hele, of sekenesse, of bildinges,	*health . . . sickness*
Of faire windes, and eek of tempestes,	
Of qualme of folk, and eek of bestes;	*disease*
Of divers transmutaciouns	*different vicissitudes*
Of estats, and eek of regiouns;	*classes . . . countries*
Of trust, of drede, of jelousie,	*fear*
Of wit, of winninge, of folie;	*wisdom*
Of plentee, and of greet famine,	
Of chepe, of derth, and of ruine;	*scarcity . . . dearth . . . ruin*
Of good or mis governement,	
Of fir, of divers accident.	*varied happenstance*[5]

(ll. 1951–76)

This sentence, to adapt the quip about an over-open mind, is so open that it needs to be closed for repairs. The list could, clearly, carry on *ad infinitum*, since there is almost no conceptual limitation in entry here, except that all this news is earthly: tidings of the micro ("rouninges and jangles") are mixed indiscriminately with news of macro significance ("Of werres, of pees").[6] The doors stand open day and night, and there is no porter discriminating who should and should not enter. The fact that the list ends with news of "divers accident" is appropriate, since the randomness of the list's non-organization is clearly designed to mirror the wholly unpredictable randomness of earthly experience. The list is not at all aggressive, but it exhibits what we shall see is the key formal marker of the aggressive list: apposition. The appositive elements are also linked, and equalized, by anaphora. Each element beginning with "Of" stands in apposition with each other such element (forty-two in all), fulfilling exactly the same grammatical function as an adjectival phrase dependent on a single "ful." And almost each of these elements begins with "of," producing a very long anaphoric sequence.

The resultant sentence is in a kind of trouble. The architectural features of the house might be expected to organize and hierarchize memory systems, in

---

5. Geoffrey Chaucer, *House of Fame*, in *Geoffrey Chaucer, The Oxford Chaucer*. For a fuller discussion of the lists in the *House of Fame*, see the essay by Wolfram R. Keller in this volume.

6. For Chaucer's sharp awareness of the potentially overwhelming infinitude of terms—and especially of technical terms—in lists, see his *Canon's Yeoman's Tale*, ll. 857–59: "To tellen al wold passen any bible / That owher is; wherfore, as for the beste / Of al thes names now wol I me reste."

the manner of ancient mnemonic techniques.⁷ But the doors and room shapes of this architectural confection, which is sixty miles long (l. 1979), scatter the contents of the house so as to defeat memory: the doors are wide open and there are plenty of "angles," or corners, which small "jangles" will occupy. The syntax of the sentence mirrors the breakdown of that filing system, since the syntax is very simple, but helplessly overloaded on a single syntactic foundation, the single main verb "is." The resultant syntax is coordinated (another key formal feature of the list, along with apposition and anaphora). The syntax and the formal features of the sentence, that is, display helplessness and lack of control. The items of news have the agency, whereas the sentence that tries to describe them is passive and infinitely plastic. It does not itself constitute a news agent.

Compare that, if you will, with the opening of Milton's *Paradise Lost* (1674), where we see the extreme opposite syntactic operations in action:

> Of Mans first disobedience, and the fruit
> Of that forbidden tree whose mortal taste
> Brought death into the world and all our woe
> With loss of *Eden,* till one greater Man
> Restore us and regain the blissful seat
> Sing Heav'nly Muse, that on the secret top
> Of *Oreb,* or of *Sinai* didst inspire
> That shepherd, who first taught the chosen seed,
> In the beginning, how the heav'ns and earth
> Rose out of *Chaos.*⁸
>
> (ll. 1–10)

The whole of world and of salvation history is embedded in this single sentence: the formation of the cosmos itself from Chaos at the beginning of time is encapsulated in the final line and a half; the Second Coming of Christ at the end of time in lines 4–5; between those events chronologically, the Fall is registered in lines 1–4, and the introduction of the Mosaic Law in line 8. Formation of clear shapes from chaos informs not only line 10, but the entire sentence, indeed, since it manages not only to isolate the key stages of salvation history, but also to place them in tense and dynamic historical relation with each other: the fall of Adam and Eve in Eden is addressed by Moses on Oreb, and will be finally resolved by Christ at the end of time; in the meanwhile, in

---

7. For the *House of Fame* as a memory machine, see Rebecca Davis, "Fugitive Poetics in Chaucer's *House of Fame,*" *Studies in the Age of Chaucer* 37 (2015): 101–32.

8. John Milton, *Paradise Lost,* ed. Gordon Teskey (New York: Norton, 2005).

the now of the poem's utterance, the Holy Spirit must inspire Milton, just as it inspired Moses.

The astonishingly powerful and satisfying effect of this sentence is produced by exceptionally muscular syntax. Hypotaxis, all subject to a single, commanding imperative ("Sing"), sets the vast historical process of past, present, and future into dynamic and intelligible relation. There is no chance whatsoever of the sentence moving out from under the control of that subordinated syntax: within subordinated clauses there are examples of coordinated pairs ("and the Fruit," "and all our woe," "or of *Sinai*"), but those syntactic escape routes are resolutely closed once the key elements are fully enumerated.

In sum, the formal features of the passage from Milton stand at the opposite extreme from the formal features of the Chaucer passage: the syntax of the Milton passage is dominated by hypotaxis; appositional units and anaphora are kept to a minimum. Potential lists are ended with a maximum of two elements (i.e., they do not become lists). Under each of these heads—apposition, anaphora, hypotactic syntax—the *House of Fame* passage manifests the opposite features. The resultant effect of the Milton passage is also, predictably, the opposite of that of the passage from Chaucer: the Chaucerian narrator emerges as the passive servant of his sentence and his scene, while Milton emerges as the commanding master of his sentence and vast scene—so much the master, indeed, that he can command the Holy Spirit. We shall observe that weakening of subject in the polemical Reformation examples we are about to consider, where the diminution of subject is deliberate and polemical.

REVOLUTIONARY MESS MANAGEMENT IN SIXTEENTH-CENTURY ENGLAND

With these formal features in focus, then, I turn to our principal subject, aggressive intra-sentence lists in revolutionary periods, and in particular in sixteenth-century English Reformation polemic. As we address the syntax of the list, we need to bring the question of freshly defined detritus into focus.

All literary works and periods can be redescribed as recycling and waste plants, taking up the materials of the past and either repurposing them for further use in the present, or else jettisoning them altogether as waste. Examples of rejected literary waste are easy to spot in many works of literature (Dante's Hell is an obvious example), no less than the evidence of recycling (an ubiquitous phenomenon, but Dante's *Commedia*, again, is a prime example).[9] This

---

9. Thus, of any number of examples of waste underlined as waste in the *Commedia*: the citation of *dolce stil nuovo* poetry by Francesca in *Inferno*, Canto 5.100–5; for recycling, see, for

routine cultural processing comes under especial pressure, however, in revolutionary moments, for reasons we observed in our introduction: the entire material and textual apparatus, and especially the sacred apparatus, of the *ancien régime* has suddenly become junk, or, even more challengingly, must now be described as such.

Take, for example, the *locus classicus* of culture destruction in the West, St. Augustine's *City of God* (early fifth century CE). Augustine zeroes in on the sites of most intense hope in any society (e.g., childbirth, grain production), and pitilessly analyzes the pantheon enlisted by polytheists to ensure success. His analysis is so relentless and becomes so absurdly precise that the entire system starts to disintegrate on account of its complexity (one god for the grain, another god for the chaff, and so on), with each name emphasized etymologically (e.g., *Nodotus* from *nodosus,* the adjectival form of *nodus,* knot) so as to underline that these supposed gods are in fact no more than mere words. Herewith an abbreviated account of Augustine's treatment of polytheistic grain protection:

> Nor could they even find a single Segetia who was worthy to be entrusted once for all with the grain in the fields (*segetes*), but as long as the seed was under ground they chose to have the goddess Seia in charge, then when it was above ground and moving toward harvest, the goddess Segetia, and when the grain was harvested and stored away, they gave the goddess Tutulina the job of guarding it safely.
>
> Who would not suppose that this Segetia was competent to care for the crop all the way from its grassy start to the ripe and solid grain in the ear? But that was not enough for men who were so enamoured of a multitude of gods that each wretched soul became the harlot of a throng of demons because she scorned the chaste embrace of the one true God. So they put Proserpina in charge of germinating seeds, the god Nodotus in charge of the joints and knots of the stems, the goddess Volutina in charge of the sheaths of the follicles, and the goddess Patelana when the sheaths open so that the ears may emerge.[10]

The aggressive list-maker is at a huge advantage promoting monotheism over the multiplicity of polytheism. Multiplicity is vulnerable against the forceful simplicity of the one; cultural multiplicity produces lists. Sixteenth-century

---

striking example, Dante's citation of Virgil's Dido (*Aeneid* 4.23) as he sees Beatrice at the summit of Purgatory (*Purgatorio* 30.48).

10. Augustine of Hippo, *City of God*, ed. D. Wiesen et al., 7 vols. (Cambridge, MA: Harvard University Press, 1957), Book 4.8, 2:31–3.

new-made Protestants saw themselves very much in the position of St. Augustine, reasserting as they did the austere prerogatives of the single God against the putatively "polytheistic" structures of the Catholic Church and its crowded multitude of saints and observances.[11] They were quick to capitalize on this potential advantage, as we shall see. They were quick to use lists.

Following the Act of Supremacy of 1534, England produced, and therefore had to deal with, a suddenly increased volume of cultural detritus. I instance just one from many possible examples of the *material* process of transforming a numinous structure into a purely material, senseless list, before turning to the junk-production work of literal syntax. The first iconoclastic legislation in England was passed in 1538.[12] All visible cult of the saints before their images was forbidden, and all images that are "abused with pilgrimages or offerings . . . ye shall, for avoiding that most detestable sin of idolatry, forthwith take down and delay [destroy]."[13] That legislation unleashed a massive program of destruction of the material fabric of saints' statues and shrines.

We can see a close-up of actions being taken across the country in a letter from Winchester to Cromwell dated in early September 1538, in the wake of the suppression of the monasteries.[14] The letter reports that "we made an end of the shrine at Winchester," meaning the shrine of St. Swithun. The letter goes on to degrade the shrine thus: "there was in it no piece of gold, nor any ring, or true stone, but all great counterfeits." That said, the letter quickly goes on to state another kind of value: "Nevertheless we think the silver alone thereof will amount near to two thousand marks." After mention of this sweetener, the letter lists others: "the cross of emeralds, the cross called Hierusalem, another cross of gold, 2 chalices of gold, with some silver plate, parcel of the portion of the vestry." All these economically precious objects having been inventoried, the letter goes back to some verbal trashing of the spiritual value of the shrine:

---

11. Treatment of the Catholic Church's saints as a revived system of polytheism is a standard *topos* of Reformation polemic. For a high-profile example, see the "Homily against the Peril of Idolatry," in Church of England, *Certain sermons or homilies* (London, 1563), RSTC, 13663: The images of the saints are a resurgence of pagan polytheism; they are nothing but "*dii tutelares* of the Gentyles idolaters, such as were Belus to the Babilonians and Assyrians" (Early English Books Online, image 54).

12. For Reformation English iconoclasm, see Margaret Aston, *England's Iconoclasts; Laws Against Images*, vol. 1 (Oxford: Clarendon Press, 1988), and Margaret Aston, *Broken Idols of the English Reformation* (Cambridge: Cambridge University Press, 2016).

13. Walter Howard Frere and William McClure Kennedy, eds., *Visitation Articles and Injunctions of the Period of the Reformation*, Alcuin Club Collections 15, 3 vols. (London: Longmans, Green, 1910), 2:38.

14. G. H. Cook, ed., *Letters to Cromwell and Others on the Suppression of the Monasteries* (London: John Baker, 1965), 197–8.

It will be worth taking down, and nothing thereof seen .... Which done, we intend ... to sweep away all the rotten bones that be called relics; which we may not omit, lest it should be thought we came more for the treasure than for the avoiding of the abomination of idolatry.[15]

This letter provides an illuminating instance of junk production in the late 1530s. The recently numinous relics must be redescribed as "the abomination of idolatry," and so visibly treated as rubbish: they must be swept up for all to see, lest the onlookers charge the iconoclasts with what must be in the minds of every reader of this letter, from Cromwell in 1538 to us in 2021; that we are really observing one kind of value (cultic) being exchanged for another (economic). The shrine is full of counterfeit treasure, but its silver is also worth two thousand marks. The letter must actively underline the cultic worthlessness so as to disguise, yet of course also to sharpen, interest in the remaining economic worth. Breaking and sweeping up the recently sacred bones is the needed sign to justify the precise calculation of the shrine's economic value. Lists form part of this process of revaluation. The demotion of cultic value justifies the promotion of economic value, which, in turn, justifies the need for a poker-faced, unsentimental inventory of other economically valuable objects.

That listing is wholly under control, governed as it is by bureaucratic protocols and by a careful balancing of two kinds of value, cultic and economic: one descends as the other rises. The little list is intra-sentence, but manageable because part of a delimited object being dismantled within a very specific timetable (finished by "3 of the clock").

What happens, however, when the intra-sentence lists are dealing with the entire Catholic Church, as seen from the vantage point of apocalyptic certainty and clarity? Here, as we shall see, the intra-sentence list takes over, incapable as the syntax of the sentence is to manage it.

We can observe this very soon after the demolition of the shrine of St. Swithun in 1538. After Cromwell's fall and execution in 1540, the newly converted Protestant John Bale fled to Antwerp. There he wrote and published *The Image of Both Churches* (published c. 1545).[16] This text presents itself as a paraphrase of the Book of Revelations, a text always guaranteed to provide fertile matter for the febrile. Bale's *Image of Both Churches* is, in fact, an extended prophecy of the victory of the True Church in England over the Church of the Antichrist. The old Church is characterized, among other things, by infinite institutional complexity. It has a bewildering array of cultic forms:

---

15. Cook, *Letters to Cromwell*, 198.
16. John Bale, *The Image of Both Churches* (London, 1570) (first published 1545), RSTC 1301.

> The Pope in his church hath ceremonies without number. None ende is there of their babling prayers, their portases, beads, temples, aulters, songes, houres, belles, Images, Organes, ornaments, Jewels, lights, oilings, shavings, religions, disguisings, diversitie of feasts, constrained vowes, fastings, processions, and pratlings, that a man would think they were proctours of Paradise.[17]

"None ende is there": the sentence, in which apposition works overtime, enacts precisely that endlessness, and prepares the way for the alliterative satirical punch at the end. Bale knows how syntax works to divest symbolic systems of numinous meaning. To destroy numinous meaning, one uses the endless list: one lumps all those numinous items together, so as both to degrade them individually, and to degrade the entire system that they constitute. Apposition and parataxis are the key syntactic instruments of devaluation: just keep adding items to the list that have exactly the same syntactic function, and the sense of the system as a whole starts to disintegrate.

We can see the same strategy at work visually in this image, "The Weight and Substaunce of Gods Most Blessed Word Against the Doctrines and Vanities of Mans Traditions." Here the essential strategy is to produce a counterintuitive visual effect: the small, single book weighs more than the voluminous and manifold stuff. Here the valuation systems are more complex than in the letter to Cromwell discussed above: the spiritual value of the Word of God outweighs the value of Catholic traditions. Fretfully faced with the appalling evidence of that surprise, the Pope helplessly pours a third form of value—the monetary weight of coins—into the floating scale.

The left-hand side of the image is simple, calm, and assured, wholly unsurprised by the counterintuitive result of the weighing. The right-hand side, by contrast, is busy, complex, and fretful in the face of science defeated by the Word of God. Different statūs of the Church (the Pope, a cardinal, an archbishop, a friar) all desperately attempt to add more and weightier things. But the very complexity of the stuff paradoxically serves only to lighten the right side with the addition of each new item. The symbolic weight of a complex system of meaning-making *diminishes* once separate elements of the system are randomly lumped together, as a set of unstructured elements.

Here the visual displacement and piling has the same effect as the appositional, intra-sentence syntax: both serve to create lightweight, ersatz

---

17. Bale, *The Image of Both Churches*, image 11. Letter forms have been modernized, here and in all citations.

FIGURE 10.1. "A Lively Picture, Describing the Weight and Substaunce of God's Most Blessed Word Against the Doctrines and Vanities of Mans Traditions," in John Foxe, *Actes and Monuments of the English Church* (London, 1576), Book 6, 795.

junk. In fact, the numinous, which might have seemed most immune from being made to look like rubbish, turns out to be especially vulnerable: it is, after all, a system of meaning-making; destroy the *structure* of meaning, and each individual numinous element is suddenly transformed into a worthless object, into bric-à-brac. As the letter to Cromwell has it, "there was in it no piece of gold, nor any ring, or true stone, but all great counterfeits."

With individual Catholic cultic items thus disaggregated from a syntactic structure, and with such items reduced, by a kind of visual apposition, to the same function, the weight of symbolic objects becomes paradoxically *less*. The lightening is caused precisely by the evacuation of symbolic meaning from the system as a whole. Laid out as individual, itemized, appositional objects—decretals, crucifixes, rosary beads, incense vases—the meaning, value, and weight of the entire system paradoxically becomes instantly lightweight. More is less. One might see the same tactic at work in Bale's sentence above: the single, aggressive subordinate clause ("that a man would think they were proctours of Paradise") effortlessly outweighs the twenty-two separate elements that precede it, by the time the meaning of those elements has been evacuated through the aggressive listing of the elements.

We are building further elements into our understanding of the way the intra-sentence list works formally. Earlier we observed the following: syntactic apposition; parataxis; potentially infinite extension; sometimes anaphora. To these features we can add memorial challenge. The list is, as we all know, a challenge for the memory, precisely because it is not part of a syntactic string. We do not know what is going to appear next from what precedes. For most of us, as we know from the unwritten shopping list, a rememberable list is about four, possibly five elements, not more. We need to isolate objects to have any chance of remembering them (this is, no doubt, why we always write shopping lists as a vertical set, rather than horizontally, joined by commas). A long list of items set syntactically as part of a sentence is destined not to be remembered; it begs to be dismissed as unmemorable in both senses.

Each item in an independent list that pretends to completeness (e.g., the shopping list, the army muster) is essential. For potentially infinite intra-sentence lists, by contrast, the more items in the list, the less important is each individual item. Bale deliberately throws miscellaneous items into his list, so as to defeat any effort to restore the items to a coherent and meaning-making whole: "oilings, shavings, religions, disguisings, diversitie of feasts, constrained vowes." The miscellaneous quality of the list produces an effect of hopelessly confused complexity that beggars the powers of memory.

The list was clearly being used deliberately, and with the same polemical strategy, by a variety of reforming figures in the 1530s. Thus Stephen Gardiner's *De vera obedientia* (1536, translated 1553) frames sentences syntactically so as to produce the same effect as Bale achieved in the sentence cited above. Gardiner says that the English have deserved their afflictions, because they have been prepared to be fed with the

> draffe of masing masses, muming matins, drousie diriges, pikepurse purgatorie, popes pardones, latine service, beades belles & baggepipes, prayeng to dead Saintes, licinge of relikes, . . . absolucion behinde the curtaine, oile & creame with other superstitious baggage, that devill and all: untill with unfeyned penitent heartes we saye with the unthriftie sonne of the Gospell: Father I have sinned against heaven, and before the, now I am not worthy to be called thy sonne.[18]

We can also see the high profile of the destructive, intra-sentence list as a polemical weapon from the fact that its targets also replicate it, in the hope of turning it back on Protestant users. Thus Thomas More charges Tyndale and

---

18. Stephen Gardiner, *De vera obedientia* (London, 1553) RSTC 11585, image 10.

his brethren of uncharitable attack on the younger brethren who are not toeing the line:

> contrary to your owne wordes [you] use [i.e. are accustomed] at your yonger brothern to laughe them to skorne, to mocke, to jeste, to checke, to chide, to brawle, & ribaldously to raile, callinge them apishe, pevisshe, popisshe, juglers, theves, murderers, bloodsupers, tormentours, and traitours, Pilatis, Cayphaas, Herodis, Annaas, & Antecristes, Judaas, hypocrites, mokenmongers, priapistes, idolatres, horemaisters, and sodomites, abominable, shameles, stark madde, and faithlesse bestes, hangemen, martyr quellers, and Criste killers, serpentes, scorpions, dremers, and very divels & finally with such venemouse wordes and other maliciouse wayes the wurste that the divell and you devise together.[19]

More attempts to mimic the style of his enemy, so as to turn the list against the enemy in much the same way as Bale turned his list against Catholics: by piling on so many items, however spectacular individual items might be, the effort is to deflate the force of the enemy attack by rehearsing its absurd exaggeration. For all the fireworks of More's list, he knows he will lose the battle of the lists: the revolutionary, who always offers simplicity, will always win the battle of the lists against the defender of the highly complex, divided, multiple structures of the *ancien régime*.[20]

John Bale, however, is the champion of the early English Reformation polemical list.[21] Bale relentlessly pursues the theme of paratactic complexity

---

19. Thomas More, *The Confutation of Tyndale's Answer*, ed. Louis A. Schuster, Richard Marius, James P. Lusardi, and Richard J. Schoeck, *The Complete Works of St. Thomas More* 8, 3 vols. (New Haven: Yale University Press, 1973), 1:59. More published the first part of the huge *Confutation of Tyndale's Answer*, which was focused on the grounds of scriptural authority, in 1532. The second part appeared in 1533. The passage is discussed in David Loewenstein, *Treacherous Faith: The Specter of Heresy in Early Modern English Literature and Culture* (Oxford: Oxford University Press, 2013), 64.

20. Already in 1515, More knows that this kind of verbal combat will be a losing game. In his letter to Martin van Dorp of that year, he foresaw the pathos of the Sisyphian labor of fighting with those who are regarded as heretics:

> the very problems with which they are assaulted afford them no end of material with which to strike back, so that the plight of both parties is very much like that of men fighting naked between heaps of stones: neither one lacks the means to strike out; neither one has the means to defend himself.

(Thomas More, *Complete Works of St. Thomas More*, vol. 15, *In Defense of Humanism: Letter to Martin Dorp, Letter to the University of Oxford, Letter to Edward Lee, Letter to a Monk*, ed. Daniel Kinney [New Haven: Yale University Press, 1986], 71.)

21. See also the essay by Alex Davis in this volume.

versus simplicity. He transfers the strategy from individual cultic forms of the Church to the structure of the Church itself. He calls the Pope the "Prince of hypocrisie," which prepares the way for an aggressive listing of the many institutional masks that the hypocritical prince uses. The Pope is the head of the "pale horse,"

> whose bodie are his Patriarkes, Cardinalles, Archebishops, Bishops, fat prebends, doctours, priestes, Abbottes, Priors, Moonks, Chanons, Friers, Nunnes, Pardoners, and Proctours, with all the sectes and and shorne swarme of perdicion, and with all those that consent with them in the Romish faith, obeying their wicked lawes, decrees, bulles, privileges, decretales, rules, tradicions, titles, pompes, degrees, blessinges, counsailes, and constitucions, contrarie to Gods trueth.[22]

Each step of a polemical Bale sentence steps on the land mine of a list. Here we have two intra-sentence, or intra-clause lists, the first laying the ground for the second. These two lists are, however, just the warm-up to yet another. Those who consent to the Pope's hypocrisy are the

> Benedictines, the Bernardines, Gerondines, Gilbertines, Celestines, Scopetines, Grandimontensers, Camaldulensers, Cruniacensers, Premonstratensers, Carthusianes, Carmelitanes, Ambrosianes, Rhodianes, Gregorianes, Purgatorianes, Guilhelmites, Jesuites, Iohannites, Hieronimites, Niniuits, Cellites, Thaborits, Templars, Hospitelers, Crucigers, Augustinianes, Dominicianes, Franciscanes, Brygidanes, Basilianes, of Josaphats valley, and of the dark alley, and suche other, with innumerable swarmes of them everye where.[23]

Bale's list goes on at such length as to defeat syntax and degenerate into absurd nonsense: "of Josaphats valley, and of the dark alley, and suche other, with innumerable swarmes." By the time the inordinate length of the list has reached this point, no structure, symbolic or otherwise, is salvageable; there is only a potentially infinite, paratactic, senseless, forgettable, rebarbative, complex list, an "innumerable swarme" of items.[24]

---

22. Bale, *The Image of Both Churches*, image 86.
23. Bale, *The Image of Both Churches*, image 121.
24. See also John Bale, *King John*, in *The Complete Plays of John Bale*, ed. Peter Happé, 2 vols. (Woodbridge: Boydell & Brewer, 1985), Act 1, ll. 441–60 (1:40–1), for a similar list, arranged metrically. *King John* can be dated to c. 1540. This speech is cited, quoted, and discussed by Davis, pp. 187–89.

EXTREME CASES

We now have the intra-sentence list focused as an especially useful tool of revolutionary polemic. Let me end with some truly spectacular intra-sentence lists from an anonymous poem written between 1529 and 1532, *The Ymage of Ipocrisy*.[25] This poem, once incorrectly attributed to John Skelton, is about 2700 lines, written in Skeltonics (two-stress rhyming couplets). The poem is a verbal *tour de force* of evangelical mockery, in which the author correctly predicts that what is regarded as treason and heresy now will soon change: "Then shall we here and se / In Christianitye, / Whether youe or we / The very traytours be."[26] I end with a discussion of this singular text by way of seeing the polemical features of the list we have already isolated in wildly exaggerated form (yes, considerably more exaggerated even than Bale's monstrous prose lists). The essence of the overall strategy with the list adds a further formal aspect of the skillfully wielded list. That formal feature is as follows: weaken the syntax by strengthening the figures of speech. Weaken the conceptual force of the sentence, that is, by surreal emphasis on its sensory features—its length, its sound.

In this passage, for example, notice how a single adverbial phrase ("with abjurations") deliberately falls down into a pothole of potentially endless adverbial phrases:

> He robbeth all nations
> With his fulminations
> And other like vexations,
> As with abjurations,
> Excommunications,
> Aggravations,
> Presentations,
> Sequestrations,
> Deprivations,
> Advocations,
> Resignations,

---

25. Anonymous, *The Ymage of Ipocrisy*, in John Skelton, *The Poetical Works of John Skelton*, ed. Alexander Dyce, 2 vols. (Cambridge: Cambridge University Press, 1843), 2:413–47. The text is printed from British Library, Lansdowne MS 794. There appears to be no early printed edition. The Dyce edition does not number lines; I cite by page number. The evidence for the date of 1529-32 is based principally on a hostile reference (435–6) to Thomas More as exercising the powers of Chancellor (1529–32).

26. Dyce, *Ymage of Ipocrisy*, 20.

> Dilapidations,
> Sustentations . . .
> And dissimulations
> With like abominations
> Of a thousand fashions.[27]

The ellipsis omits thirty lines of identically metered legal ecclesiastical formulae. Each line contains a two-stressed word, each an ecclesiastical legal instrument, and all are in apposition; they all rhyme. Even as they seem to end ("With like abominations / Of a thousand fashions"), they leap back into life almost immediately ("His trialitees and pluralitees / Be full of qualities; / His tottes and quottes / Be full of blottes: / With quibes and quaries / Of inventataries, / Of testamentaries, / And of mortuaries").[28] That pyrotechnic bonfire of the vanities is just the first of many. The next takes up the list of ecclesiastical orders on which Bale seems to have drawn later in the decade, but wickedly seasons it with diabolical additions: "Some be Stellifers, / And some be Ensifers, / Some Lucifers / Some Crucifers."[29] But wait: these are just the curtain raisers for the ultimate bonfire of absurdity, the endless processional list of the friars, where scatology pushes the entire, already weakened, structure over into the waste disposal system. The sentence begins with "Then," but we must wait eighty-three lines before a main verb. Each of the intervening lines consists of the name of an order of friars, mixing actual orders with orders satirically invented for mocking intent:

> Then fryer Dominike
> And freyer Demonike,
> Fryer Cordiler
> And fryer Bordiler,
> Fryer Jacobine
> Fryer Augustine,
> And fryer Incubine,
> And fryer Succubine,
> Fryer Carmelite,
> And Fryer Hermelite,
> Fryer Minorite,
> And fryer Ipocrite. . . .

---

27. Dyce, *Ymage of Ipocrisy*, 427.
28. Dyce, *Ymage of Ipocrisy*, 427.
29. Dyce, *Ymage of Ipocrisy*, 441.

> With an hundred more
> Could I name by ro.³⁰

Needless to say, the sentence (whose ellipsis already omits *sixty-nine lines*), carries on, but lowers the linguistic register further to produce scatological and/or abusive Latin orders: "Squalidi laudati / Foedi effeminati, / Falsi falsati, / Fuci fucati, / Culi cacati, / Balbi braccati, / Mimi merdati, / Larvi larvati" (with sixteen more to come).

The syntax of such sentences holds, but its capacity to invest the words with sense is entirely overtaken and hollowed out by the meaning and sensory effect of the words themselves: the meaning is offensive, and made so by the relentless hammering of stress patterns, alliteration, and rhyme, so relentless as to evacuate the words of meaning, and to render numinous words vulnerable to attack by insolent jibe (e.g., Minorite/Ipocrite). This is, to be sure, childish word play, but in the context of the immediate pre-Reformation context, highly charged. So far from being the passive servant of his potentially infinite intra-sentence lists, this author launches the potentially infinite list, as Bale will soon afterwards, as a polemical missile.

---

30. Dyce, *Ymage of Ipocrisy*, 443.

CONTRIBUTORS

SUZANNE CONKLIN AKBARI is Professor of Medieval Studies at the Institute for Advanced Study in Princeton, New Jersey. She has written books on optics and allegory (*Seeing through the Veil*) and European views of Islam and the Orient (*Idols in the East,* 2010), and edited collections on travel literature (*Marco Polo,* 2010), Mediterranean Studies (*A Sea of Languages,* 2016), and somatic histories (*The Ends of the Body,* 2015), as well as *How We Write* (2015) and *How We Read* (2019). Her most recent book is *The Oxford Handbook of Chaucer* (2020), co-edited with James Simpson. Akbari is finishing up a monograph called *Small Change: Metaphor and Metamorphosis in Chaucer and Christine de Pizan,* and working on another one, *The Shape of Time,* on premodern ideas of periodization. A co-editor of the *Norton Anthology of World Literature,* Akbari co-hosts a literature podcast called *The Spouter Inn.* She's involved in two collaborative projects on global medieval studies, "The Book and the Silk Roads" and "Practices of Commentary."

ALEXIS KELLNER BECKER is Assistant Professor of Literatures in English at Ithaca College in Ithaca, New York, where she teaches medieval literature, poetry, and the histories and structure of the English language. Her research focuses on the entanglements of medieval reading, labor, and the environment, and has appeared in *New Medieval Literatures* and the *Open Access Companion to the Canterbury Tales.* She is completing a book project entitled *Land and Literacies in Medieval Britain,* which shows how the management of the land is both a material precondition for and an obsession of medieval British reading and writing.

INGO BERENSMEYER is Professor of Modern English Literature at LMU Munich. He previously held positions at the Universities of Giessen and Ghent. He has published widely on English literature from the sixteenth to the twenty-first century, and his current research interests are in literary theory, textual studies and book history, and authorship studies. His most recent book is *Literary Culture in Early Modern England, 1630–1700: Angles of Contingency* (De Gruyter, 2020). He has co-edited the *Cambridge Handbook of Literary Authorship* (2019) and edited a *Handbook of English Renaissance Literature* (De Gruyter, 2019), which includes a chapter on *The Faerie Queene*. His current book project is a study of the changing representation of literary authorship in the modern novel.

EVA VON CONTZEN is Professor of English literature, including the literatures of the Middle Ages, at the University of Freiburg, Germany. Since 2017, she is the principal investigator for the project "Lists in Literature and Culture: Towards a Listology (LISTLIT)," funded by the European Research Council. Apart from lists, her research interests include narrative theory, medieval saints' legends, the history of the epic catalogue, and cognitive literary studies. Her publications include the monograph *The Scottish Legendary: Towards a Poetics of Hagiographic Narration* (Manchester University Press, 2016), as well as co-edited volumes on *Enacting the Bible in Late Medieval and Early Modern Drama* (Manchester University Press, 2020, with Chanita Goodblatt) and *Sanctity as Literature in Medieval Britain* (Manchester University Press, 2015, with Anke Bernau).

ALEX DAVIS is Senior Lecturer in English at the University of St Andrews. He is the author of *Chivalry and Romance in the English Renaissance* (2003), *Renaissance Historical Fiction* (2011), and *Imagining Inheritance from Chaucer to Shakespeare* (2020), and he is one of the editors of the MHRA Tudor and Stuart Translations edition of *Erasmus in English, 1523–1584* (2022).

ANDREW JAMES JOHNSTON is Professor of Medieval and Renaissance English Literature at the Freie Universität Berlin. He is the author of *Performing the Middle Ages from* Beowulf *to* Othello (Brepols, 2008). His co-edited collections include *The Medieval Motion Picture* (Palgrave Macmillan, 2014, with Margitta Rouse and Philipp Hinz); *The Art of Vision: Ekphrasis in Medieval Literature and Culture* (The Ohio State University Press, 2015, with Ethan Knapp and Margitta Rouse); *Love, History and Emotion in Chaucer and Shakespeare* (Manchester University Press, 2016, with Russell West-Pavlov and Elisabeth Kempf); and *Material Remains: Reading the Past in Medieval and Early Modern British Literature* (The Ohio State University Press, 2021, with Jan-Peer Hartmann). His latest article is entitled "The Aesthetics of 'Wawes Grene': Planets, Paintings and Politics in Chaucer's *Knight's Tale*," in Helen Fulton, ed., *Chaucer and Italian Culture* (University of Wales Press, 2021).

WOLFRAM R. KELLER teaches English literature at Freie Universität Berlin. His research interests include medieval and early modern insular literature as well as contemporary Canadian and Scottish literature. He is the author of *Selves &*

Nations: The Troy Story from Sicily to England in the Middle Ages (2008), editor of *Challenging Canadian Multiculturalism* (2012), and co-editor of *"A Fantastic and Abstruse Latinity?" Hiberno-Continental Cultural and Literary Relations in the Middle Ages* (2017) and *Perfect Harmony and Melting Strains: Transformations of Music in Early Modern Culture Between Sensibility and Abstraction* (2021).

KATHRYN MOGK WAGNER is Director of Academic Programming at the Center for Christianity and Scholarship at Duke University. Her current research project explores how fourteenth- and fifteenth-century English texts represent and theorize Latin liturgical performance, recuperating value from unintelligibility. Her broader interests include liturgical theology, postcritical reading, and liberal arts pedagogy.

MARTHA RUST is Associate Professor of English at New York University and the author of *Imaginary Worlds in Medieval Books: Exploring the Manuscript Matrix* (Palgrave, 2007). Her current book project is entitled *Lists and the Poetics of Reckoning in Middle English Culture*.

JAMES SIMPSON is Donald P. and Katherine B. Loker Professor of English at Harvard University. Educated at the universities of Melbourne and Oxford, he was formerly Professor of Medieval and Renaissance English at the University of Cambridge. His most recent books are *Reform and Cultural Revolution*, volume 2 in the *Oxford English Literary History* (Oxford University Press, 2002); *Burning to Read: English Fundamentalism and its Reformation Opponents* (Harvard University Press, 2007); *Under the Hammer: Iconoclasm in the Anglo-American Tradition* (Oxford University Press, 2010); and *Permanent Revolution: The Reformation and the Illiberal Roots of Liberalism* (Harvard University Press, 2019).

INDEX

Abelard, Peter, 86n17. See also *Planctus Dinae*
Achilleid (Statius), 116, 165n41
Adage (Erasmus), 175n7
Æðelræd, 19
Aeneid (Virgil), 118, 137, 141–42, 156, 202n9
Aesop, 179
affordance, 8, 53, 156; afford, 5
Agricola, Rudolph, 178
Akbari, Suzanne, 9, 12, 82n10, 95n30
Alboin, 38
Alciato, Andrea, 158n10
Alexander the Great, 38
Alexander, Philip S., 98, 98n3
alienation, 12, 58, 68, 71–73
Alighieri, Dante, 118, 118n12, 162–63, 170, 201. See also *Divine Comedy*
Allegorical Interpretations of Genesis (Philo), 11, 99–103, 99nn5–6, 100n7, 101nn9–11, 102nn13–14, 109
Allen, Marillene, 158n8, 158n13, 162nn27–28, 163n29
alliteration, 16, 22–23, 25–27, 29, 31, 62, 68, 71, 125–26, 188, 205, 212

"Alma chorus Domini," 60–63, 72
Almandal, 69
Ambrisco, Alan S., 130n44
Amodio, Mark C., 37n7
Amsler, Mark E., 137n3, 145n36, 149n47, 150n50
Analecta Hymnica, 60, 64–67, 67n25, 67nn27–28, 72, 73n48. See also "Alma chorus Domini;" "Christe Salvator;" "Deus pater piissime;" "De nominee Iesu;" "Fortis El et Eloi"
Andrews, Charles McLean, 21n32
Anglicus, Bartholomaeus, 138. See also *De proprietatibus rerum*
Apollonius, 124. See also *Argonautica*
apposition, 197, 199–201, 205–7, 211–12
Apuleius, 52–53
Aquinas, Thomas, 69–70, 69n34, 140, 140n17
Arcadia (Sannazaro), 163
Areford, David S., 114n32
Argonautica (Apollonius), 124
Ariosto, Ludovico, 163. See also *Orlando furioso*

• 217 •

Aristotle, 136, 140, 140n16
Arnovick, Leslie, 68, 68n32
Ars notoria, 69–70
As You Like It (Shakespeare), 158
"As a Mydsomer Rose" (Lydgate), 113–14, 113n29, 114n30
Aston, Margaret, 192–93, 192n51, 203n12
Attila the Hun, 38, 44
Auerbach, Erich, 39n13
Augustine, 69, 69n33, 202–3, 202n10. See also *City of God*
authority, 5, 7, 12, 19, 28, 31, 34, 46, 52, 115, 118, 120, 130, 134, 178, 181, 187, 191, 208n19
Avalon, Hugh of, 81–82
Avila, Teresa of, 77

Bacon, Francis, 175, 175n8
Bakker, Egbert J., 39n13
Baldwin, T. W., 174, 174n2, 179n16
Bale, John, 12–13, 173–74, 174nn4–5, 186–92, 187nn42–43, 188nn44–45, 198, 204–12, 204n16, 205n17, 209nn22–24. See also *Image of Both Churches, The*; *King Johan*; *vocacyon of Johan Bale, The*
Banham, Debby, 21, 21n31, 25n41, 27n52, 29n60
Barney, Stephen A., 5, 5nn14–16, 100, 100n8, 104n17, 118–19, 118n13, 119n15, 137, 137n5, 142n28
Barnicle, Mary Elizabeth, 121, 121n22, 121n24, 122n27, 123, 123nn31–32
Barthes, Roland, 191–92, 192n49
Baswell, Christopher, 131, 131n45, 132n47
Bata, Ælfric, 30–31
Bately, Janet, 26n44
Batman vppon Bartholome (Batman), 167
Bawcutt, Priscilla, 137n3, 145n37, 148, 148n43, 149n48
Becker, Alexis, 10, 12
Bede, 85n17
Beilin, Elaine, 159n15
Belknap, Robert, 4n10, 137n4
Benjamin Major (Saint Victor), 78, 78n5
Benjamin Minor (Middle English), 9, 12, 75–77, 80–91, 80n6, 93–96

Benjamin Minor (Saint Victor), 75, 78, 78n5, 80, 82
Benson, David, 125, 125n36, 128, 128n41, 130n43, 131n46
Benson, Larry D., 116n2, 137n6
Beowulf, 36, 39n13, 40, 45n22, 51–53
Berensmeyer, Ingo, 9, 11–12, 196n1
Bergen, Henry, 120n18
Bernau, Anke, 6, 6n19, 140n20
Bethurum, Dorothy, 26n44
Bible, 55, 67, 71, 75, 78, 85, 90, 92–93, 97–100, 97n2, 102–103, 105, 107, 109, 114, 167, 204; New Testament, 55, 55n1, 67, 71, 167, 204; Old Testament, 55, 55n1, 75, 78, 85, 90, 92–93, 97–100, 97n2, 102–103, 105, 107, 109, 114, 167
Bicknell, Alexander, 168–69, 168nn48–49. See also *Prince Arthur*
Bland, Mark, 164n35
Blatt, Thora Balslev, 188, 189n46
Bloch, Erich, 42n18
Blume, Clemens, 103n16
Boccaccio, Giovanni, 116, 156, 162, 165n40. See also *Filostrato*; *Teseida*
Boethius, 91–92, 142. See also *Consolation of Philosophy*
Bogost, Ian, 33n72
Boitani, Piero, 156n2, 159n18
Boke named the gouernour (Elyot), 179
Bonaventure, 78, 78n3. See also *Itinerarium mentis in Deum*
boredom, 9, 12
Borges, Jorge Luis, 6, 6n22, 7
Borlik, Todd Andrew, 159n17, 161nn21–23
Borsuk, Amaranth, 171n59
Bose, Mishtooni, 91, 91n25
Brandes, Hermann, 126n35
Brayford, Susan, 97–98, 97nn1–2, 98n4, 114, 114n31
Bremmer, Rolf H., Jr., 38, 38n10
Brewer, J. S., 180n20
Brie, Friedrich, 119n18, 123n29
Britnell, Richard H., 139n13
Bundy, Murray W., 138n8

Bunyan, John, 196n3. See also *Pilgrim's Progress*

Caesar, Gaius Julius, 37–38, 51, 170
Cagliari, Lucifer of, 188
Cain, Christopher M., 36n4
Calinescu, Matei, 52, 53n39
Cameron, Angus, 27n50
Campbell, Gordon, 156, 156n1
Campbell, Kirsty, 91n23
Cannon, Christopher, 196n1
Canterbury Tales (Chaucer), 4, 156, 159, 168, 199n6
Carlson, David R., 140n19
Carruthers, Mary, 119n14, 143n30, 151n55
Cary, Susan E., 101n12
catalogue, 2, 4, 8–12, 26–27, 32, 42, 44, 58, 115, 119, 119nn16–17, 121–24, 126–32, 134, 143n31, 147, 155–57, 156n2, 159–64, 159n18, 167–71, 169n51, 176, 188–89, 192, 196, 196n1; epic, 10–12, 115, 119, 119n16, 121, 124, 131, 134, 143n31, 155–57, 162, 169, 169n51, 171; of heroes, 119, 122, 126, 147; of ships, 2, 12, 121–24, 126, 129–30, 132, 156; of trees, 9, 11, 155–56, 160–63, 168
Cato, the Elder, 16n4. See also *De agri cultura*
Cave, Terence, 176, 176n10
Celle, Peter of, 85n17. See also *De disciplina claustrali*
Chakrabarty, Dipesh, 42n18, 48–49, 48n24
Chambers, Raymond Wilson, 35n1, 37, 37n9
Charles II, 158
charm, 18, 18n15, 61–63, 68; "Letter to Charlemagne," 61–62; "Prayer of Charlemagne," 61, 63
Chastel d'amur (Grosseteste), 94, 95n30
Chaucer, Geoffrey, 2–5, 9–10, 12, 115–20, 116n2, 117n7, 130–41, 130n43, 137n6, 141n25, 143, 143n31, 144n32, 145, 148–49, 152, 155–56, 159–62, 159n18, 160n19, 164–68, 164 fig. 8.1, 165n42, 166 table 8.1, 167 fig. 8.2, 196, 196n1, 198, 199nn5–6, 201. See also *Canterbury Tales*; "The Former Age"; *House of Fame*; *Legend of Good Women*; *Parliament of Fowls*; *Troilus and Criseyde*
Cité des dames (de Pizan), 91

City of God (Augustine), 202
Clairvaux, Bernard of, 85n17. See also *S. Bernardi opera omnia*
Clanchy, M. T., 27n52
Claudian, 116, 162, 165nn39–40, 165n42, 170. See also *De raptu Proserpinae*
Clerk of Whalley, John, 125–28, 125nn34–35, 134. See also *'Gest Hystoriale' of the Destruction of Troy*
Clifford, Margaret, 159
Cloud of Unknowing, 80
Cole, Andrew, 32, 32n69
Coleman, Christopher, 184n33
Colet, John, 176–77
"Colin Clouts Come Home Againe" (Spenser), 158
Collinson, Patrick, 183n29
Colloquy (Eynsham), 29–30
Colonne, Guido delle, 116, 119–20, 125–27, 131–33, 143. See also *Historia destructionis Troiae*
Columella, Lucius Junius, Moderatus, 16n4. See also *Rei rusticae libri*
Combellack, C. R. B., 123, 123n28, 123n30
Compendium historiae in genealogia Christi (Poitiers), 76n1
Consolation of Philosophy (Boethius), 91
Constable, Giles, 81n8
Contzen, Eva von, 4n10, 8n28; 10–12, 21, 56n3, 135, 137n4, 143n31, 150n50, 156n1, 156n4, 173
Cook, G. H., 203n14, 204n15
Cook, Patrick, 159n16
Cooper, Helen, 117, 117nn5–7, 118nn9–10
Cooper, Lisa H., 3n5, 4n9, 29, 29n61
Cranmer, Thomas, 186
Crick, Julia, 19n19
"Christe Salvator," 66
Cromwell, Gregory, 174
Cromwell, Thomas, 11, 173–74, 174nn3–4, 180–90, 180nn20–21, 184n37, 193, 203–6
Culex (pseudo-Virgil), 165n39
Culler, Jonathan, 156n3

D'Asti, Bruno, 85n17

Da Rold, Orietta, 15n3
Dahan, Gilbert, 86n17
Damasus I, 59
Damian, Peter, 85n17
Damrosch, David, 50–52, 50n31, 52nn36–38, 53n40, 54
Dares, 116, 116n1, 119, 121–22, 129, 131–33, 143. See also *De excidio Troiae historia*
Davis, Alex, 10–13, 196n1, 208n21, 209n24
Davis, Rebecca, 142n28, 200n7
De agri cultura (Cato), 16n4
De bello Troiano (Exeter), 156
De Copia (Erasmus), 10–12, 174–79
De disciplina claustrali (Celle), 85n17
De excidio Troiae historia (Dares), 116
de Insulis, Alanus, 91. See also *Plaint of Nature*
de Lorris, Guillaume, 86. See also *Roman de la Rose*
de Meun, Jean, 3. See also *Roman de la Rose*
De mystica theologia (pseudo-Dionysius), 77, 80
"De nominee Iesu," 72–73
de Pizan, Christine, 91–92. See also *Cité des dames*
De proprietatibus rerum (Anglicus), 138
De raptu Proserpinae (Claudian), 116, 165nn39–40, 165n42
de Sainte-Maure, Benoît, 119, 121. See also *Roman de Troie, Le*
De vera obedientia (Gardiner), 207
de Voragine, Jacobus, 104n18. See also *Golden Legend, The*
"De Vulneribus Christi," 103–105, 103n16, 107–8, 107n20. See also *Omnibus consideratis*
Doleželová, Lucie, 3n4
Decretum Gelasianum, 59–60
defamiliarization, 57, 73, 192
Defence of Poesy (Sidney), 163–64
Delaney, Sheila, 118n10
Deonise Hid Divinite, 80
"Description of Cooke-ham, The" (Lanyer), 159

"Deus pater piissime," 64
Dictys, 116, 119, 131, 133, 143. See also *Ephemeris belli Troiani*
Dinshaw, Carolyn, 42n18
Discoverie of Witchcraft (Scot), 63
Divine Comedy (Alighieri), 162, 201, 201n9
Dobschütz, Ernst von, 59n8
Doctor Faustus (Marlowe), 157–58
Donaldson, David, 119n18, 126n39
Donet (Pecock), 93–94, 94n28
Donoghue, Daniel, 33n71
Dorp, Martin van, 208n20
Douglas, Gavin, 9, 12, 135–36, 140–41, 145, 145n37, 148, 152. See also *Palice of Honour*
Douie, Decima L., 82n9
Drayton, Michael, 158. See also *Poly-Olbion*
Dreves, Guido M., 103n16
Drout, Michael D. C., 36n2
Dryden, John, 168, 168n47
Duffy, Eamon, 61, 61n14, 72, 72n47, 109n23, 192, 192n50
Duncan-Jones, Katherine, 161, 165n37
Dyce, Alexander, 210nn25–26, 211nn27–29, 212n30
Dyer, Christopher, 16, 16n7

Ebin, Lois, 145n36, 146n38
Eco, Umberto, 3n6, 4n10, 6n23, 21, 21n29, 31nn64–65
Eden, 9, 11, 97–100, 103–4, 108–9, 114, 200; four rivers of, 9, 11, 97–98, 100, 104, 114
Edward II (Marlowe), 158
Edwards, Robert R., 138n11, 143n30
Eisenstadt, Shmuel N., 49, 49n26
elegy, 42
Elizabeth I, 158, 189
Elliot, Elizabeth, 151nn52–53
Elton, G. R., 180n20, 181–87, 181n22, 182nn23–27, 183n29, 184n36, 185nn38–40
Elyot, Thomas, 179, 179nn18–19. See also *Boke named the gouernour*
enlistment, 1, 2n1
Eormanric, 35, 37, 43, 47
Ephemeris belli Troiani (Dictys), 116

Erasmus of Rotterdam, Desiderius, 10–11, 173–79, 174n3, 175nn6–7, 177nn11–13, 178n15, 181, 186. See also *Adage*; *De Copia*

Eriugena, John Scotus, 77

Esolen, Anthony M., 162n28

Etymologies (Seville), 29, 58–60, 66

Exeter, Joseph of, 156. See also *De bello Troiano*

Eynsham, Ælfric of, 25n41, 29–31. See also *Colloquy*; *Glossary*; *Grammar*

Faerie Queene (Spenser), 12, 155, 162–69, 164n35

Fairfax, Edward, 168

Fairhall, James, 171n57

Faith, Rosamond, 15n1, 17n9, 20, 20n23, 20n28, 21n31, 25n41, 26n44, 27n52, 28n54, 29n60

family tree, 9, 76, 90–91, 93–95

Farmer, Hugh, 82n9

Favreau, Robert, 67n29

Federico, Sylvia, 120n19

Fell, Christine, 23n35, 24, 24n39, 28n55, 29, 29n58

Fewer, Colin, 130n44

Filostrato (Boccaccio), 116

Finkmann, Simone, 121n26

Finlayson, John, 125n35

Folower to the Donet (Pecock), 93, 95n31

Forde, Baldwin of, 86n17. See also *Opera*

Forest, John, 190

"Former Age, The" (Chaucer), 3

"Fortis El et Eloi," 64–65

Foucault, Michel, 6–7, 6n24, 7n25

Fox, Denton, 135–36, 135n1, 147n40

Foxe, John, 206 fig. 10.1

Fradenburg, Louise Olga, 141n24

Frank, Roberta, 39n13, 40, 40n15, 43n20, 51, 52n35, 53, 53n41

Franklin-Brown, Mary, 4n8

Frere, Walter Howard, 203n13

Friedman, Susan Stanford, 49–50, 49nn28–29, 50n32

Fulk, R. D., 36n4

Fyler, John, 142n27

Gabler, Hans Walter, 171n57

Gardarn, Derfel, 190

Gardiner, Mark, 24, 24n40, 26n46, 28n55, 29, 29n57

Gardiner, Stephen, 207, 207n18. See also *De vera obedientia*

genealogy, 9, 12, 18, 20, 76, 81, 91–92, 94, 96

Georgics (Virgil), 166n43

Gerefa, 10, 12, 15–18, 15n2, 20–34, 22n34, 26n44

Gerusalemme liberate (Tasso), 168

'Gest Hystoriale' of the Destruction of Troy (Clerk of Whalley), 119, 125–28, 125n35, 134

Gillingham, Robert George, 29n59

global modernism, 35–37, 42, 48, 50–51, 54

Glossary (Eynsham), 25n41, 29–31

glossary, 25n41, 29–31. See also *Glossary* (Eynsham)

Gobbitt, Thomas, 15n2, 16–18, 16n5, 17n10, 18nn13–14, 19n21, 20–21, 20n25, 20n27, 22nn33–34, 27–28, 32n67

Golden Legend, The (de Voragine), 104, 104n18

Goody, Jack, 32n70, 49, 49n27, 173, 173n1, 176, 176n9, 179–81, 193

Graeber, David, 183n30

Grafton, Anthony, 177–78, 178n14, 186

Grammar (Eynsham), 29–30

Gray, Douglas, 109nn23–24, 110n26, 113n28

Greenblatt, Stephen, 52n37

Greenlee, John Wyatt, 27n51

Griffin, Nathaniel E., 123n29, 126n40

Grosseteste, Robert, 77, 94–96, 95n30. See also *Chastel d'amur*; *Tabula*; *Templum Dei*

Gulliver's Travels (Swift), 197n3

Gwara, Scott, 30n63

Hadfield, Andrew, 163n32, 164n35

Hamerow, Helena, 25n43

Hamilton, A. C., 167

Hamlet (Shakespeare), 159

Happé, Peter, 187n43, 188–89
Harriot, Thomas, 157, 157n6
Harris, Ian, 183n29
Hartmann, Jan-Peer, 41–42, 42n17
Hartog, François, 39, 39n12
Harvey, E. Ruth, 138n8
Harvey, P. D. A., 16–17, 16n4, 16n6, 17nn11–12, 26, 26nn44–45, 26n47, 27n48, 114n32
Hasler, Anthony J., 147n40, 148n42, 150n51
Hayot, Eric, 169
Heal, Felicity, 140n22
Hebring, Rosanne, 61n13
Heng, Geraldine, 120n19
Heninger, S. K. Jr., 163n33
Henry V, 130, 133
Henry VIII, 174, 179–81, 179n16, 186, 189
Heroides (Ovid), 142
Hiley, David, 60nn9–10
Hill, David, 21n31
Historia destructionis Troiae (Colonne), 119
Historia Regum Britanniae (Monmouth), 116–17, 117n4
Hodgson, Phyllis, 80n6, 82n11, 84nn13–14, 85nn15–16, 86n18, 87n19
Hoffman, Frank G., 138n11
Homer, 1, 39, 39n13, 116, 118, 121n26, 122, 143, 170, 196, 196n2. *See also Iliad*; *Odyssey*
Honeyman, Chelsea, 137n2, 145n36, 147n39
Horace, 116, 116n3, 163, 163n31, 170. *See also Satires*
Horae Eboracenses, 55, 62
House of Fame (Chaucer), 5, 9–10, 12, 115–19, 116n2, 117n7, 130, 130n43, 134–37, 139, 141–45, 152, 198–201, 199n5, 200n7
household, 8–10, 27, 28n54, 135–36, 138–43, 146–47, 149–50, 182–86, 183nn28–29, 191
Howe, Nicholas, 6, 6n20, 25n43, 35n1, 44, 44n21, 45n22, 156n2
Hundred Good Pointes of Husbandrie, A (Tusser), 159

Iliad (Homer), 1, 121, 156, 167, 196
Image of Both Churches, The (Bale), 204–9
Ingledew, Francis, 120n19

Irvine, Susan, 19n19
Italicus, Silius, 165n39, 165n42. *See also Punica*
Itinerarium mentis in Deum (Bonaventure), 78
Izmirlieva, Valentina, 57n5, 63–64, 63n19, 64n22

Jakobson, Roman, 5, 5n15
James IV, 152
Janowitz, Naomi, 59n7
Jardine, Lisa, 177–78, 178n14, 186
Jeay, Madeleine, 6, 6n21
Jerome, 59–60, 59n6, 63–66, 72
John of the Cross, 77
Johnston, Andrew James, 9–11, 135, 148–49, 148n45, 149n46, 151
Joyce, James, 170, 171n57, 197n3. *See also Ulysses*

Kantorowicz, Ernst, 184
Karnes, Michelle, 83, 83n12, 141n26
Kato, Takako, 15n3
Kaye, Joel, 139nn14–15
Keiser, George R., 3n5
Keller, Wolfram, 9–10, 12, 120n20, 141n25, 144n32, 199n5
Kelly, Thomas Forrest, 2n2
Kempe, Margery, 42n18
Kendall, Elliot, 140n22
Kennedy, William McClure, 203n13
Keynes, Simon, 19n18
Kieckhefer, Richard, 69n38
Kihlman, Erica, 60n10, 61n11
King Johan (Bale), 174, 186–92, 187n43, 209n24
King, John N., 174n5
Klaassen, Frank, 63n18, 69n37, 70n39
Klapisch-Zuber, Christiane, 76n1
Knott, Betty I., 175n7
Kratzmann, Gregory, 137n2, 145n35, 147nn39–40, 149n48

Lanyer, Aemilia, 159. *See also* "Description of Cooke-ham, The"

Laud Troy Book, 119, 128–30, 134
Laurence, Stephen, 101n12
Lawton, David, 125n35, 131n46
Le Goff, Jacques, 140n18
Legend of Good Women (Chaucer), 149, 149n48
Leland, John, 198
Lemanski, Stanley, 19, 19nn21–22, 20n24, 31
Levine, Caroline, 8, 8nn28–29, 56, 56n2
Lewis, Charlton T., 108n22
Lewis, Flora, 103n16
Libellus de re herbaria (Turner), 159
Liber iuratus Honorii, 69
Liber Razielis, 70
Liber Theysolius, 70
Liebermann, Felix, 22n33, 27
Lily, William, 179n17
Lipton, Sara, 82n10
Little, Katherine C., 7–8, 8n27, 31n66, 49n30
Lobsien, Verena O., 139n12
Loewenstein, David, 208n19
Lollius, 116–17, 143
Lowry, Todd, 140n17
Luborsky, Ruth Samson, 163n33
Lucan, 116, 170
Lydgate, John, 103, 113–14, 119, 123, 130–4, 130n43, 131n46. *See also* "As a Mydsomer Rose;" *Siege of Thebes*; *Troy Book*
Lynch, Kathryn L., 117n7, 138, 138n7, 138nn10–11

MacCracken, Henry Noble, 113n29
MacCulloch, Diarmaid, 180n21, 184, 184nn34–35, 190n47
Mainberger, Sabine, 4n10
Maitland, Frederic William, 19, 19n20, 28, 28n56
Malinowski, Bronislaw, 68, 68n31
Malone, Kemp, 35n1, 40n14, 51n34
Marcella, 59
Margolis, Eric, 101n12
Marlowe, Christopher, 157–58, 158n7, 158n11. *See also Doctor Faustus*; *Edward II*
Martin, Joanna, 147n39

Matthews, David, 2, 2n3, 5, 6n18, 140n20
Maurus, Hrabanus, 85n17
McConica, James Kelsey, 174n3
McCusker, Honor, 186, 186n41
McDonald, Nicola F., 121n23, 124
McGuire, Brian, 78n5, 82n9
McRae, Andrew, 158n12
Meecham-Jones, Simon, 117, 117n4, 117n8
Merchant of Venice, The (Shakespeare), 159
Mercia, Offa of, 37, 47
Meritt, Herbert Dean, 27, 27n49, 28n55
Metamorphoses (Ovid), 156, 165n40
Meyer-Lee, Robert J., 131n46
Mikkers, Edmond, 85n17
Miller, Edwin Shepard, 191–92, 191n48
Miller, T. S., 5n17, 118n14
Millet, Bella, 116n3
Milton, John, 170, 198, 200–201, 200n8. *See also Paradise Lost*
Minnis, A. J., 117n7
Miskimin, Alice, 145n35, 148n44, 152
Monmouth, Geoffrey of, 116–17, 143. *See also Historia Regum Britanniae*
More, Thomas, 207–8, 208nn19–20, 210n25
Morgan, Nigel, 104n16, 111n27
Mormando, Franco, 72n45
Moss, Amanda, 90, 91n22
Moyes, J., 103n16, 105, 105n19, 107
Mueller, Alex, 120n21, 125, 125n35, 125n37, 128
Müller, Miriam, 16n8
Muscatine, Charles, 4–5, 4nn11–13

Nagle, Brendan, 183n28
Naismith, R. G. R., 27n52
Natural History (Pliny), 167
negative theology, 75, 77, 80; negation, 57
Neidorf, Leonard, 51, 51nn33–34
Neves, João César Das, 140n17
New Herball, A (Turner), 159
Newman, Barbara J., 85n17
Niles, John D., 36–38, 36nn5–6, 37n8, 39n13, 42, 42n19
Norton-Smith, J., 147n40

O'Brien, Bruce, 18n17, 19n19
Odyssey (Homer), 39n13
Old Arcadia (Sidney), 12, 155, 160–61, 163–69, 164n35
Olsan, Lea, 62n15, 63n17
Olson, Sherri, 30n62
Omnibus consideratis, 104–105, 109–11, 113–114
Opera (Forde), 86n17
Opitz, Christian Nikolaus, 94n29
Orlando furioso (Ariosto), 163
Oschinsky, Dorothea, 16n6
Othello (Shakespeare), 159
Ovid, 116, 118, 131, 142, 144, 151–52, 156, 162, 165n38, 165n40, 167, 170. See also *Heroides*; *Metamorphoses*

Page, R. I., 28, 28n55
Palice of Honour (Douglas), 9, 12, 135–37, 141, 145–53, 145n35, 145n37, 148n44, 149n48
Palmén, Ritva, 78n5, 83, 83n12
Panton, George A., 119n18, 126n39
Paradise Lost (Joyce), 198, 200–201
Paris, Matthew, 76
Parkes, M. B., 16n8
Parkinson, David J., 137n2, 147, 148n41, 149n47, 150n49
Parliament of Fowls (Chaucer), 152, 156, 159–60, 162, 164, 196, 196n1
Patterson, Lee, 130n44, 144n33
Pearsall, Derek, 130n43, 131n46, 133, 133n48
Pecock, Reginald, 76, 90–96, 91nn23–24, 92n26, 94n28, 95n31. See also *Donet*; *Folower to the Donet*; *Repressor*; *Reule of Crysten Religioun*
performative, 7, 11–12, 56, 59–61, 68, 71
Pfaff, R. W., 71n44, 72n46
Phaedrus (Plato), 167
Phillips, Christopher, 63n18
Philo, 11, 99–104, 99nn5–6, 100n7, 101nn9–11, 102nn13–14, 107–10, 113. See also *Allegorical Interpretations of Genesis*
Piers Plowman (Langland), 3
Pilgrim's Progress (Bunyan), 196n3
Plaint of Nature (de Insulis), 91

Planctus Dinae (Abelard), 86n17
Plato, 99n5, 101, 167. See also *Phaedrus*; *Republic*
Pliny, 167. See also *Natural History*
Poitiers, Peter of, 76, 76n1. See also *Compendium historiae in genealogia Christi*
Pollock, Frederick, 19, 19n20
Pollux, Julius, 177
Poly-Olbion (Drayton), 158
Ponsonby, William, 164, 164n35
Poole, R. G., 22n34, 28n55
Poos, L. R., 3, 3n7
Porter, David, 30n63
Powell, Kathryn, 18n16, 20n26
Pratt, R. A., 116n3
Praz, Mario, 158n9
Prince Arthur (Bicknell), 168–69
Prudentius, 86. See also *Psychomachia*
Pseudo-Dionysius, 77–78, 80. See also *De mystica theologia*
Pseudo-Virgil, 165n39. See also *Culex*
Psychomachia (Prudentius), 86
Punica (Italicus), 165n39, 165n42
Putter, Ad, 159n18, 171n59

Quadripartitus, 17–19, 26, 30
Quinn, David, 157n6

Rabelais, François, 175
Rabin, Andrew, 18n15, 26n44
Radday, Yehuda T., 98
Rashi, 97
Rastall, Richard, 60n10
Rectitudines singularum personarum, 15–20, 15n2, 19n22, 22n34, 26–27, 29–33
Reformation, 6, 8, 10–12, 62, 77, 174, 178, 181, 186, 195, 197, 201, 203nn11–12, 208, 212
Register of the Great Seal of Scotland, 1306–1424, The, 27n53
Rei rusticae libri (Columella), 16n4
Reitz, Christiane, 121n26
Remien, Peter, 169
Repressor (Pecock), 93

Republic (Plato), 99n5
Reule of Crysten Religioun (Pecock), 76–77, 91–94, 91n24, 92n26
Richard II, 185
Richards, Mary P., 19n18
Riga, Peter, 85n17
Rolle, Richard, 71
Rollman, David A., 36n3
Roman de la Rose, 3, 86, 156
Roman de Troie, Le (de Sainte-Maure), 119
Rosemann, Philipp W., 95n30
Rouse, Margitta, 148–49, 148n45, 149n46, 151
Ruffolo, Lara, 5n17, 116n2, 118n11
Rust, Martha, 3, 3n7, 9, 11

S. Bernardi opera omnia (Clairvaux), 85n17
Sabapathy, John, 32, 32n68
Saint Victor, Richard of, 75, 78, 80, 82. See also *Benjamin Major*; *Benjamin Minor*
Sammons, Benjamin, 121n26
Sandquist, Brigitte L., 171n57
Sannazaro, Jacopo, 163–64. See also *Arcadia*
Satires (Horace), 163
Sawley, Stephen of, 85n17
Scanlon, Larry, 131n44
Schniedewind, William W., 32n70
Schroeder, Joy A., 85n17
Scipmen, 20
Scot, Reginald, 63. See also *Discoverie of Witchcraft*
Scott-Warren, Jason, 157n5
Seege or Batayle of Troye, The, 119, 121–24, 134
Sege of Troye, The, 123
"Seventy-Two Names of God, The," 64
Seville, Isidore of, 29, 58–61, 64–67, 97. See also *Etymologies*
Shakespeare, William, 159, 175. See also *As You Like It*; *Hamlet*; *Merchant of Venice, The*; *Othello*
Sharp, Tristan, 85n17
Shepheardes Calender (Spenser), 163
Shippey, Tom, 39n13
Short, Charles, 108n22

Sicard, Patrice, 78n4
Sidney, Mary, 161, 164, 167
Sidney, Sir Philip, 9, 12, 155–56, 160, 161n20, 161n24, 163–69, 163n32, 164 fig. 8.1, 164nn34–35, 165n37, 166 table 8.1, 167 fig. 8.2, 171. See also *Defence of Poesy*; *Old Arcadia*
Siege of Thebes (Lydgate), 131n44
Siena, Bernardino of, 71–72
Simpson, James, 10–13, 21, 91n24, 120n21, 125, 126n38, 128, 131n44, 135, 144n34, 160n18, 173, 187, 196n1, 196n3, 198n4
Simpson, W. Sparrow, 67n24, 67n26
Skelton, John, 5, 210, 210n25
Skemer, Don C., 57n4, 61n12, 63n20, 65n23
Slavin, Arthur J., 183n29
Spearing, A. C., 151n54
Speculum novitii, 85n17
Spenser, Edmund, 9, 12, 155–56, 158, 158n14, 162–71, 162nn25–26, 163n30, 163n32, 164 fig. 8.1, 164nn35–36, 165n39, 166 table 8.1, 167 fig. 8.2, 168n45, 170. See also "Colin Clouts Come Home Againe;" *Faerie Queene*; *Shepheardes Calender*; *Virgil's Gnat*
Spivak, Gayatri Chakravorty, 48–49, 49n25
Stäheli, Urs, 7–8, 7n26
Stanbury, Sarah, 3, 3n7
Starkey, David, 184n33
Statius, 116, 162, 165nn40–41, 170. See also *Achilleid*; *Thebaid*
Strohm, Paul, 130n44, 131n44
Stubb, William, 183n29
Studer, John, 131n46
Summit, Jennifer, 198n4
Suso, Heinrich, 71
Swan, Mary, 15n3, 19n19
Swanton, Michael, 22n34
Swift, Jonathan, 197n3. See also *Gulliver's Travels*
syntax, 60, 66, 74, 195–98, 200–201, 203–5, 209–10, 212

Tabula (Grosseteste), 94–96, 95n30
Tasso, Torquato, 168, 168n46, 170. See also *Gerusalemme liberata*

Taylor, Cheryl, 80, 80n7
Templum Dei (Grosseteste), 94, 95n30
temporality, 10, 36, 39, 41–42, 42n18 44–45, 47, 51, 53–54, 176
Teseida (Boccaccio), 156, 165n40
Thebaid (Statius), 116, 165n40
Thornbury, Emily, 47n23
thula, 37, 39, 44, 47
Tout, T. F., 183n29
Tractatus trium cantorum, 61
Traub, Valerie, 42n18
Treharne, Elaine, 15n3, 19n19
Trevisa, John, 138, 138n9
Trilling, Renée R., 36n1
Troilus and Criseyde (Chaucer), 116–17, 131
Trojan War, 11–12, 115–16, 120–22, 124–27, 131, 134
Troy Book (Lydgate), 119, 123, 130–34, 130n43
Tuke, Sir Brian, 182
Turner, William, 159. See also *A New Herball*; *Libellus de re herbaria*
Turville-Petre, Thorlac, 125, 125n33
Tusser, Thomas, 159. See also *A Hundred Good Pointes of Husbandrie*
Tyndale, William, 207

Ulysses (Joyce), 170–71, 197n3
Upton, John, 163n31, 165n41, 166n43, 167, 167n44, 170, 170nn55–56, 171n58

Vankeerbergen, Bernadette C., 130n43
Véronèse, Julien, 69nn35–36, 70nn40–43
Versnel, H. S., 68, 68n30
Victorines, 78, 78n5
Virgil, 116, 118, 131, 141–42, 144, 156, 162, 166–67, 166n43, 170, 202n9. See also *Aeneid*; *Georgics*

Virgil's Gnat (Spenser), 165n39
Visser, Edzard, 121n26
vocabulary, 8, 10, 15–16, 29, 32, 40, 80, 175–76. See also household
vocacyon of Johan Bale, The (Bale), 188

Wagner, Kathryn Mogk, 9–12
Wallace, David, 140n21
Waswo, Richard, 116n3
Waters, Dagmar, 184n32
Waters, Tony, 184n32
Watson, Nicholas, 77n2
Weber, Max, 183–84, 183n29, 183n31, 184n32
Weiskott, Eric, 42n19
White, Hayden, 38n11
White, Paul Whitfield, 174n4
Widsith, 9–11, 35–48, 38n11, 39n13, 40n14, 42nn19–20, 45n22, 47n23, 51–54
Wilson, Edward, 125n34
Windet, John, 164n35
wisdom poetry, 5, 35–36, 42
Witalisz, Władysław, 120n19
Wolf, Kordula, 116n1
Wolfe, John, 164n35
Wood, Diana, 139nn13–14
Wordsworth, Christopher, 62n16
Wormald, Jenny, 141n23
Wormald, Patrick, 18n16, 26n44
Wülfing, J. Ernst, 119n18, 129n42
Wulfstan, 25, 26n44

Yates, Frances A., 143n30
Ymage of Ipocrisy, The, 12, 210–12, 210nn25–26, 211nn27–29, 212n30
Young, Francis M., 107n21

Zirker, Angelika, 159n16

INTERVENTIONS: NEW STUDIES IN MEDIEVAL CULTURE
Ethan Knapp, Series Editor

Interventions: New Studies in Medieval Culture publishes theoretically informed work in medieval literary and cultural studies. We are interested both in studies of medieval culture and in work on the continuing importance of medieval tropes and topics in contemporary intellectual life.

Enlistment: Lists in Medieval and Early Modern Literature
EDITED BY EVA VON CONTZEN AND JAMES SIMPSON

Women's Friendship in Medieval Literature
EDITED BY KARMA LOCHRIE AND USHA VISHNUVAJJALA

Courtly and Queer: Deconstruction, Desire, and Medieval French Literature
CHARLIE SAMUELSON

Continental England: Form, Translation, and Chaucer in the Hundred Years' War
ELIZAVETA STRAKHOV

Material Remains: Reading the Past in Medieval and Early Modern British Literature
EDITED BY JAN-PEER HARTMANN AND ANDREW JAMES JOHNSTON

Translation Effects: Language, Time, and Community in Medieval England
MARY KATE HURLEY

Talk and Textual Production in Medieval England
MARISA LIBBON

Scripting the Nation: Court Poetry and the Authority of History in Late Medieval Scotland
KATHERINE H. TERRELL

Medieval Things: Agency, Materiality, and Narratives of Objects in Medieval German Literature and Beyond
BETTINA BILDHAUER

Death and the Pearl Maiden: Plague, Poetry, England
DAVID K. COLEY

Political Appetites: Food in Medieval English Romance
AARON HOSTETTER

Invention and Authorship in Medieval England
ROBERT R. EDWARDS

Challenging Communion: The Eucharist and Middle English Literature
JENNIFER GARRISON

Chaucer on Screen: Absence, Presence, and Adapting the Canterbury Tales
EDITED BY KATHLEEN COYNE KELLY AND TISON PUGH

Chaucer, Gower, and the Affect of Invention
STEELE NOWLIN

Fragments for a History of a Vanishing Humanism
EDITED BY MYRA SEAMAN AND EILEEN A. JOY

The Medieval Risk-Reward Society: Courts, Adventure, and Love in the European Middle Ages
WILL HASTY

The Politics of Ecology: Land, Life, and Law in Medieval Britain
    EDITED BY RANDY P. SCHIFF AND JOSEPH TAYLOR

The Art of Vision: Ekphrasis in Medieval Literature and Culture
    EDITED BY ANDREW JAMES JOHNSTON, ETHAN KNAPP, AND MARGITTA ROUSE

Desire in the Canterbury Tales
    ELIZABETH SCALA

Imagining the Parish in Late Medieval England
    ELLEN K. RENTZ

Truth and Tales: Cultural Mobility and Medieval Media
    EDITED BY FIONA SOMERSET AND NICHOLAS WATSON

Eschatological Subjects: Divine and Literary Judgment in Fourteenth-Century French Poetry
    J. M. MOREAU

Chaucer's (Anti-)Eroticisms and the Queer Middle Ages
    TISON PUGH

Trading Tongues: Merchants, Multilingualism, and Medieval Literature
    JONATHAN HSY

Translating Troy: Provincial Politics in Alliterative Romance
    ALEX MUELLER

Fictions of Evidence: Witnessing, Literature, and Community in the Late Middle Ages
    JAMIE K. TAYLOR

Answerable Style: The Idea of the Literary in Medieval England
    EDITED BY FRANK GRADY AND ANDREW GALLOWAY

Scribal Authorship and the Writing of History in Medieval England
    MATTHEW FISHER

Fashioning Change: The Trope of Clothing in High- and Late-Medieval England
    ANDREA DENNY-BROWN

Form and Reform: Reading across the Fifteenth Century
    EDITED BY SHANNON GAYK AND KATHLEEN TONRY

How to Make a Human: Animals and Violence in the Middle Ages
    KARL STEEL

Revivalist Fantasy: Alliterative Verse and Nationalist Literary History
    RANDY P. SCHIFF

Inventing Womanhood: Gender and Language in Later Middle English Writing
    TARA WILLIAMS

Body Against Soul: Gender and Sowlehele *in Middle English Allegory*
    MASHA RASKOLNIKOV

www.ingramcontent.com/pod-product-compliance
Lightning Source LLC
Chambersburg PA
CBHW020123240426
43673CB00038B/578